THE GLORIES OF MARY

Translated from the original Italian of
St. Alphonsus Maria de Liguori,
Founder of the Congregation of the Most Holy Redeemer

The Glories of Mary

This new and improved translation of *The Glories of Mary*,
having been duly examined, is hereby approved of.

John Joseph Hughes
Archbishop of New York
New York, Jan. 21, 1852

The Glories of Mary by St. Alphonsus de Liguori is comprised of two parts.
The present publication is *Part I: Commentaries on the* Salve Regina.

America Needs Fatima

Think of what the saints have done
for their neighbor because they
loved God. But what saint's love for God
can match Mary's love? She loved
Him more in the first moment of her
existence than all the saints and
angels ever loved Him or will love Him.
Just as there is not one among
all the blessed who loves God as
Mary does, so there is no one, after
God, who loves us as much as this
most loving Mother.
—St. Alphonsus Maria de Liguori

CONTENTS

CHAPTER 1   **Salve, Regina, Mater misericordiæ!**   ♦ *Hail Queen, Mother of Mercy!*

CHAPTER 2   **Vita, dulcedo**   ♦ *Our Life, Our Sweetness*

CHAPTER 3   **Spes nostra, salve**   ♦ *Hail, Our Hope*

CHAPTER 4   **Ad te clamamus exules filii Evæ**
♦ *To Thee Do We Cry, Poor Banished Children of Eve*

PREFACE TO THE AMERICAN EDITION

The edition of the "Glories of Mary" now presented to the Catholic public of America is the first complete translation of the work ever made into the English language. We trust that it will be found to retain the spirit of the learned and saintly author, and that it will be welcomed by the faithful in this country with the same delight which it has universally called forth in Catholic Europe.

PROTEST OF THE AUTHOR

In obedience to the decrees of Urban VIII, of holy memory, I protest that I do not intend to attribute any other than purely human authority to all the miracles, revelations, graces, and incidents contained in this book; neither to the titles holy or blessed applied to the servants of God not yet canonized; except in cases where these have been confirmed by the holy Roman Catholic Church, and by the holy Apostolic See, of whom I profess myself an obedient son; and therefore to their judgment I submit myself and whatever I have written in this book.

Mother of Good Counsel of Genazzano. 19th century engraving.

PETITION OF THE AUTHOR
TO JESUS AND MARY

My most loving Redeemer and Lord Jesus Christ, I thy poor servant, knowing how pleasing to thee are those who seek to glorify thy most holy mother, whom thou lovest so much, and dost so much desire to see loved and honored by all men, I propose to publish this book of mine which treats of her glories. I know not to whom I could commend it but to thee, who hast so much at heart the glory of this mother. To thee, then, I present and dedicate it. Receive this little offering of my love for thee and thy beloved mother. Take it under thy protection, and pour into the hearts of those who read it the light of confidence in this immaculate Virgin, and the warmth of a burning love for her, in whom thou hast placed the hope and refuge of all the redeemed. And for the reward of this, my poor effort, give me, I pray thee, that love for Mary with which I have desired to inflame, by this my little work, the hearts of all those who read it.

To thee also I appeal, oh my sweetest Lady and mother Mary. Thou knowest that in thee, next to Jesus, I have placed all hope of my eternal salvation, since all the good I have received, my conversion, my vocation to leave the world, and whatever other graces have been given me by God, I acknowledge them all as coming through thee. Thou knowest that to see thee loved by all as thou dost deserve, and to offer thee some token of gratitude, I have always sought to proclaim thee everywhere, in public and in private, and to inspire all men with a sweet and salutary devotion to thee. I hope to continue to do so for the remainder of my life, even to my last breath. But I see by my advanced age and declining health that the end of my pilgrimage and my entrance into eternity are drawing near; therefore, I hope to give to the world, before my death, this little book of mine which may continue to proclaim thee for me, and also may excite others to publish thy glories and the great mercy which thou dost exercise towards thy devoted servants. I hope, my most beloved queen, that this my poor offering, although it falls so far short of thy merit, may be pleasing to thy grateful heart, since it is wholly a gift of love. Extend, then, that most kind hand of thine with which thou hast delivered me from the world and from hell, and accept it and protect it as belonging to thee. But I ask this reward for my little offering, that henceforth I may love thee more, and that all into whose hands this work shall fall, may be inflamed with thy love, so that immediately their desire may increase to love thee, and see others love thee also; and that they may engage with all ardor in proclaiming and promoting, as far as possible, thy praise, and confidence in thy most holy intercession. Thus I hope, thus may it be.

TO THE READER

I n order that this little work of mine may not be exposed to censure from very fastidious critics, I have thought it best to place in a clearer light some of the propositions which it contains, and which may seem too bold, or perhaps obscure. I here enumerate some of them, and if others, my dear reader, should come under your eye, I pray you to consider them as meant and spoken by me according to the sense of true and sound theology, and of the holy Roman Catholic Church, whose obedient son I profess myself. In the Introduction, referring to Chapter 5 of the book, I have said that God has ordained that all graces should come to us through the hands of Mary. Now this is a very consoling truth for souls tenderly attached to the most holy Mary, and for poor sinners who desire to be converted. Nor should this appear to anyone inconsistent with sound theology, since its author, St. Augustine, puts it forth as a general statement, that Mary has shared, by means of her charity, in the spiritual birth of all the members of the Church.[1]

A well-known author, whom no one will suspect of exaggeration or of fanciful and overheated devotion, adds, that as Jesus Christ really formed his Church on Calvary, it is plain that the holy Virgin really co-operated with him, in a peculiar and excellent manner, in its formation.[2] And for the same reason it may be said, that if she brought forth Jesus Christ, the head of the Church, without pain, she did not bring forth the body of this head without pain. Hence she commenced on Calvary to be, in a particular manner, mother of the whole Church. To say all in a few words, Almighty God, in order to glorify the mother of the Redeemer, has ordained that her great charity should intercede for all those for whom her divine Son offered and paid the superabundant ransom of his precious blood, in which alone is our *salvation, life* and *resurrection*. It is on the basis of this doctrine and whatever belongs to it that I have undertaken to establish my propositions,[3] which the saints in their affecting colloquies with Mary, and in their fervent

---

1. Mater quidem spiritu non capitis nostri, quod est ipse salvator, ex quo magis illa spiritualiter natu est; quia omnes, qui in eum crediderint, in quibus et ipsa est, recte filii sponsi appellantur; sed plane mater membrorum ejus (quæ nos sumus) quia cooperata est charitate, ut fideles in Ecclesia nascerentur, qui illius capitis membra sunt. Lib. de Sancta Virginitate, cap 6.
2. M. Nicole, Instr. theol. and mor. on the Lord's Prayer, the Angelical Salutation, etc., Instr. 5, c. 2.
3. Part 1, c. 6, § 2, c. 7, 8, § 2, c. 9.

discourses concerning her, have not hesitated to assert: when an ancient father, quoted by the celebrated Vincenzo Contensone, has written: The fullness of grace was in Christ as the head from which it flows, but in Mary as the neck through which it is transmitted.[4] This is plainly taught by the angelic Doctor, St. Thomas, who confirms all the foregoing in these words: The blessed Virgin is called full of grace in three ways. . . .The third, in reference to its overflowing upon all men. For great is it in each saint if he hath enough of grace for the salvation of many; but this would be the greatest, if he had enough for the salvation of all men; and it is so with Christ and the blessed Virgin, for in every danger we may obtain salvation through the glorious Virgin. Hence, cant. 4, v. 4 *a thousand bucklers*—that is, remedies against dangers—*hang upon her:* "Mille clypei pendent ex ea." Hence in every virtuous work we can have her aid, and, therefore, she herself says, in me is all hope of life and of virtue: "*In me omnis spes vitæ et virtutes.*"[5]

---

4. In Christo fuit plenitudo gratiæ, sicut in capite influente, in Maria vero, sicut in collo transfundente. Theolog. mentis et cordis, Tom. 2, Lib. 10. Dissert. 6, c. 1. Speculat. 2. in Reflexiones.
5. Dicitur autem Beata Virgo plena gratiæ, quantum ad tria . . . Tertio quo ad refusionem in omnes homines. Magnum enim est in quolibet sancto, quando habet tantum de gratia quod sufficit ad salutem multorum; sed quando haberet tantum, quod sufficeret ad salutem omnium hominum de mundo, hoc esset maximum; et hoc est in Christo et in Beata Virgine. Nam in omni periculo potes salutem obtinere ab ipsa Virgine gloriosa. Unde cantic. 4. *Mille clypei*, id est remedia contra pericula, *pendent ex ea.* Item in omni opere virtutis potes eam habere in adjutorium; et ideo dicit ipsa. Eccli. xxiv. 25.

INTRODUCTION WHICH OUGHT TO BE READ

My dear reader and brother in Mary, since the devotion which has urged me to write, and now moves you to read this book, renders us both happy children of this good mother, if you ever should hear any one say that I could have spared this labor, there being so many learned and celebrated books that treat of this subject, answer him, I pray you, in the words of Francone the abbot, which we find in the Library of the Fathers, that the praise of Mary is a fountain so full that the more it extends, the fuller it becomes, and the fuller it becomes the more it extends;[1] which signifies, that the blessed Virgin is so great and sublime, that the more we praise her, the more there is to praise. So that St. Augustine says: All the tongues of men, even if all their members were changed to tongues, would not be sufficient to praise her as she deserves.[2]

I know that there are innumerable books, both great and small, which treat of the glories of Mary; but as these are rare or voluminous, and not according to my plan, I have endeavored to collect in a small space, from all the authors at my command, the most select and pithy sentences of the Fathers and theologians, in order to give devout persons an opportunity, with little effort or expense, to inflame their ardor by reading of the love of Mary, and especially, to present materials to priests which may enable them to excite by their sermons devotion to the divine mother.

Worldly lovers are accustomed to mention frequently and to praise the persons beloved, that these may be praised and applauded also by others; then how poor must we suppose the love of those to be who boast of being lovers of Mary, but who seldom remember to speak of her, and inspire the love of her also in others! Not so the true lovers of our most lovely Lady: they would praise her everywhere, and see her loved by all the world; and therefore in public and in private, wherever it is in their power, they endeavor to kindle in the hearts of all, those blessed flames of love with which theirs are burning for their beloved queen.

---

1. Laus Mariæ fons est indeficiens, qui quanto amplius tenditur, tanto amplius impletur; quanto amplius impletur, tanto amplius dilatatur.
2. Etiamsi omnium nostrum membra verterentur in linguas eam laudare sufficiret nullus. Ap. B. Dion. Carth.

But that every one may be persuaded of how great benefit it is to himself and the people to promote devotion to Mary, let us hear what the Fathers say of it. St. Bonaventure declares that those who are devoted to publishing the glories of Mary, are secure of paradise; and Richard of St. Laurence confirms this by saying, that to honor the queen of angels is to acquire life everlasting;[3] since our most grateful Lady, adds the same author, pledges herself to honor in the other life him who promises to honor her in this;[4] and is there any one ignorant of the promise made by Mary herself to those who engage in promoting the knowledge and love of her upon the earth? "They that explain me shall have life everlasting,"[5] as the holy Church applies it on the festival of her Immaculate Conception. Exult, exult! oh my soul! said St. Bonaventure, who was so assiduous in proclaiming the praises of Mary, and rejoice in her, because many good things are prepared for those who praise her; and since all the Holy Scriptures, he added, speak in praise of Mary, let us endeavor always with heart and tongue to celebrate this our divine mother, that we may be conducted by her to the kingdom of the blessed.[6]

We are told in the revelations of St. Bridget, that the blessed Emingo, Bishop, being accustomed to begin his sermons with the praises of Mary, the Virgin herself appeared one day to the saint, and said to her: "Tell that prelate who is accustomed to commence his discourses with my praises, that I will be his mother, and that I will present his soul to God, and that he shall die a good death;"[7] and he indeed died like a saint, in prayer and in celestial peace. Mary appeared before his death to another religious, a Dominican, who was accustomed to terminate his sermons by speaking of her. She defended him from the assaults of the demons, comforted him, and bore away with her his happy soul.[8]

The devout Thomas à Kempis represents Mary as commending to her Son those who publish her praise, and saying, "Oh, my Son, have compassion on the souls of thy lovers, and of those who speak in my praise."[9]

As far as the advantage of the people is concerned, St. Anselm says, that the sacred womb of Mary, having been made the way of salvation for

---

3. Honorare Mariam est thesaurizare vitam ctcrnam. De Laud. v. c. 2.
4. Honorificantes se in hoc sæculo honorificabit in futuro.
5. Qui elucidant me, vitam eternam habebunt. Eccli. xxiv, 81.
6. Exulta, exulta, anima mea, et lætare in illa; quia multa bona sunt laudatoribus præparata. Si enim omnes scripturæ loquuntur de ea. Deiparam perpetuo corde et lingua celebremus, ut ab ipsa ad gaudia eterna perducamur.
7. Revel. cap. 14.
8. Ap. P. Auriem.
9. Fili miserere animæ amatoris tui et laudatoris mei. Serm. 20, ad Nov.

sinners, sinners cannot but be converted and saved by discourses in praise of Mary.[10] If the assertion is true and incontrovertible, as I believe it to be, and as I shall prove, in the fifth chapter of this book, that all graces are dispensed by the hand of Mary alone, and that all those who are saved, are saved solely by means of this divine mother; it may be said, as a necessary consequence, that the salvation of all depends upon preaching Mary, and confidence in her intercession. We know that St. Bernardine of Sienna sanctified Italy; St. Dominic converted many provinces; St. Louis Bertrand, in all his sermons, never failed to exhort his hearers to practice devotion towards Mary; and many others also have done the same.

I find that Father Paul Segneri, the younger, a celebrated missionary, in every mission preached a sermon on devotion to Mary, and this he called his favorite sermon. And we can attest, in all truth, that in our missions, where we have an invariable rule not to omit the sermon on our Lady, no discourse is so profitable to the people, or excites more compunction among them, than that on the mercy of Mary. I say *on the mercy of Mary:* for St. Bernard says, we may praise her humility, and marvel at her virginity; but being poor sinners, we are more pleased and attracted by hearing of her mercy; for to this we more affectionately cling, this we more often remember and invoke.[11] Therefore in this little book, leaving to other authors the description of the other merits of Mary, I have confined myself especially to treating of her great compassion and her powerful intercession; having collected, as far as possible, with the labor of years, all that the holy Fathers and the most celebrated authors have said of the mercy and power of Mary; and because these attributes of the blessed Virgin are wonderfully set forth in the great prayer of the *Salve Regina*, approved by the Church and required by her to be recited the greater part of the year by all the clergy, secular and regular, I have undertaken to explain in separate discourses this most devout prayer.

Devout reader, if this little work of mine pleases you, as I hope it will, I pray you to commend me to the holy Virgin, that I may obtain great confidence in her protection. Ask for me this grace, and I will ask the same for you, whoever you may be, who bestow on me this charity. Oh, blessed is he who clings with love and confidence to those two anchors of salvation,

---

10. Quomodo fieri potest ut ex memoria laudum ejus salus non proveniat peccatorum, cujus uterus facta est via ad peccatores salvandos? S. Ans. Lib. 3, de Exc. V. cap. 1.
11. Laudamus humilitatem, miramur virginitatem; sed miseris sapit dulcius misericordia; misericordiam amplectimur carius, recordamur sæpius, crebrius invocamus. Serm. 4, de Assump.

Jesus and Mary! He certainly will not be lost. Let us both say, oh my reader, with the devout Alphonso Rodriguez: Jesus and Mary, my sweet loves, for you I will suffer, for you I will die; may I be wholly yours, may I be in nothing my own.[12] May we love Jesus and Mary, and become saints, since we can aspire and hope for no greater happiness than this. Farewell, till we meet in heaven at the feet of this sweet mother and her dearly beloved Son, to praise them, to thank them, and love them, in their immediate presence through all eternity. Amen.

PRAYER TO THE BLESSED VIRGIN
TO OBTAIN A GOOD DEATH

Oh Mary, sweet refuge of miserable sinners, at the moment when my soul departs from this world, my sweetest mother, by the grief that thou didst endure when thou wast present at the death of thy Son upon the cross, then assist me with thy mercy. Keep far from me my infernal enemies, and come thyself to take my soul and present it to my eternal Judge. Do not abandon me, oh my queen. Thou, next to Jesus, must be my comfort in that dreadful moment. Entreat thy Son that in His goodness, He will grant me the favor to die clasping thy feet, and to breathe out my soul in His sacred wounds, saying, Jesus and Mary, I give you my heart and my soul.

---

12. Jesus et Maria, amores mei dulcissimi, pro vobis patiar, pro vobis moriar; sim totus vester, sim nihil meus. Ap. Auriem Aff. sc.

ON THE SALVE REGINA

It treats of the various and abundant graces which the mother of God bestows on her devoted servants, in several discourses of the Salve Regina.

Mary Help of Christians. Basilica of Maria Auxiliadora, Turin, Italy.

CHAPTER 1

Salve, Regina, Mater misericordiæ
Hail Queen, Mother of mercy

SECTION 1
Of the great confidence we should have
in Mary, because she is the Queen of Mercy

The Holy Church justly honors the great Virgin Mary, and would have her honored by all men with the glorious title of queen, because she has been elevated to the dignity of mother of the King of kings. If the Son is king, says St. Athanasius, his mother must necessarily be considered and entitled queen.[1] From the moment that Mary consented, adds St. Bernardine of Sienna, to become the mother of the Eternal Word, she merited the title of queen of the world and all creatures.[2] If the flesh of Mary, says St. Arnold, abbot, was the flesh of Jesus, how can the mother be separated from the Son in his kingdom? Hence it follows that the regal glory must not only be considered as common to the mother and the Son, but even the same.[3]

If Jesus is the king of the whole world, Mary is also queen of the whole world:[4] therefore, says St. Bernardine of Sienna, all creatures who serve God ought also to serve Mary; for all angels and men, and all things that are in heaven and on earth being subject to the dominion of God, are also subject to the dominion of the glorious Virgin.[5] Hence Guerric, abbot, thus addresses the divine mother: Continue, Mary, continue in security to reign; dispose, according to thy will, of every thing belonging to thy Son, for thou, being mother and spouse of the King of the world, the kingdom and power over all creatures is due to thee as queen.[6]

Mary, then, is queen; but let all learn for their consolation that she is

---

1. Si ipse Rex est qui natus est de Virgine, mater, quæ eum genuit, Regina et Domina proprie ac vere censetur. Serm. de Deip.
2. Iunc autem Virgo in illo consensu meruit primatum orbis, dominum mundi, sceptrum regni super omnes creaturas. Tom. 2. cap. 51.
3. Neque a dominatione filii Mater potest esse sejuncta, una est Mariæ et Christi caro. Filii gloriam cum Matre, non tam communem judico, quam eamdem. S. Arnol. de Laud. Virg.
4. Regina constituta, totum jure possidet filii regnum. Rupert, abb.
5. Tot creaturæ serviunt gloriosæ Virgini, quot serviunt Trinitati; omnes namque creaturæ sive angeli, sive homines, et omnia quæ sunt in cœlo et in terra, quia omnia sunt divino imperio subjecta, gloriosæ Virgini sunt subjectæ. Tom. 2, cap. 61.
6. Perge Maria, perge secura in bonis filii tui; fiducialite age tamquam regina, mater regis et sponsa; tibi debetur regnum et potestas.

a mild and merciful queen, desiring the good of us poor sinners. Hence the holy Church bids us salute her in this prayer, and name her the *Queen of Mercy*. The very name of queen signifies, as blessed Albertus Magnus remarks, compassion, and provision for the poor; differing in this from the title of empress, which signifies severity and rigor. The greatness of kings and queens consists in comforting the wretched as Seneca says.[7] So that whereas tyrants, in reigning, have only their own advantage in view, kings should have for their object the good of their subjects. Therefore at the consecration of kings their heads are anointed with oil, which is the symbol of mercy, to denote that they, in reigning, should above all things cherish thoughts of kindness and beneficence towards their subjects.

Kings should then principally occupy themselves with works of mercy, but not to the neglect of the exercise of justice towards the guilty, when it is required. Not so Mary, who, although queen, is not queen of justice, intent upon the punishment of the guilty, but queen of mercy, solely intent upon compassion and pardon for sinners. Accordingly, the Church requires us explicitly to call her queen of mercy. The High Chancellor of Paris, John Gerson, meditating on the words of David, "These two things have I heard, that power belongeth to God, and mercy to thee, O Lord,"[8] says, that the kingdom of God consisting of justice and mercy, the Lord has divided it: he has reserved the kingdom of justice for himself, and he has granted the kingdom of mercy to Mary, ordaining that all the mercies which are dispensed to men should pass through the hands of Mary, and should be bestowed according to her good pleasure.[9] St. Thomas confirms this in his preface to the Canonical Epistles, saying that the holy Virgin, when she conceived the divine Word in her womb, and brought him forth, obtained the half of the kingdom of God by becoming queen of mercy, Jesus Christ remaining king of justice.[10]

The eternal Father constituted Jesus Christ king of justice, and therefore made him the universal judge of the world; hence the prophet sang: "Give to the king thy judgment, Oh God; and to the king's son thy justice."[11] Here a learned interpreter takes up the subject and says: Oh Lord, thou hast given to thy Son thy justice, because thou hast given to the mother

---

7. Hoc reges habent magnificum, prodesse miseris.
8. Duo hæc audivi, quia potestas Dei est, et tibi, Domine, misericordia. Psal. lxi. 12.
9. Regnum Dei consistit in potestate et misericordia; potestate Deo remanente, cessit quodammo-do misericordiæ pars matri regnanti. Psal. iii. Tr. 4, S. Magn.
10. Quando filium Dei in utero concepit, et post modum peperit, dimidiam partem regni Dei impe-travit, ut ipsa sit regina misericordiæ, ut Christus est rex justitiæ.
11. Deus judicium tuum regi da; et justitiam tuam filio regis. Psal. lxxi. 2.

of the king thy mercy.[12] And St. Bonaventure happily varies the passage above quoted by saying: Give to the king thy judgment, Oh God, and to his mother thy mercy.[13] Ernest, Archbishop of Prague, also says that the eternal Father has given to the Son the office of judging and punishing, and to the mother the office of compassionating and relieving the wretched.[14] Therefore the Prophet David predicted that God himself, if I may thus express it, would consecrate Mary queen of mercy, anointing her with the oil of gladness,[15] in order that all of us miserable children of Adam might rejoice in the thought of having in heaven that great queen, so full of the unction of mercy and pity for us; as St. Bonaventure says: Oh Mary, so full of the unction of mercy and the oil of pity, that God has anointed thee with the oil of gladness![16]

And how well does blessed Albertus Magnus here apply the history of Queen Esther, who was indeed a type of Our Queen Mary! We read in the fourth chapter of the Book of Esther, that in the reign of King Assuerus, there went forth, throughout his kingdom, a decree commanding the death of all the Jews. Then Mardochai, who was one of the condemned, committed their cause to Esther that she might intercede with the king to obtain the revocation of the sentence. At first Esther refused to take upon herself this office, fearing that it would excite the anger of the king more. But Mardochai rebuked her, and bade her remember that she must not think of saving herself alone, as the Lord had placed her upon the throne to obtain salvation for all the Jews: "Think not that thou mayest save thy life only, because thou art in the king's house, more than all the Jews."[17] Thus said Mardochai to Queen Esther, and thus might we poor sinners say to our Queen Mary, if she were ever reluctant to intercede with God for our deliverance from the just punishment of our sins. Think not that thou mayest save thy life only, because thou art in the king's house, more than all men. Think not, oh Lady, that God has exalted thee to be queen of the world, only to secure thy own welfare; but also that thou, being so greatly elevated, mayest the more compassionate and the better relieve us misera-

---

12. Quia misericordiam tuam dedisti Matri Regis.
13. Deus judicium tuum regi da, et misericordiam tuam matri ejus.
14. Pater omne judicium dedit filio, et omne officium misericordiæ dedit matri.
15. Unxit te Deus oleo lætitiæ. Psal. xliv. 8.
16. Maria, plena unctione misericordiæ et oleo pietatis; propterea unxit te Deus oleo lætitiæ. In spec. cap. 7.
17. Ne putes quod animam tuam tantun liberes, quia in domo regis es præ cunctis Judæis. Esth. iv. 15.

ble sinners. Assuerus, when he saw Esther before him, affectionately inquired of her what she had come to ask of him: "What is thy petition?" Then the queen answered, "If I have found favor in thy sight, oh king, give me my people for which I request."[18] Assuerus heard her, and immediately ordered the sentence to be revoked. Now, if Assuerus granted to Esther, because he loved her, the salvation of the Jews, will not God graciously listen to Mary, in his boundless love for her, when she prays to him for those poor sinners who recommend themselves to her and says to him: If I have found favor in thy sight, oh King, my King and my God, if I have ever found favor with Thee (and well does the divine mother know herself to be the blessed, the fortunate, the only one of the children of men who found the grace lost by man; she knows herself to be the beloved of her Lord, more beloved than all the saints and angels united), give me my people for which I request: if thou lovest me, she says to him, give me, oh my Lord, these sinners in whose behalf I entreat Thee. Is it possible that God will not graciously hear her? Is there any one who does not know the power of Mary's prayers with God? The law of clemency is on her tongue.[19] Every prayer of hers is as a law established by our Lord, that mercy shall be exercised towards those for whom Mary intercedes. St. Bernard asks, why does the Church name Mary *Queen of Mercy*? and answers, Because we believe that she opens the depths of the mercy of God, to whom she will, when she will, and as she will; so that not even the vilest sinner is lost, if Mary protects him.[20]

But it may, perhaps, be feared that Mary disdains interposing in behalf of some sinners, because she finds them so laden with sins? Perhaps the majesty and sanctity of this great queen should alarm us? No, says St. Gregory, in proportion to her greatness and holiness are her clemency and mercy towards sinners who desire to amend, and who have recourse to her.[21] Kings and queens inspire terror by the display of their majesty, and their subjects fear to enter their presence; but what fear, says St. Bernard, can the wretched have of going to this queen of mercy since she never shows herself terrible or austere to those who seek her, but all sweetness

18. Quæ est petitio tua? Si inveni gratiam in oculis tuis o rex, dona mihi populum meum, pro quo obsecro.
19. Lex clementiæ in lingua ejus. Prov. xxxi. 26.
20. Quod divinæ pietatis abyssum cui vult, quando vult et quomodo vult, creditur aperire; ut nemo tam enormis peccator pereat, cui sancta sanctorum pratrocinii suffragia præstat. In Salve Regina.
21. Maria quanto altior et sanctior, tanto clementior et dulcior circa conversos peccatores. Lib. 1, ep. 47.

and kindness?[22] Mary not only gives, but she herself presents to us milk and wool: the milk of mercy to inspire us with confidence, and wool to shield us from the thunderbolts of divine justice!

Suetonius narrates of the Emperor Titus, that he never could refuse a favor to any one who asked it, and that he even sometimes promised more than he could perform; and he answered to one who admonished him of this, that a prince should not dismiss any one from his presence dissatisfied. Titus said this, but, in reality, was perhaps often either guilty of falsehood, or failed in his promises. But our queen cannot lie, and can obtain whatever she wishes for her devoted servants. She has a heart so kind and compassionate, says Blosius, that she cannot send away dissatisfied any one who invokes her aid.[23] But, as St. Bernard says, how couldst thou, oh Mary, refuse succor to the wretched, when thou art queen of mercy? And who are the subjects of mercy, if not the miserable? Thou art the queen of mercy, and I the most miserable of all sinners; if I, then, am the first of thy subjects, then thou shouldst have more care of me than of all others.[24]

Have pity on us, then, oh queen of mercy, and give heed to our salvation; neither say to us, oh most holy Virgin, as St. Gregory of Nicomedia would add, that thou canst not aid us because of the multitude of our sins, when thou hast such power and pity that no number of sins can ever surpass it! Nothing resists thy power, since thy Creator and ours, while he honors thee as his mother, considers thy glory as his own, and exulting in it, as a Son, grants thy petitions as if he were discharging an obligation.[25] By this he means to say, that though Mary is under an infinite obligation to her Son for having elected her to be his mother yet it cannot be denied that the Son also is greatly indebted to his mother for having given him his human nature; whence Jesus, as if to recompense Mary as he ought, while he enjoys this his glory, honors her especially by always graciously listening to her prayers.

How great then should be our confidence in this queen, knowing how powerful she is with God and at the same time how rich and full of mercy; so much so that there is no one on earth who does not share in the mercies

---

22. Quid ad Mariam accedere trepidat humana fragilitas? Nihil austerum in ea, nihil terribile; tota suavis est, omnibus offerens lac et lanam. Super Sign. Magn.
23. Ita benigna est, ut neminem tristem redire sinat. Lib. 4, c. 12.
24. Tu es regina misericordiæ, et ego miserrimus peccator, subditorum maximus. Rege nos ergo, o regina misericordiæ. In Salv. Reg.
25. Habes vires insuperabiles, ne clementiam tuam superet multitudo peccatorum. Nihil tuæ resistet potentiæ; tuam enim gloriam creator existimat esse propriam, et filius in ea exultans, quasi exsolvens debitum, implet petitiones tuas. Or. de exitu B. V.

and favors of Mary! This the blessed Virgin herself revealed to St. Bridget: "I am," she said to her, "the queen of heaven and the mother of mercy; I am the joy of the just, and the gate of entrance for sinners to God; neither is there living on earth a sinner who is so accursed that he is deprived of my compassion; for everyone, if he receives nothing else through my intercession, receives the grace of being less tempted by evil spirits than he otherwise would be; no one, therefore," she added, "who is not entirely accursed" (by which is meant the final and irrevocable malediction pronounced against the damned), "is so entirely cast off by God that he may not return and enjoy his mercy if he invokes my aid. I am called by all the mother of mercy, and truly the mercy of God towards men has made me so merciful towards them." And then she concluded by saying, "Therefore he shall be miserable, and forever miserable in another life, who in this, being able, does not have recourse to me, who am so compassionate to all, and so earnestly desire to aid sinners."[26]

Let us then have recourse, let us always have recourse to this most sweet queen, if we would be sure of our salvation; and if the sight of our sins terrifies and disheartens us, let us remember that Mary was made queen of mercy for this very end, that she might save by her protection the greatest and most abandoned sinners who have recourse to her. They are to be her crown in heaven, as her divine spouse has said: "Come from Lebanon, my spouse, come from Lebanon, come; thou shalt be crowned from the dens of the lions, from the mountains of the leopards."[27] And what are these dens of wild beasts and monsters, if not miserable sinners, whose souls become dens of sins, the most deformed monsters? Now, by these same sinners, as Rupert, the abbot, remarks, who are saved by thy means, oh great Queen Mary, thou wilt be crowned in heaven; for their salvation will be thy crown, a crown indeed worthy and fit for a queen of mercy;[28] and let the following example illustrate this.

---

26. Ego regina cœli; ego mater misericordiæ; ego justorum gaudium et aditus peccatorum ad Deum. Nullus est adeo maledictus, qui quamdiu vivit careat misericordia mea; quia propter ne levius tentatur a dæmonibus, quam alias tentaretur. Nullus est ita abjectus a Deo, nisi fuerit omnino maledictus, qui si me invocaverit, non revertatur ad Deum, et habiturus, sit misericordiam. Ego vocor ab omnibus mater misericordiæ, et vere misericordia illius misericordem me fecit. Ideo miser erit qui ad misericordem, cum possit, non accedit. Rev. Lib. 1, cap. 6.
27. Veni de Libano, sponsa mea, veni de Libano, veni; coronaberis ... de cubilibus leonum, de montibus pardorum. Cant. 4, 8.
28. De talium leonem cubiculis tu coronaberis. Eorum salus corona tua erit. Rup. Vid. l. 3., in Cant.

EXAMPLE

We read in the life of sister Catherine, an Augustinian nun, that in the place where that servant of God lived, there lived also a woman named Mary, who, in her youth, was a sinner, and obstinately persevered in her evil courses, even to extreme old age. For this she was banished by her fellow-citizens, forced to live in a cave beyond the limits of the place, and died in a state of loathsome corruption, abandoncd by all, and without the sacraments; and on this account was buried in a field, like a beast. Now sister Catherine, who was accustomed to recommend very affectionately to God the souls of those who had departed this life, after learning the miserable death of this poor old woman, did not think of praying for her, as she and every one else believed her already among the damned. Four years having past, a soul from purgatory one day appeared to her, and said, "Sister Catherine, how unhappy is my fate! you commend to God the souls of all those who die, and for my soul alone you have had no pity." "And who are you?" said the servant of God. "I am," answered she, "that poor Mary who died in the cave." "How! are you saved?" exclaimed sister Catherine. "Yes, I am saved," she said, "by the mercy of the Virgin Mary." "And how?" "When I saw death drawing near, finding myself laden with sins, and abandoned by all, I turned to the mother of God and said to her, Lady, thou art the refuge of the abandoned, behold me at this hour deserted by all; thou art my only hope, thou alone canst help me; have pity on me. The holy Virgin obtained for me the grace of making an act of contrition; I died and am saved, and my queen has also obtained for me the grace that my pains should be abridged, and that I should, by suffering intensely for a short time, pass through that purification which otherwise would have lasted many years. A few masses only are needed to obtain my release from purgatory. I pray thee cause them to be offered for me, and I promise to pray God and Mary for thee." Sister Catherine immediately caused those masses to be said for her, and that soul, after a few days, appeared to her again, more brilliant than the sun, and said to her, "I thank thee, sister Catherine: behold I am now going to paradise to sing the mercy of God and pray for thee."

PRAYER

Oh Mother of my God and my Lady Mary, as a poor wounded and loath-some wretch presents himself to a great queen, I present myself to thee, who art the queen of heaven and earth. From the lofty throne on which thou art seated, do not disdain, I pray thee, to cast thy eye upon me, a poor sinner. God hath made thee so rich in order that thou mayest succor the needy, and hath made thee queen of mercy that thou mayest help the miserable, look upon me, then, and have pity on me. Look upon me, and do not leave me until thou hast changed me from a sinner into a saint. I see I merit nothing, or rather I merit for my ingratitude to be deprived of all the graces which, by thy means, I have received from the Lord. But thou, who art the mother of mercy, dost not require merits, but miseries, that thou mayest succor those who are in need; and who is more poor and more needy than I?

Oh glorious Virgin, I know that thou, being queen of the universe, art also my queen; and I, in a more especial manner, would dedicate myself to thy service; that thou mayest dispose of me as seemeth best to thee. There-fore I say to thee with St. Bonaventure, Oh, Lady, I submit myself to thy control, that thou mayest rule and govern me entirely. Do not leave me to myself.[29] Rule me, oh my queen, and do not leave me to myself. Command me, employ me as thou wilt, and punish me if I do not obey thee, for very salutary will be the punishments that come from thy hand. I would esteem it a greater thing to be thy servant than Lord of the whole earth. *Thine I am, save me!*[30] Accept me, oh Mary, for thy own and attend to my salvation, as I am thine own. I no longer will be my own, I give myself to thee. And if hitherto I have so poorly served thee, having lost so many good occasions of honoring thee, for the time to come I will unite myself to thy most loving and most faithful servants. No one from this time henceforth shall surpass me in honoring and loving thee, my most lovely queen. This I promise, and I hope to perform with thy assistance. Amen.

---

29. Domina, me tuæ dominationi volo committere ut me plenarie regas et gubernes. Non mihi me relinquas.
30. Tuus sum ego, salvum me fac.

SECTION 2
How much greater should be our
confidence in Mary, because she is our Mother

Not by chance, nor in vain, do the servants of Mary call her mother, and it would seem that they cannot invoke her by any other name, and are never weary of calling her mother; mother, indeed, for she is truly our mother, not according to the flesh, but the spiritual mother of our souls and of our salvation. Sin, when it deprived our souls of divine grace, also deprived them of life. Hence, when they were dead in misery and sin, Jesus our Redeemer came with an excess of mercy and love to restore to us, by his death upon the cross, that lost life, as he has himself declared: "I am come that they may have life, and may have it more abundantly."[31] *More abundantly*, because, as the theologians teach us, Jesus Christ by his redemption brought us blessings greater than the injury Adam inflicted upon us by his sin; he reconciled us to God, and thus became the father of our souls, under the new law of grace, as the prophet Isaiah predicted: "The Father of the world to come, the Prince of peace."[32] But if Jesus is the father of our souls, Mary is the mother; for, in giving us Jesus, she gave us the true life; and offering upon Calvary the life of her Son for our salvation, she then brought us forth to the life of divine grace.

At two different times, then as the holy Fathers show us, Mary became our spiritual mother; the first when she was found worthy of conceiving in her virginal womb the Son of God, as the blessed Albertus Magnus says.

St. Bernardine of Sienna more distinctly teaches us that when the most holy Virgin, on the annunciation of the angel, gave her consent to become mother of the eternal Word, which he awaited before making himself her Son, she by this consent even from that time demanded of God, with lively affection, our salvation; and she was so earnestly engaged in obtaining it, that from that time she has borne us, as it were, in her womb, as a most loving mother.[33]

St. Luke says, speaking of the birth of our Savior, that Mary "brought forth her first-born son."[34] Therefore, says a certain writer, if the evangelist affirms

---

31. Veni, ut vitam habeant et abundantius habeant. Joan. x. 10.
32. Pater futuri sæculi, princeps pacis. Isa. ix. 6.
33. Virgo per hunc consensum in incarnatione filii omnium salutem vigorosissime expetiit et procuravit; et omnium salvationi per hunc consensum se dedicavit, ita ut ex tunc omnes in suis visceribus bajulat, tanquam verissima mater filios suos. Tr. de B. V. serm. 6.
34. Peperit filium suum primogenitum. Luc. cap. ii. 7.

that Mary brought forth her first-born, is it to be supposed that she afterwards had other children? But the same author adds: if it is of faith that
Mary had no other children according to the flesh except Jesus, then she
must have other spiritual children, and these we are.[35] Our Lord revealed
this to St. Gertrude, who, reading one day the passage of the Gospel just
quoted, was troubled, not knowing how to understand it, that Mary being
mother of Jesus Christ alone, it could be said that he was her first-born. And
God explained it to her, by telling her that Jesus was her first-born according
to the flesh, but men were her second-born according to the spirit.

And this explains what is said of Mary in the holy Canticles: "Thy belly
is as a heap of wheat, set about with lilies."[36] St. Ambrose explains this
and says: Although in the pure womb of Mary there was only one grain of
wheat, which was Jesus Christ, yet it is called a heap of grain, because in
that one grain were contained all the elect, of whom Mary was to be the
mother.[37] Hence, William the Abbot wrote, Mary, in bringing forth Jesus,
who is our Savior and our life, brought forth all of us to life and salvation.[38]

The second time in which Mary brought us forth to grace was, when on
Calvary, she offered to the eternal Father with so much sorrow of heart the
life of her beloved Son for our salvation. Wherefore, St. Augustine asserts,
that, having then co-operated by her love with Christ in the birth of the
faithful to the life of grace, she became also by this co-operation the spiritual mother of us all, who are members of our head, Jesus Christ.[39] This is also
the meaning of what is said of the blessed Virgin in the sacred Canticles:
"They have made me the keeper in the vineyards; my vineyard I have not
kept."[40] Mary, to save our souls, was willing to sacrifice the life of her Son,[41]
as William the Abbot remarks. And who was the soul of Mary, but her Jesus,
who was her life and all her love? Wherefore St. Simeon announced to her
that her soul would one day be pierced by a sword of sorrow;[42] which was

35. Si primogenitus, ergo alii filii secuti sunt secundogeniti? Carnales nullos habet B. Virgo, præter
    Christum; ergo spirituales habeat necesse est.
36. Venter tuus sicut acervus tritici, vallatus liliis. Cant. vii. 2.
37. Unum granum frumenti fuit in utero Virginis, Christus Dominus; et tamen acervus tritici dic-
    itur, quia granum hoc virtute omnes electos continet, ut ipse sit primogenitus in multis fratri-
    bus. De Instit.Virg.
38. In illo uno fructu, in uno salvatore omnium Jesu plurimos Maria peperit ad salutem. Pariendo
    vitam, multos peperit ad vitam. In Cant. iv. 13.
39. Illa spiritu mater est membrorum salvatoris, quia cooperata est charitate, ut fideles in ecclesia
    nascerentur. De Virg. cap. 6.
40. Posuit me custodem in vineis; vineam meam non custodivi. Cant. l. 5.
41. Ut multas animas salvas faceret, animam suam morti exposuit.
42. Et tuam ipsius animam doloris gladius pertransibit. Luc. ii. 35.

the very spear that pierced the side of Jesus, who was the soul of Mary. And then she in her sorrow brought us forth to eternal life; so that we may all call ourselves children of the dolors of Mary. She, our most loving mother, was always and wholly united to the divine will; whence St. Bonaventure remarks, that when she saw the love of the eternal Father for men, who would have his Son die for our salvation, and the love of the Son in wishing to die for us, she too, with her whole will, offered her Son and consented that he should die that we might be saved, in order to conform herself to that exceeding love of the Father and Son for the human race.[43]

It is true that, in dying for the redemption of the world, Jesus wished to be alone. I have trodden the wine-press alone,[44] "Torcular calcavi solus." But when God saw the great desire of Mary to devote herself also to the salvation of men, he ordained that by the sacrifice and offering of the life of this same Jesus, she might co-operate with him in the work of our salvation, and thus become mother of our souls. And this our Savior signified, when, before expiring, he saw from the cross his mother and the disciple St. John both standing near him, and first spoke to Mary: Behold thy son, "Ecce filius tuus;"[45] as if he said to her: Behold the man who, by the offering thou hast made of my life for his salvation, is already born to grace. And then turning to the disciple, he said: Behold thy mother, "Ecce mater tua."[46] By which words, says St. Bernardine of Sienna, Mary was then made mother not only of St. John, but of all men, for the love she bore them.[47] On this account, as Silveira observes, St. John himself, when recording this fact in his Gospel, wrote, "After that he said to the disciple: 'Behold thy mother.'"[48] Let it be remarked that Jesus Christ did not say this to John, but to the disciple, to signify that the Savior appointed Mary for common mother of all those who, being Christians, bear the name of his disciples.[49]

I am the mother of fair love,[50] "Ego sum mater pulchræ dilectionis," said Mary; because her love, as an author remarks, which renders the souls of men beautiful in the eye of God, prompts her, as a loving mother, to receive us for her children.[51] And as a mother loves her children, and watches over

---

43. Nullo modo dubitandum est, quia Mariæ animus volut etiam tradere filium suum pro salute generis humani, ut mater per omnia conformis fieret Patri et Filio.
44. Isa. lxiii. 3.
45. Joan. xix. 26.
46. Deinde dicit discipulo: Ecce mater tua. Joan. xix. 27.
47. In Joanne intelligimus omnes, quorum B. Virgo per dilectionem facta est mater. Tom. 1, Serm. 55.
48. Deinde dicit discipulo: Ecce mater tua. Joan. xix. 27.
49. Joanne est nomen particulare, discipulus commune, ut denotatur quod Maria omnibus detur in matrem.
50. Ego sum mater pulchræ dilectionis. Eccli. xxiv. 24.
51. Quia tota es amor erga nos, quos in filios recepit. Paciucch. de B. V.

their welfare, so thou, oh our most sweet queen, lovest us, and dost procure our happiness, says St. Bonaventure.[52]

Oh, happy those who live under the protection of a mother so loving and so powerful! The prophet David, although Mary was not yet born, besought of God salvation, by dedicating himself to Mary as her son, and thus prayed: "Save the son of thy handmaid."[53] "Whose handmaid?" asks St. Augustine,[54] "she who says: Behold the handmaid of the Lord."[55] And who, says Cardinal Bellarmine, who would dare to snatch these children from the bosom of Mary, where they have taken refuge from their enemies? What fury of hell or of passion can conquer them, if they place their trust in the protection of this great mother?[56] It is narrated of the whale, that when she sees her young in peril, from the tempest or their pursuers, she opens her mouth and receives them into her bowels. Just so, says Novarino, does this compassionate mother of the faithful, when the tempest of the passions is raging. She then, with maternal affection, protects them as it were in her bowels, and continues to shelter them until she has placed them in the secure haven of paradise.[57] Oh, most loving mother! Oh, most compassionate mother, be ever blessed! and may that God be ever blessed, who has given us thee as a mother, and as a secure refuge in all the dangers of this life. The blessed Virgin herself revealed this to St. Bridget, saying: "As a mother who sees her son exposed to the sword of the enemy, makes every effort to save him, thus do I, and will I ever do for my children, sinful though they be, if they come to me for help."[58] Behold, then, how in every battle with hell we shall always conquer, and certainly conquer, if we have recourse to the mother of God and our mother, always repeating: "We fly to thy protection, oh holy mother of God; we fly to thy protection, oh holy mother of God."[59] Oh, how many victories have the faithful obtained over hell, by having recourse to Mary with this short but powerful prayer! That great servant of God, Sister Mary of the Crucifixion, a Benedictine nun, by this means always conquered the evil spirits.

---

52. Nonne plus sine comparatione nos diligis, ac bona nostra procuras, quam mater carnalis?
53. Salvum fac filium ancillæ tuæ. Psal. lxxxv. 16.
54. Cujus ancillæ?
55. Quæ dit; Ecce ancilla Domini. In Psal. lxxxv.
56. Quam bene nobis erit sub præsidio tantæ matris? Quis detrahere audebit de sinu ejus? Quæ nos tentatio, aut turbatio superare poterit confidantes in patrocinio matris Dei et nostræ? Bell., de sept verb.
57. Fidelium piissima mater, furente tentationum tempestate, materno affectu eos, velut intra viscera propria receptos protegit, donec in beatum portum reponat. V. cap. 14, exc. 81.
58. Ita ego facio, et faciam omnibus peccatoribus misericordiam meam potentibus. Lib. 4, c. 38.
59. Sub tuum præsidium confugimus, sancta Dei genetrix.

Be joyful then, all ye children of Mary; remember that she adopts as her children all those who wish her for their mother. Joyful; for what fear have you of being lost when this mother defends and protects you? Thus says St. Bonaventure: Every one who loves this good mother and trusts in her protection should take courage and repeat: What do you fear, oh my soul? The cause of thy eternal salvation will not be lost, as the final sentence depends upon Jesus, who is thy brother, and upon Mary who is thy mother.[60] And St. Anselm, full of joy at this thought, exclaims, in order to encourage us: Oh, blessed confidence! Oh, secure refuge! The mother of God is my mother also. With what certainty may we hope, since our salvation depends upon the sentence of a good brother and of a kind mother![61] Hear, then, our mother who calls us, and says to us; "Whosoever is a little one, let him come to me."[62] Little children have always on their lips the word mother, and in all the dangers to which they are exposed, and in all their fears, they cry mother, Ah, most sweet Mary! Ah, most loving mother! this is exactly what thou dost desire; that we become little children, and always call upon thee in our dangers, and always have recourse to thee, for thou wishest to aid and save us, as thou hast saved all thy children who have had recourse to thee.

EXAMPLE

In the history of the foundations of the Company of Jesus, in the kingdom of Naples, is related the following story of a noble youth of Scotland, named William Elphinstone. He was a relation of King James. Born a heretic, he followed the false sect to which he belonged; but enlightened by divine grace, which showed him his errors, he went to France, where, with the assistance of a good Jesuit father, who was like himself a Scotchman, and still more by the intercession of the blessed Virgin, he at length saw the truth, abjured heresy, and became a Catholic. He went afterwards to Rome, where a friend of his found him one day very much afflicted, and weeping. He asked him the cause, and he answered, that in the night his

---

60. Dic, anima mea, cum magna fiducia: Exultabo et lætabor, quia quicquid judicabitur de me pendet ex sententia fratris et matris meæ.
61. O beata fiducia, O tutum refugium! Mater Dei est mater mea. Qua certitudine igitur debemus sperare, quoniam salus de boni fratris et piæ matris pendet arbitrio! In Depr. ad. V.
62. Si quis est parvulus, veniat ad me. Prov. ix. 4.

mother had appeared to him and said: "My son, it is well for thee that thou hast entered the true Church; I am already lost, because I died in heresy." From that time he became more fervent in his devotion to Mary, chose her for his mother, and by her was inspired to become a religious. He made a vow to do so, but being ill, he went to Naples to restore his health by a change of air. But the Lord ordered it so that he should die in Naples, and die a religious; for, having become dangerously ill soon after his arrival there, he by prayers and tears obtained from the superiors admittance, and when about receiving the viaticum, he made his vows in presence of the blessed sacrament, and was enrolled in the society. After this, in the tenderness of his feelings, he gave thanks to his mother Mary for having rescued him from heresy, and brought him to die in the true Church, and in a religious house in the midst of his brethren. Therefore, he exclaimed: "Oh! how glorious it is to die in the midst of so many angels!" Being exhorted to take a little rest, he answered: "Ah, this is not the time to rest when the end of my life is drawing near." Before dying, he said to the persons present: "Brethren, do you not see the angels of heaven around me?" One of the religious having heard him murmuring something to himself, asked him what he had said. He answered, that his angel-guardian had revealed to him that he should be in purgatory but a short time, and would soon enter paradise. Then he began again to talk with his sweet mother Mary, and repeating the word, mother, mother, he tranquilly expired, like a child falling asleep in the arms of its mother. Soon after, it was revealed to a devout religious that he had already entered paradise.

PRAYER

Oh, my most holy mother, how is it possible that, having so holy a mother, I should be so wicked? A mother so inflamed with love to God, and that I should so love creatures? A mother so rich in virtue, and that I should be so poor? Oh, my most amiable mother! I no longer deserve, it is true, to be thy son, because by my bad life I have rendered myself unworthy. I am content if thou wilt accept me as thy servant. I am ready to renounce all the kingdoms of the earth, to be admitted among the lowest of thy servants. Yes, I am content, but do not forbid me to call thee my mother. This name wholly consoles me, melts me, and reminds me of my obligation to love thee. This name encourages me to confide in thee. When I am the most terrified at the thought of my sins and of the divine justice, I feel myself comforted by the remembrance that thou art my mother. Permit me, then, to call thee my mother, my sweetest mother. Thus I call thee, and thus I will ever call thee. Thou, next to God, shalt always be my hope, my refuge, and my love, in this valley of tears. And thus I hope to die, commending my soul, at the last moment, into thy sacred hands, saying: "My mother, my mother Mary, help me, have pity on me." Amen.

SECTION 3
How great is the love of our Mother for us

If, then, Mary is our mother, let us consider how much she loves us. The love of parents for their children is a necessary love, and for this reason, as St. Thomas observes,[63] children are commanded in the divine law to love their parents; but there is no command, on the other hand, given to parents to love their children, for love towards one's own offspring is a love so deeply planted in the heart by nature herself, that even the wild beasts, as St. Ambrose says, never fail to love their young.[64] It is said that even tigers, hearing the cry of their whelps when they are taken by the hunters, will plunge into the sea to swim after the vessels where they are confined. If, then, says our most loving mother Mary, even tigers cannot forget their young, how can I forget to love you, my children? And, she adds, even if it should happen that a mother could forget her child, it is not possible that I can forget a soul which is my child.[65]

Mary is our mother, not according to the flesh, but by love: "I am the mother of fair love."[66] Hence she becomes our mother only on account of the love she bears us; and she glories, says a certain author, in being the mother of love; because, having taken us for her children, she is all love towards us.[67] Who can describe the love of Mary for us miserable creatures? Arnold of Carnotensis says that, at the death of Jesus Christ, she ardently desired

---

63. Opusc. 60, cap. 4.
64. Natura hoc bestiis infundit, ut catulos parvulos ament. Lib. 6, Exa. c. 4.
65. Nunquid oblivisci potest mulier infantem suum, ut non misereatur filio uteri sui? Et si illa oblita fuerit ego tamen non obliviscar tui. Isa. xlix. 15.
66. Ego mater pulchræ dilectionis. Eccl. xxiv. 24.
67. Se dilectionis esse matrem gloriatur, quia tota est amor erga nos, quos in filios recepit. Paciucch.

to die with her Son for our sake.[68] So that, as St. Ambrose adds, when her Son hung dying on the cross, Mary offered herself to his murderers, that she might give her life for us.[69]

But let us consider the reasons of this love, for thus we shall better understand how this good mother loves us. The first reason of the great love that Mary bears to men, is the great love she bears to God. Love to God and man is contained in the same precept, as St. John has written: "This commandment we have from God, that he who loveth God, love also his brother;"[70] so that one increases as the other increases. Hence what have the saints not done for love of the neighbor, because they have loved God so much? They have gone so far as to expose and lose liberty and even life for his salvation. Let us read what St. Francis Xavier did in India, where, for the sake of the souls of those barbarians, he climbed mountains, and exposed himself to innumerable dangers to find those wretched beings, in the caverns where they dwelt like wild beasts, and to lead them to God. St. Francis de Sales, to convert the heretics of the province of Chablais, risked his life by crossing a river every day for a year, on his hands and knees, upon a frozen beam, that he might go to the other side to preach to those stubborn men. St. Paulinus became a slave, to obtain liberty for the son of a poor widow. St. Fidelis, to bring the heretics of a certain place back to God, willingly consented, in preaching to them, to lose his life. The saints, then, because they have loved God so much, have done much for love of the neighbor. But who has loved God more than Mary? She loved God more, in the first moment of her life, than all the saints and angels have loved him in the whole course of theirs; as we shall consider at length, when we speak of the virtues of Mary. She herself revealed to sister Mary of the Crucifixion,[71] that the fire of love with which she burned for God was so great, that it would in a moment inflame heaven and earth; and that, in comparison to it, all the flames of the burning love of the seraphim were as cool breezes. Therefore, as there is none among the blessed spirits who loves God more than Mary; so there is, and can be none, except God, who loves us more than this our most loving mother. If the love of all mothers for their children, of all husbands for their wives, and of all saints and

68. Flagrabat Virgo æstuante charitate incensa, ut pro humani generis salute simul cum prole pro-
    funderet vitam. Tract de. Verb. Dom.
69. Pendebat in cruce filius, mater persecutoribus se offerebat. De Inst. Virg. c. 7.
70. Hoc mandatum habemus a Deo, ut qui diligit Deum, diligat et fratrem suum. 1 Joan. iv. 21.
71. Vita, Lib. 2, cap. 5.

angels for their devoted servants, were united, it would not be so great as the love that Mary bears to one soul alone. Father Nierembergh says that the love which all mothers have borne to their children is a shadow when compared with the love which Mary bears to any one of us. Truly she alone loves us more, he adds, than all the angels and saints united.

Moreover, our mother loves us much, because we have been commended to her as children by her beloved Jesus, when, before expiring, he said to her: "Woman, behold thy son;"[72] signifying by the person of John, all men, as we have before remarked. These were the last words of her Son to her. The last remembrances left by beloved friends at the moment of their death are greatly valued, and the memory of them is never lost. Moreover, we are children extremely dear to Mary, because we cost her so much suffering. Those children are much dearer to a mother whose lives she has preserved;—we are those children, for whom, that we may have the life of grace, Mary suffered the pain of sacrificing the dear life of her Jesus; submitting, for our sake, to see him die before her eyes in cruel torments. By this great offering of Mary we were then born to the life of divine grace. So, then, we are children very dear to her, because we were redeemed at such a cost of suffering. Accordingly, as we read of the love which the eternal Father has manifested for men by giving his own Son to death for us, "God so loved the world as to give his only-begotten Son,"[73] as St. Bonaventure remarks, it may be said of Mary also, that she so loved us as to give her only-begotten Son.[74] And when did she give him to us? She gave him to us, says Father Nierembergh, when first she consented to his death; she gave him to us, when others deserted him through hatred or through fear, and she alone could have defended, before the judges, the life of her Son. We can easily believe that the words of so wise and tender a mother would have had a great power, at least with Pilate, to induce him to abstain from condemning to death a man whom he knew and declared innocent. But no, Mary would not utter even one word in favor of her Son, to prevent his death, upon which our salvation depended; finally, she gave him to us again at the foot of the cross, in those three hours when she was witnessing his death;

---

72. Mulier ecce filius tuus.
73. Sic Deus dilexit mundum, ut filium suum unigenitum daret. Joan. iii. 16.
74. Sic Maria dilexit nos, ut filium suum unigenitum daret.

because then, at every moment, she was offering up for us his life, with
the deepest grief, and the greatest love for us, at the cost of great trouble and suffering, and with such firmness, that if executioners had been
wanting, as St. Anselm and St. Antoninus tell us, she herself would have
crucified him in obedience to the will of the Father, who had decreed he
should die for our salvation. And if Abraham showed a similar fortitude
in consenting to sacrifice his son with his own hands, we must believe
that Mary would certainly have done the same, with more resolution, as
she was holier, and more obedient than Abraham. But to return to our
subject. How grateful should we be to Mary, for an act of so much love!
for the sacrifice she made of the life of her Son, in the midst of so much
anguish, to obtain salvation for us all! The Lord, indeed, rewarded Abraham for the sacrifice he was prepared to make to him of his son Isaac;
but what can we render to Mary for the life of her Jesus, as she has given
us a Son more noble and beloved than the son of Abraham? This love of
Mary, says St. Bonaventure, greatly obliges us to love her, seeing that she
has loved us more than any other created being loves us, since she has
given for us her only Son, whom she loved more than herself.[75]

And from this follows another reason why we are so much beloved by
Mary: because she knows that we have been purchased by the death of
Jesus Christ. If a mother should see a servant redeemed by a beloved son
of hers, by twenty years of imprisonment and suffering, for this reason
alone how much would she esteem that servant! Mary well knows that
her Son came upon earth solely to save us miserable sinners, as he himself declared: "I have come to save what was lost."[76] And to save us he has
consented to lay down his life for us: "Becoming obedient unto death."[77]
If Mary, then, had little love for us, she would slightly value the blood
of her Son, which was the price of our salvation. It was revealed to St.
Elizabeth, the nun, that Mary, from the time she was in the temple, was
always praying that God would quickly send his Son to save the world.
Now, how much more certainly must we believe that she loves us, after
she has seen us so greatly prized by her Son, that he deigned to purchase
us at such a cost!

---

75. Nulla post eam creatura ita per amorem nostrum exardescet, quæ filium suum unicum, quem
    multo plus se amavit, nobis dedit, et pro nobis obtulit.
76. Veni salvum facere, quod perierat. Luc. xix. 10.
77. Factus obediens usque ad mortem. Phil. ii. 8.

And because all men have been redeemed by Jesus, Mary loves and favors all. She was seen by St. John clothed with the sun: "And there appeared a great wonder in heaven, a woman clothed with the sun."[78] She is said to be clothed with the sun, because, as "There is no one that can hide himself from his heat,"[79] so there is no one living on the earth who is deprived of the love of Mary. From the heat of the sun, as it is explained by the venerable Raymond Jordan, who through humility called himself the Idiot, that is, from the love of Mary.[80] And who, says St. Anthony, can comprehend the care which this loving mother has of us all? Therefore, to all she offers and dispenses her mercy.[81] For our mother has desired the salvation of all, and has co-operated with her Son in the salvation of all.

It is certain that she is concerned for the whole human race, as St. Bernard affirms;[82] hence the practice of some devout servants of Mary is very useful, who, as Cornelius à Lapide relates, have the habit of praying our Lord to grant them those graces which the blessed Virgin is seeking for them, using these words: "Oh Lord, give me what the most holy Virgin Mary is asking for me."[83] And this is well, as à Lapide adds, for our mother desires greater things for us than we think of asking for ourselves.[84] The devout Bernardine de Bustis says, that Mary is more desirous to do us good, and bestow favors upon us, than we are to receive them.[85] Therefore blessed Albertus Magnus applies to Mary the words of wisdom: "She preventeth them that covet her, so that she first showeth herself unto them."[86] So great is the love, says Richard of St. Laurence, which this good mother bears us, that when she perceives our necessities, she comes to relieve them. She hastens before she is invoked.[87]

If Mary, then, is good to all, even to the ungrateful and negligent, who have but little love for her, and seldom have recourse to her, how much more loving must she not be to those who love her and often invoke her!

---

78. Et signum magnum apparuit in cœlo, mulier amicta sole. Apoc. xii. 1.
79. Non est qui se abscondet a calore ejus. Psal. xviii. 7.
80. A calore ejus, idest a dilectione Mariæ.
81. O quanta cura est Virgini matri de nobis! Omnibus aperit sinum misericordiæ suæ.
82. Constat pro universo genere humano fuisse solicitam. Hom. 2. Mis.
83. Domine, da mihi, quod pro me postulat Ss. Virgo Maria.
84. Ipsa enim majora optat, quam nos optare possumus.
85. Plus ipsa desiderat facere tibi bonum, et largiri gratiam quam tu accipere concupiscas. Mar. 1. Serm. 5.
86. Præoccupat qui se concupiscunt, ut illis se prior ostendat. Sap. vi. 14.
87. Prius occurrit, quam invocetur. Ric. in Cant. iv. 5.

"She is easily seen by them that love her."[88] Oh, how easy it is, exclaims the same blessed Albertus, for those who love Mary to find her, and find her full of love and pity! "I love them that love me,"[89] she assures us, and declares that she cannot but love those who love her. And although our most loving lady loves all men as her children, yet, says St. Bernard, she recognizes and loves especially those who most tenderly love her. Those happy lovers of Mary, as the Idiot asserts, are not only loved, but served by her.[90]

Leonard the Dominican, as we read in the chronicles of his order, who was accustomed to recommend himself two hundred times a day to this mother of mercy, when he was on his death-bed, saw one beautiful as a queen by his side, who said to him: "Leonard, do you wish to die and come to my Son and me?" "Who are you?" answered the religious. "I am the mother of mercy," replied the Virgin; "you have many times invoked me, and now I come to take you: let us go to paradise." On that same day Leonard died, and we hope that he followed her to the kingdom of the blessed.

"Ah, most sweet Mary, blessed is he who loves you!" the venerable brother John Berchmans, of the Society of Jesus, used to say: "If I love Mary, I am sure of perseverance, and I shall obtain from God whatsoever I wish." And this devout youth was never satisfied with renewing his intention, and often repeated to himself, "I will love Mary, I will love Mary."

Oh, how much this our good mother exceeds all her children in affection, even if they love her to the extent of their power! "Mary is always more loving than her lovers," says St. Ignatius, martyr.[91] Let us love her as much as St. Stanislaus Kostka, who loved this his dear mother so tenderly, that when he spoke of her, every one who heard him desired to love her also; he invented new titles by which he honored her name; he never commenced an action without first turning to her image and asking her blessing; when he recited her office, her rosary, and other prayers, he repeated them with such affectionate earnestness, that he seemed speaking face to face with Mary; when he heard the Salve Regina sung, his soul and even his countenance was all on fire; when asked one day by a father of the society, as they were going together to visit an altar of the blessed Virgin, how much he loved

---

88. Facile invenitur ab his qui diligunt illam. Sap. vi. 18.
89. Ego diligentes me diligo. Prov. viii. 17.
90. Inventa Maria Virgine, invenitur omne bonum. Ipsa namque diligit diligentes se, immo sibi servientibus servit. De contempl. Virgin. in Prolog.
91. Semper Maria cum amantibus est amantior. Ep. ad., Ep. aur.

her, "Father," he answered, "what can I say more than she is my mother?" And that father tells us how the holy youth spoke these words with such tender emotion of voice, countenance, and heart, that he appeared not a man, but an angel discoursing the love of Mary.

Let us love her as much as blessed Hermann, who called her his beloved spouse, whilst he also was honored by Mary with the same name. As much as St. Philip Neri, who felt wholly consoled in merely thinking of Mary, and on this account named her his delight. As much as St. Bonaventure, who not only called her his lady and mother, but, to show the tender affection he bore her, went so far as to call her his heart and his soul: Hail, lady, my mother; yea, my heart, my soul."[92] Let us love her as much as her great lover St. Bernard, who loved his sweet mother so much, that he called her "the ravisher of hearts:"[93] whence the saint, in order to express to her the ardent love he bore her, said to her, "Hast thou not stolen my heart?"[94] Let us name her our beloved mistress, as St. Bernardine of Sienna named her, who went every day to visit her before her sacred image, in order to declare his love in the tender colloquies he held with his queen. When he was asked where he went every day, he answered that he went to find his beloved. Let them love her as much as St. Aloysius Gonzaga, who burned continually with so great love of Mary, that as soon as he heard the sound of the sweet name of his dear mother, his heart kindled, and a flame perceptible to all, lighted up his countenance. Let us love her like St. Francis Solano, who, distracted by a holy passion for Mary, sometimes went with a musical instrument to sing of love before her altar, saying that, like earthly lovers, he was serenading his beloved queen.

Let us love her as so many of her servants have loved her, who had no way left of manifesting their love to her. Father Jerome of Trexo, of the Society of Jesus, delighted in calling himself the slave of Mary, and as a mark of his servitude went often to visit her in a church: and what did he do there? He watered the church with the tears of that tender love which he felt for Mary; then he wiped them with his lips, kissing that pavement a thousand times, remembering that it was the house of his beloved mistress. Father Diego Martinez, of the same society, who, on account of his devotion to our Lady, on the feasts of Mary, was carried by angels to heaven, that he might

---

92. Ave Domina, mater mea; imo cor meum, anima mea.
93. Raptrix cordium.
94. Nonne rapuisti cor meum?

see with how much devotion they were celebrated there, said, "Would that I had all the hearts of the angels and the saints to love Mary as they love her. Would that I had the lives of all men, to devote them all to the love of Mary!" Let others love her as Charles the son of St. Bridget loved her, who said that he knew of nothing in the world which gave him so much consolation as the thought of how much Mary was beloved by God; and he added, that he would accept every suffering rather than that Mary should lose, if it were possible for her to lose it, the least portion of her greatness; and if the greatness of Mary were his, he would renounce it in her behalf, because she was more worthy of it. Let us desire to sacrifice our life in testimony of our love to Mary, as Alphonso Rodriguez desired to do. Let us, like Francesco Binanzio, a religious, and Radagunde, wife of King Clotaire, engrave with sharp instruments of iron upon our breast the sweet name of Mary. Let us, with red-hot iron, impress upon our flesh the beloved name, that it may be more distinct and more enduring, as did her devoted servants Battista Archinto and Agostino d'Espinosa, both of the Company of Jesus. If, then, the lovers of Mary imitate, as much as possible, those lovers who endeavor to make known their affection to the person beloved, they can never love her so much as she loves them. I know, oh Lady, said St. Peter Damian, how loving thou art, and that thou lovest us with unconquerable love.[95] The venerable Alphonso Rodriguez, of the Society of Jesus, was once standing before an image of Mary; and there burning with love for the most holy Virgin, broke forth into these words: "My most amiable mother, I know that thou lovest me, but thou dost not love me so much as I love thee." Then Mary, as if wounded in her love, spoke to him from that image and said: "What dost thou say—what dost thou say, oh Alphonso? Oh, how much greater is the love I bear thee than the love thou bearest me! Know that the distance from heaven to earth is not so great as from my love to thine."

With how much reason, then, did St. Bonaventure exclaim: Blessed are those whose lot it is to be faithful servants and lovers of this most loving mother![96] For this most grateful queen is never surpassed in love by her devoted servants.[97] Mary, in this respect, imitating our loving Redeemer Jesus Christ, makes by her favors a twofold return to him who loves her. I

95. Scio, Domina, quia amantissima es et amas nos amore invincibili. Serm. 1, de Nat. B. V.
96. Beati quorum corda diligunt Mariam! Beati qui ei famulantur!
97. Nunquam in hoc certamine a nobis vincitur. Amorem redhibet, et præterita beneficia semper novis adauget. Paciucch. de B. Virg.

will exclaim, then, with the enamored St. Anselm: May my heart languish, may my soul melt with your never-failing love.[98] May my heart always burn and my soul be consumed with love for you, oh Jesus, my beloved Savior, oh my dear mother Mary. Grant then, oh Jesus and Mary, since without your grace I cannot love you, grant to my soul, not through my merits, but through yours, that I may love you as you deserve. Oh, God! the lover of men, thou hast died for thy enemies, and canst thou deny to him who asks it, the grace of loving thee and thy mother?[99]

EXAMPLE

It is narrated by Father Auriemma,[100] that a poor shepherdess loved Mary so much that all her delight was to go to a little chapel of our Lady, on a mountain, and there in solitude, while her sheep were feeding, to converse with her beloved mother and pay her devotion to her. When she saw that the figure of Mary, in relief, was unadorned, she began, by the poor labor of her hands, to make a drapery for it. Having gathered one day some flowers in the fields, she wove them into a garland, and then ascending the altar of that little chapel, placed it on the head of the figure, saying: "Oh, my mother, I would that I could place on thy head a crown of gold and gems; but as I am poor, receive from me this poor crown of flowers, and accept it as a token of the love I bear thee." Thus this devout maiden always endeavored to serve and honor her beloved Lady. But let us see how our good mother, on the other hand, rewarded the visits and the affection of her child. She fell ill, and was near her end. It happened that two religious passing that way, weary with travelling, stopped to rest under a tree; one fell asleep and the other watched, but both had the same vision. They saw a company of beautiful virgins, and among them there was one who, in loveliness and majesty, surpassed the rest. One of the brothers addressed her, and said: "Lady, who art thou? And where art thou going?" "I am the mother of God," she replied, "and I am going to the neighboring village, with these holy virgins, to visit a

---

98. Vestri continuo amore langueat cor meum, liquefiat anima mea. In Depr. ad V.
99. Date itaque supplicanti animæ meæ, non propter meritum meum sed propter meritum vestrum, date illi quantum digni estis amorem vestrum. O amator hominum, tu potuisti reos tuos usque ad mortem amare, et poteris roganti amorem tui et matris tuæ negare? Lec. cit.
100. Affett. Scamb. tom. 2, cap. 7.

dying shepherdess, who has many times visited me." She spoke thus and disappeared. These two good servants of God proposed to each other to go and visit her also. They went towards the place where the dying maiden lived, entered a small cottage, and there found her lying upon a little straw. They saluted her, and she said to them: "Brothers, ask of God that he may permit you to see the company that surrounds me." They were quickly on their knees, and saw Mary, with a crown in her hand by the side of the dying girl, consoling her. Then those holy virgins began to sing, and with that sweet music the blessed soul was released from the body. Mary crowned her, and took her soul with her to paradise.

PRAYER

Oh Lady, Ravisher of hearts! I would exclaim with St. Bonaventure; who, with the love and favor thou dost bestow upon thy servants, dost ravish their hearts; take my miserable heart also, which desires so earnestly to love thee. Thou, oh my mother, with thy beauty hast enamored a God, and hast drawn him from heaven into thy bosom, and shall I live without loving thee? No. I will say to thee with thy loving child John Berchmans: "I will never rest until I have attained a tender love for my mother Mary."[101] No, I will not rest until I am certain of having obtained a love—a constant and tender love for thee, my mother, who hast loved me with so much tenderness even when I was so ungrateful towards thee. And where should I now be if thou, oh Mary, hadst not loved me, and obtained so many favors for me? If then thou hast loved me so much when I did not love thee, how much more may I confide in thy goodness, now that I love thee? I love thee, oh my mother, and would wish for a heart capable of loving thee, for all those unhappy beings who do not love thee. Would that my tongue could praise thee with the power of a thousand tongues, in order to make known thy greatness, thy holiness, thy mercy, and thy love, with which thou lovest those who love thee. If I had riches, I would employ them all for thy honor; if I had subjects, I would make them all thy lovers; for thee and for thy glory I would give my life, if it were required. I love thee, oh my mother,

101. Nunquam quiescam, donec habuero tenerum amorem erga matrem meam Mariam.
102. Amor aut similes invenit, aut facit. Aristot.

but at the same time I fear that thou dost not love me, for I have heard that love makes lovers like those they love.[102] If then I find myself so unlike to thee, it is a proof that I do not love thee. Thou so pure, I so unclean; thou so humble, I so proud; thou so holy, I so sinful. But this, oh Mary, is to be thy work; since thou lovest me, make me like unto thyself. Thou hast the power to change the heart; take then mine and change it. Let the world see what thou canst do for those who love thee. Make me holy—make me worthy of thy Son. Thus I hope; thus may it be.

SECTION 4
Mary is also mother of penitent sinners

Mary assured St. Bridget that she was mother not only of the just and innocent, but also of sinners, provided they wish to amend.[103] When a sinner becomes penitent, and throws himself at her feet, he finds this good mother of mercy more ready to embrace and aid him than any earthly mother could be. This St. Gregory wrote to the princess Matilda: "Desire to cease from sin, and I confidently promise you that you will find Mary more prompt than an earthly mother in thy behalf."[104] But whoever aspires to be the son of this great mother, must first leave off sinning, and then let him hope to be accepted as her son. Richard, commenting upon the words, "Then rose up her children,"[105] remarks, that first comes the word rose up, *surrexerunt*, and then children, *filii*; because he cannot be a son of Mary who does not first rise from the iniquity into which he has fallen.[106] For, says St. Peter Chrysologus, he who does works contrary to those of Mary, by such conduct denies that he wishes to be her son.[107] Mary is humble, and will he be proud? Mary is pure, and will he be impure? Mary is full of love, and will he hate his neighbor? He proves that he is not, and does not wish to be the son of this holy mother, when he so much disgusts her with his life. The sons of Mary, repeats Richard of St. Laurence, are her imitators in chastity, humility, meekness, mercy.[108] And how can he who so much disgusts her with his life, dare to call himself the son of Mary? A certain sinner

---

103. Ego sum quasi mater omnium peccatorum volentium se emendare. L. 4, Rev. c. 138.
104. Pone finem a voluntate peccandi, et invenies Mariam—indubitanter promitto—promptiorem carnali matre in tui dilectione. L. 4, Ep. 47.
105. Surrexerunt filii ejus. Prov. xxxi. 28.
106. Nec dignus est, qui in mortali peccato est, vocari filius tantæ matris.
107. Qui genetricis non facit opera, negat genus.
108. Filii Mariæ imitatores ejus, in castitate, humilitate, mansuetudine, misericordia.

once said to Mary, "Show thyself a mother;"[109] but the Virgin answered him, "Show thyself a son."[110] Another, one day, invoked this divine mother, calling her mother of mercy. But Mary said to him, "When you sinners wish me to aid you, you call me mother of mercy, and yet by your sins make me the mother of misery and grief." "He is cursed of God that angereth his mother."[111] His mother—that is, Mary, remarks Richard.[112] God curses every one who afflicts this his good mother, by his bad life or his willfulness.

I have said willfulness, for when a sinner, although he may not have left his sins, makes an effort to quit them, and seeks the aid of Mary, this mother will not fail to assist him, and bring him to the grace of God. This St. Bridget once learned from Jesus Christ himself, who, speaking with his mother, said: "Thou dost aid those who are striving to rise to God, and dost leave no soul without thy consolation."[113] While the sinner, then, is obstinate, Mary cannot love him; but if he finds himself enchained by some passion which makes him a slave of hell, and will commend himself to the Virgin, and implore her with confidence and perseverance to rescue him from his sin, this good mother will not fail to extend her powerful hand, she will loose his chains, and bring him to a state of safety. It is a heresy, condemned by the sacred Council of Trent, to say that all the prayers and works of a person in a state of sin are sins. St. Bernard says that prayer is the mouth of a sinner, although it is without supernatural excellence, since it is not accompanied by charity, yet is useful and efficient in obtaining a release from sin; for, as St. Thomas teaches,[114] the prayer of the sinner is indeed without merit, but it serves to obtain the grace of pardon; for the power of obtaining it is based not upon the worth of him who prays, but upon the divine bounty, and upon the merits and promise of Jesus Christ, who has said, "Every one that asketh receiveth."[115] The same may be said of the prayers offered to the divine mother. If he who prays, says St. Anselm, does not deserve to be heard, the merits of Mary, to whom he commends himself, will cause him to be heard.[116] Hence St. Bernard exhorts every sinner to pray to Mary and to feel great confidence in praying to her; because if he does not deserve what

109. Monstra te esse matrem.
110. Monstra te esse filium. Ap. Aur.
111. Maledictus a Deo qui exasperat matrem suam. Eccli. iii, 18.
112. Matrem suam, idest Mariam.
113. Conanti surgere ad Deum tribuis auxilium, et neminem relinquis vacuum a tua consolatione.
114. 2, 2, qu. 178, a. 2, ad 1.
115. Omnis qui petit, accipit. Luc. xi. 10.
116. Si merita invocantis non merentur, ut exaudiatur; merita tamen matris intercedunt, ut exaudiatur.

he demands, yet Mary obtains for him, by her merits, the graces which she asks of God for him.[117] The office of a good mother, says the same saint, is this: if a mother knew that her two sons were deadly enemies, and that one was plotting against the life of the other, what would she do but endeavor in every way to pacify him? Thus, says the saint, Mary is mother of Jesus, and mother of man; when she sees any one by his sin an enemy of Jesus Christ, she cannot endure it, and makes every effort to reconcile them.[118] Our most indulgent lady only requires the sinner to commend himself to her, and have the intention to reform. When she sees a sinner coming to implore mercy at her feet, she does not regard the sins with which he is laden, but the intention with which he comes. If he comes with a good intention, though he have committed all the sins in the world, she embraces him, and this most loving mother condescends to heal all the wounds of his soul; for she is not only called by us the mother of mercy, but she really is such, and shows herself such by the love and tenderness with which she succors us. The blessed Virgin herself expressed all this to St. Bridget, when she said to her, "However great may be a man's sins, when he turns to me, I am immediately ready to receive him; neither do I consider how much he has sinned, but with what intention he comes; for I do not disdain to anoint and heal his wounds, because I am called, and truly am, the mother of mercy."[119]

Mary is the mother of sinners who desire to be converted, and as a mother she cannot but compassionate them, and it even seems that she regards the woes of her poor children as her own. When the woman of Canaan implored Jesus Christ to liberate her daughter from the demon which tormented her, she said: "Have mercy on me, oh Lord, thou son of David; my daughter is grievously troubled by a devil."[120] But as the daughter, not the mother, was tormented by the devil, it would seem that she should have said, "Oh Lord, have mercy on my daughter," not "have mercy upon me;" but no, she said, "Have mercy upon me,"[121] and with reason, for all the miseries of children are felt as their own by their mothers. Exactly thus Mary prays God, says Richard of St. Laurence, when she commends to him a

---

117. Quia indignus erat, cui donaretur, datum est Mariæ, ut per illam acciperes quicquid haberes. Serm. 3, in Virg. Nat.
118. O felix Maria, tu mater rei, tu mater judicis; cum sis mater utriusque, discordias inter tuos filios nequis sustinere. In Depr. ad V.
119. Quantumcumque homo peccat, statim parata sum recipere revertentem; nec attendo quantum peccaverit, sed cum quali intentione redit; nam non dedignor ejus plagas ungere, et sanare, quia vocor et vere sum mater misericordiæ. Rev. l. c. 23.
120. Miserere mei. Domine Fili David, filia mea male a dæmonio vexatur. Matth. xv. 22.
121. Miserere mei.

sinner who has recommended himself to her: "Have mercy upon me."[122] It is as if she said to him, My Lord, this poor creature, who is in sin, is my child; have pity on him, not so much on him as on me who am his mother. Oh, would to God that all sinners would have recourse to this sweet mother, for all would certainly be pardoned by God. Oh Mary, exclaims St. Bonaventure, in wonder; thou dost embrace, with maternal affection the sinner who is despised by the whole world! neither dost thou leave him until he is reconciled to his Judge![123] The saint here intends to say that the sinner who remains in sin is hated and rejected by all men; even insensible creatures, fire, air, the earth would punish him, and inflict vengeance upon him in order to repair the honor of their insulted Lord. But if this wretch has recourse to Mary, does she banish him from her presence? No: if he comes asking for help, and intending to amend, she embraces him with the affection of a mother, and does not leave him until she has reconciled him to God by her powerful intercession, and re-established him in his grace.

We read in the Second Book of Kings,[124] that the wise woman of Thecua said to David: "My Lord, I had two sons, and for my misfortune one has killed the other; so that I have already lost a child; justice would now take from me my other and only son; have pity on me a poor mother, and do not let me be deprived of both my children." Then David had compassion on this mother, and liberated the criminal, and restored him to her.[125] It appears that Mary offers the same petition when God is angry with a sinner, who has recourse to her: Oh my God, she says to him, I had two sons, Jesus and man; man has killed my Jesus on the cross; thy justice would now condemn man; my Lord, my Jesus is dead; have mercy upon me, and if I have lost one, do not condemn me to lose the other also. Ah, God assuredly does not condemn those sinners who have recourse to Mary, and for whom she prays; since God himself has given these sinners to Mary for her children. The devout Lanspergius puts these words into the mouth of our Lord: I have commended sinners to Mary as her children. Wherefore she is so watchful in the performance of her office that she permits none

---

122. Maria clamat pro anima peccatrice; miserere mei. De Laud. V. n. 6.
123. O Maria, peccatorem toti mundo despectum, materno affectu complecteris! nec deseris, quousque miserum judici reconcilies. In spec. c. 5.
124. C. xiv.
125. Mariæ peccatores in filios commendavi, propterea adeo est sedula, ut, officio suo satisfaciens neminem eorum, qui sibi commissi sunt, præcipue illam invocantium, perire sinat, sed quantum valet, omnes mihi reducat. V. 1. 4, Min. Op.

to be lost who are committed to her care, especially those who invoke her, and uses all her power to lead them back to me. And who can describe, says Blosius, the goodness, the mercy, the fidelity, and the charity with which this our mother strives to save us, when we invoke her aid?[126] Let us prostrate ourselves, then, says St. Bernard, before this good mother, let us cling to her sacred feet, and leave her not until she gives us her blessing, and accepts us for her children.[127] Who could distrust the goodness of this mother? said St. Bonaventure. Though she should slay me, I will hope in her; and, confident in my trust, I would die near her image, and be saved.[128] And thus should every sinner say who has recourse to this kind mother: Oh my Lady and mother, I deserve for my faults that thou shouldst banish me from thy presence, and shouldst punish me for my sins; but even if thou shouldst cast me off and slay me, I shall never lose confidence in thee and in thy power to save me. In thee I entirely confide, and if it be my fate to die before some image of thine, recommending myself to thy compassion, I should have a certain hope of my salvation, and of going to praise thee in heaven, united to all thy servants who called upon thee for aid in death, and are saved. Let the following example be read, and let the reader judge if any sinner can distrust the mercy and love of this good mother, if he has recourse to her.

EXAMPLE

It is narrated by Belluacensis that in Ridolio, a city of England, in the year 1430, there lived a young nobleman named Ernest, who gave all his patrimony to the poor, and entered a monastery, where he led so holy a life that he was greatly esteemed by his superiors, particularly for his special devotion to the most holy Virgin. It happened that a pestilence prevailed in that city and the citizens had recourse to that monastery to ask the prayers of the monks. The abbot ordered Ernest to go and pray

---

126. Hujus matris bonitas, misericordia, fidelitas, charitas erga homines tanta est ut nullis verbis explicari possit.
127. Beatis illius pedibus persolvamur; teneamus eam, nec dimittamus donec benedixerit nes. In Sign. Mag.
128. Etiamsi occiderit me, sperabo in eum; et tutus confidens juxta ejus imaginem mori desidero, et salvus ero.

before the altar of Mary, and not to quit it until she had given him an answer. The youth remained there three days, and received from Mary, in answer, some prayers, which were to be said. They were said, and the plague ceased. It happened afterwards that this youth became less ardent in his devotion to Mary; the devil assailed him with many temptations, especially to impurity, and to a desire to flee from the monastery; and having neglected to recommend himself to Mary, he resolved to take flight by casting himself from the wall of the monastery; but passing before an image of the Virgin which stood in the corridor, the mother of God spoke to him, and said: "My son, why do you leave me?" Ernest was overwhelmed with surprise, and, filled with compunction, fell on the earth, saying: "My Lady, behold, I have no power to resist, why do you not aid me?" And the Madonna replied: "Why have you not invoked me? If you had sought my protection, you would not have been reduced to this; from this day commend yourself to me, and have confidence." Ernest returned to his cell; but the temptations were renewed, yet he neglected to call upon Mary for assistance. He finally fled from the monastery, and leading a bad life, he went on from one sin to another, till he became an assassin. He rented an inn, where in the night he murdered unfortunate travelers and stripped them of all they had. One night, among others, he killed the cousin of the governor of the place, who, after examination and trial, condemned him to the gallows. But during the examination, a young traveler arrived at the inn, and the host, as usual, laid his plans and entered his chamber to assassinate him: but on approaching the bed, he finds the young man gone and a Christ on the cross, covered with wounds, in his place. Our Lord, looking compassionately at him, said: "Is it not enough that I have died once for thee? Dost thou wish to slay me again? Do it, then; lift thy hand and kill me!" Then the poor Ernest, covered with confusion, began to weep, and exclaimed: "Oh Lord, behold me ready to return to thee, who hast shown me so much mercy." He immediately left the inn to go back to the monastery and do penance; but the officers of justice overtook him on the way, he was carried before the judge, and in his presence confessed all the murders he had committed. He was at once condemned to death, without even being allowed time for confession. He commended himself to Mary. He was hung upon the gallows, but the Virgin prevented his death. She herself released him, and said to him: "Return to the monastery; do penance; and when you shall see in my hand a paper containing the pardon of thy sins, then prepare to die. Ernest returned, and having related all to the abbot, did great penance. After many years, he saw in the hand of Mary the paper containing his pardon; he then prepared for his last end, and died a holy death.

PRAYER

Oh Mary, sovereign queen, and worthy mother of my God, most holy Mary! Finding myself so vile, so laden with sin, I dare not approach thee and call thee mother. But I cannot let my miseries deprive me of the consolation and confidence I feel in calling thee mother. I know that I deserve to be rejected by thee, but I pray thee to consider what thy son Jesus has done and suffered for me; and then cast me from thee if thou canst. I am a poor sinner who, more than others, have despised the divine Majesty; but the evil is already done. To thee I have recourse: thou canst help me; oh, my mother, help me. Do not say that thou canst not aid me, for I know that thou art omnipotent, and dost obtain whatever thou desireth from thy God. If then thou sayest that thou canst not help me, at least tell me to whom I must have recourse for succor in my deep distress. With St. Anselm, I will say to thee, and to thy Son: Have pity on me, oh thou, my Redeemer, and pardon me, thou my mother, and recommend me to pardon; or teach me to whom I may have recourse, who is more compassionate than you, and in whom I may have more confidence. No, neither in heaven nor on earth can I find one who has more compassion for the miserable, or who can aid me more than you. Thou, oh Jesus, art my father, and thou, oh Mary, art my mother. You love those who are the most wretched, and you seek to save them. I am worthy of hell, and of all beings the most miserable; you need not to seek me, neither do I ask you to seek me; I present myself to you with a sure hope that I shall not be abandoned by you. Behold me at your feet; my Jesus, pardon me; my Mary, help me.

The White Virgin. 14th century, anonymous. Cathedral of Toledo, Spain.

CHAPTER 2

Vita, dulcedo
Our life, our sweetness

SECTION 1
Mary is our life, because she obtains for us the pardon of our sins

In order to understand rightly the reason why the holy Church calls Mary our life, we must consider that as the soul gives life to the body, so divine grace gives life to the soul; for a soul without grace, though nominally alive, in truth is dead, as we find in the Apocalypse: "Thou hast the name of being alive, and thou art dead."[1] As Mary, then, obtains for sinners, by her intercession, the gift of grace, she restores them to life. The holy Church applies to her the following words of Proverbs: "They that in the morning early watch for me, shall find me."[2] They shall find me, or, according to the Septuagint, "they shall find grace."[3] Hence, to have recourse to Mary is to find the grace of God; for, as immediately follows: "He who finds me shall find life, and shall receive from God eternal salvation."[4] Listen, as St. Bonaventure exclaims here upon these words, listen, all ye who desire the kingdom of God; honor the Virgin Mary, and ye shall have life and eternal salvation.[5]

St. Bernardine of Sienna says, that God did not destroy man after his fall, because of the peculiar love that he bore his future child Mary. And the saint adds, that he doubts not all the mercy and pardon which sinners receive under the Old Law, was granted them by God solely for the sake of this blessed Virgin.[6]

Therefore St. Bernard exhorts us, if we have been so unfortunate as to lose divine grace, to strive to recover it, but to strive through Mary; for if we have lost it, she has found it:[7] and hence she is called by this saint,

---

1. Nomen habes quod vivas, et mortuus es. Apoc. iii. 1.
2. Qui mane vigilant ad me, invenient me. Prov. viii. 17.
3. Invenient me, invenient gratiam.
4. Qui me invenerit, inveniet vitam, et hauriet salutem a Domino.
5. Audite, audite qui cupitis regnum Dei; Virginem Mariam honorate, et invenietis vitam et salutem eternam.
6. Omnes indulgentias factas in Veteri Testamento non ambigo Deum fecisse solum propter hujus benedictæ puellæ Virginis reverentiam, et amorem. Tom. 4, serm. 61, c. 8.
7. Quæramus gratiam, et per Mariam quæramus. Serm. de Aquæd.

"The finder of grace."[8] This the angel Gabriel expressed for our consolation, when he said to the Virgin, "Fear not, Mary, for thou hast found grace."[9] But if Mary had never been without grace, how could the angel say to her that she had found it? A thing is said to be found when it has been lost. The Virgin was always with God and with grace; she was even full of grace, as the Archangel himself announced when he saluted her, "Hail! full of grace, the Lord is with thee."[10] If, then, Mary did not find grace for herself, for whom did she find it? Cardinal Hugo answers, when commenting upon the above passage, that she found it for sinners who had lost it. Let sinners, then, says the devout writer, who have lost grace, flee to Mary; with her they will certainly find it; and let them say: Oh Lady, what is lost must be restored to him who has lost it; this grace which thou hast found is not thine, thou hast never lost it; it is ours, for we have lost it, and to us thou shouldst restore it.[11] In connection with which, Richard of St. Laurence remarks: If then we desire to find the grace of God, let us go to Mary, who has found it, and always finds it.[12] And since she ever has been, and ever will be, dear to God, if we have recourse to her, we certainly shall find it. She says, in the holy Canticles, that God has placed her in the world to be our defense,[13] and therefore she is ordained to be the mediatrix of peace between the sinner and God. "I am become in his presence as one finding peace."[14] By which words St. Bernard gives encouragement to the sinner, and says: Go to this mother of mercy, and show her the wounds which thy sins have inflicted upon thy soul. Then she will certainly pray her Son that he may pardon thee by the milk with which she has nourished him, and the Son who loves her so much will certainly hear her.[15] So, too, the holy Church teaches us to pray the Lord to grant us the powerful intercession of Mary, that we may arise from our sins, in the following prayer: "Grant us, oh merciful God strength against all our weakness; that we who celebrate the memory of the holy mother of God,

---

8. Inventrix gratiæ.
9. Ne timeas Maria, invenisti gratiam. Luc. i. 30.
10. Ave gratia plena, Dominus tecum.
11. Currant ergo, currant peccatores ad Virginem qui gratiam amiserant peccando, et eam invenient apud ipsam. Secum dicant; Redde nobis rem nostram, quam invenisti.
12. Cupientes invenire gratiam quæramus inventricem gratiæ, quæ, quia semper invenit frustrari non poterit. De Laud. V. 1. 2.
13. Ego murus et ubera mea sicut turris. Cant. viii. 10.
14. Ex quo facta sum coram eo quasi pacem reperiens. Cant. viii. 10.
15. Vade ad matrem misericordiæ, et ostende illi tuorum plagas peccatorum; et ita ostendet pro te ubera. Exaudiet utique matrem filius.

may, by the help of her intercession, arise again from our iniquities."[16]

Justly, then, does St. Lawrence Justinian call her the hope of evil-doers, "spes delinquentium," since she alone can obtain their pardon from God. St. Bernard rightly names her the ladder of sinners, "Peccatorum scala;" since she, this compassionate queen, offers her hand to poor fallen mortals, leads them from the precipice of sin, and helps them to ascend to God. St. Augustine rightly calls her the only hope of us sinners, since by her means alone we hope for the remission of all our sins.[17] And St. John Chrysostom repeats the same thing, namely, that sinners receive pardon only through the intercession of Mary.[18] Whence the saints in the name of all sinners thus salute her: Hail! mother of God and ours; Heaven where God dwells; Throne from which the Lord dispenses all graces; always pray to Jesus for us, that by thy prayers we may obtain pardon in the day of account, and the glory of the blessed in heaven.[19] Finally, Mary is rightly called aurora: "Who is she that cometh forth as the morning rising?"[20] Because, as Pope Innocent says, aurora is the end of night, and the beginning of day, well is the Virgin Mary, who is the end of vices and the beginning of virtues, designated as aurora.[21] And the same effect which the birth of Mary produced in the world, devotion to her produces in the soul; she puts an end to the night of sin, and leads the soul into the way of virtue. Hence, St. Germanus says: Oh mother of God, thy protection is immortal! thy intercession is life.[22] And in his sermon on the *Zone of the Virgin*,[23] the saint says that the name of Mary, to him who pronounces it with affection, is either the sign of life, or that soon he will have life.

Mary sang: "For behold, from henceforth all nations shall call me blessed."[24] On this account, says St. Bernard, all nations shall call thee blessed, because all thy servants by thy means shall obtain the life of grace and eternal glory.[25] "In thee sinners find pardon, and the just perseverance,

---

16. Concede, misericors Deus, fragilitati nostræ præsidium; ut qui sanctæ Dei Genitricis memoriam agimus, intercessionis ejus auxilio a nostris iniquitatibus resurgamus.
17. Tu es spes unica peccatorum, quia per te speramus veniam omnium delictorum. Serm. 18, de Sanctis.
18. Per hanc peccatorum veniam consequimur.
19. Ave igitur mater, Cœlum, Thronus, Ecclesiæ nostræ Decus; assidue precare Jesum, ut per te misericordiam invenire in die judicii, et quæ reposita sunt iis qui diligunt Deum bona consequi possimus. In Offic. Nat. B. M., die 5.
20. Quæ est ista, quæ progreditur quasi aurora consurgens? Cant. vi. 9.
21. Cum aurora sit finis noctis, et origo diei, vere per auroram designatur Maria Virgo, quæ fuit finis vitiorum, et origo virtutum. Serm. 2 de Assump. B. V.
22. Serm. 3, in Dorm. B. V.
23. De Zona Virgin.
24. Ecce enim ex hoc beatam me dicent omnes generationes. Luc. i. 48.
25. Ex hoc beatam te dicent omnes generationes, quæ omnibus generationibus vitam et gloriam genuisti. Serm. 2, in Pentec.

and afterwards life eternal."[26] Do not despair, as the devout Bernardine de Bustis says, oh sinners, although you have committed all possible sin, but confidently have recourse to this Lady, for you will find her hands full of mercies. Then he adds: Mary is more desirous to bestow favors upon you than you are to receive them.[27]

By St. Andrew of Crete, Mary is called "The security of divine pardon."[28] By this is meant, that when sinners have recourse to Mary that they may be reconciled to God, God assures them of pardon, and gives them the assurance by also giving them the pledge of it. And this pledge is Mary, whom he has given us for our advocate, by whose intercession, in virtue of the merits of Jesus Christ, God pardons all sinners who place themselves under her protection. It was revealed to St. Bridget by an angel, that the holy prophets were full of joy when they learned that God, by the humility and purity of Mary, would become reconciled to sinners, and receive into his favor those who had provoked his wrath.[29]

No sinner need ever fear that he shall be rejected by Mary, if he has recourse to her mercy. No, for she is mother of mercy; and as such, desires to save the most miserable. Mary is that happy ark in which he who takes refuge will never suffer the shipwreck of eternal ruin; "arca in qua naufragium evadimus." Even the brutes were saved in the time of the deluge in the ark of Noah; so, under the mantle of Mary, even sinners are saved. St. Gertrude one day saw Mary with her mantle extended, beneath which many wild beasts, lions, bears, and tigers had sheltered themselves; and Mary not only did not cast them from her, but received them with pity and caressed them. And by this the saint understood, that the vilest sinners, when they flee to Mary, are not cast out, but welcomed and saved from eternal death. Let us enter, then, into this ark, and seek refuge under the mantle of Mary; for she certainly will not reject us, and will surely save us.

---

26. In te peccatores veniam, justi gratiam inveniunt in eternum. Serm. de Nat. B. V.
27. O peccator ne diffidas etiamsi commisisti omnia peccata; sed secure ad istam gloriosissimam Dominam recurras. Invenies eam in manibus plenam misericordia, et largitate; plus enim ipsa desiderat facere tibi bonum, et largiri gratiam, quam tu acciperi concupiscas. Serm. 5, de N. M.
28. Fidejussio divinarum reconciliationum, quæ dato pignore fit.
29. Exultabant autem prænoscentes, quod ipse Dominus ex tua humilitate et vitæ puritate, O Maria stella præfulgida, placaretur, et quod reciperet eos in suam gratiam, qui ipsum ad iracundiam provocaverunt. Serm. Ang. c. 9.

EXAMPLE

It is narrated by Father Bevius,[30] of a very sinful person named Helen, that having gone to church she accidentally heard a sermon on the rosary. As she went out she bought one but carried it hidden, so that it should not be seen. Afterwards, she began to recite it; and although she recited it without devotion, the most holy Virgin infused into her heart such consolation and sweetness in it, that she could not cease repeating it. And by this she was inspired with such a horror of her evil life, that she could find no peace, and was forced, as it were, to go to confession. She confessed with so much contrition, that the confessor was amazed. Having finished her confession, she went immediately before an altar of the blessed Virgin, to thank her advocate; she recited her rosary, and the divine mother spoke to her from her image, and said: "Helen, you have too long offended God and me; henceforth change your life, and I will bestow upon you many of my favors." The poor sinner in confusion, answered: "Ah, most holy Virgin, it is true that hitherto I have been very sinful, but thou, who art all-powerful, assist me; I give myself to thee, and will pass the remainder of my life in doing penance for my sins." Assisted by Mary, Helen bestowed all her goods upon the poor, and commenced a rigorous penance. She was tormented by dreadful temptations, but she continued to recommend herself to the mother of God; and always, with her aid, came off victorious. She was favored also with many supernatural graces, as visions, revelations, and prophecies. At last, before her death, of which she had been warned a few days previously by Mary, the Virgin herself came with her Son to visit her; and in death, the soul of this sinner was seen, in the form of a beautiful dove, ascending to heaven.

PRAYER

Behold, oh mother of my God, Mary, my only hope, behold at thy feet a miserable sinner, who implores thy mercy. Thou art proclaimed and called by the whole Church, and by all the faithful, the refuge of sinners; thou

---

30. His. della SS. Virg.

then art my refuge; it is thine to save me. Thou knowest how much thy
Son desires our salvation.[31] Thou, too, knowest what Jesus Christ suffered
to save me. I offer to thee, oh my mother, the sufferings of Jesus; the cold
which he endured in the stable, the steps of his long journey into Egypt,
his toils, his sweat, the blood that he shed, the torments which caused his
death before thy eyes upon the cross; show thy love for this Son, whilst I,
for the love of him, beg thee to aid me. Extend thy hand to a fallen creature, who asks pity of thee. If I were a saint, I would not ask for mercy; but
because I am a sinner, I have recourse to thee, who art the mother of mercies. I know that thy compassionate heart finds consolation in succoring
the wretched, when thou canst aid them, and dost not find them obstinate
in their sins. Console, then, to-day thy own compassionate heart, and console me; for thou hast a chance to save me, a poor wretch condemned to
hell; and thou canst aid me, for I will not be obstinate. I place myself in thy
hands; tell me what I must do, and obtain for me strength to do it, and I will
do all I can to return to a state of grace. I take refuge beneath thy mantle.
Jesus Christ wishes me to have recourse to thee, that, for thy glory and his,
since thou art his mother, not only his blood, but also thy prayers, may aid
me to obtain salvation. He sends me to thee that thou mayest assist me.
Oh Mary, I hasten to thee, and in thee I trust. Thou dost pray for so many
others, pray, and say also one word for me. Say to God, that thou desirest
my salvation, and God certainly will save me. Tell him that I am thine; this
is all I ask from thee.

SECTION 2
Mary is again our life, because she obtains for us perseverance

Final perseverance is a divine gift so great that, as the holy Council
of Trent has declared, it is a wholly gratuitous gift and one that cannot
be merited by us. But, as St. Augustine teaches us, all those obtain perseverance from God who ask it of him; and as Father Suarez says, they
infallibly obtain it if they are diligent to the end of life in praying for it;
because, as Cardinal Bellarmine writes: This perseverance is daily to be
sought, that it may be daily obtained.[32] Now, if it is true, which I consider

---

31. Scis dulcissima Dei mater, quantum placeat benedicto filio tuo salus nostra. Guill. Paris.
32. Quotidie petenda est, ut quotidie obtineatur.

certain, according to the present very general opinion, as I shall presently demonstrate in Chapter 5—if it is true that all the graces which are bestowed on us by God pass through the hands of Mary, it must also be true that only through Mary can we hope for and obtain this great gift of perseverance. And we certainly shall obtain it, if, with confidence, we always ask it of Mary. She herself promises this grace to all those who serve her faithfully in this life. "They that work by me shall not sin; they that explain me shall have life everlasting:"[33] which words the holy Church puts into the mouth of Mary on the Feast of her Conception.

In order that we may be preserved in the life of divine grace, spiritual strength is necessary to resist all the enemies of our salvation. Now, this strength can only be obtained by means of Mary: Mine is this strength, says Mary: "Mea est fortitudo." God has intrusted this gift to my hand, that I may bestow it on my devoted servants. "By me kings reign:" "Per me reges regnant."[34] By me my servants reign, and rule their senses and their passions, and thus make themselves worthy of reigning eternally in heaven. Oh, what strength have the servants of this great Lady to conquer all the temptations of hell! Mary is that tower spoken of in the holy Canticles: "Thy neck is as the tower of David, which is built with bulwarks: a thousand bucklers hang upon it, all the armor of valiant men."[35] She is like a strong tower of defense for her lovers, who take refuge with her in the day of battle; in her all her devoted servants find shields and weapons of every kind to defend themselves against the powers of hell.

For this reason, the most holy Virgin is called a plane-tree: "As a plane-tree by the water in the streets was I exalted."[36] This passage is explained by Cardinal Hugo, who tells us that the plane-tree has leaves like shields.[37] And by this is explained the defense that Mary affords those who take refuge with her. The blessed Amadeus gives another explanation, and says that she is called a plane-tree, because, as the plane-tree, with its shade, protects the traveler from the heat of the sun and from the rain, so, under the mantle of Mary, men find shelter from the heat of their passions and the fury of temptations.[38]

---

33. Qui operantur in me, non peccabunt; qui elucidant me, vitam eternam habebunt. Eccli. xxiv. 30, 31.
34. Prov. viii. 15. In Festo S. Mariæ ad nives.
35. Sicut turris David collum tuum, quæ edificata est cum propugnaculis; mille clypei pendent ex ea, omnis armatura fortium. Cant. iv. 4.
36. Quasi platanus exaltata sum juxta aquam in plateis. Eccli. xxiv. 19.
37. Platanus habet folia scutis similia.
38. Virgo ramorum extensione se ubique expandit, ut filios Adæ ab æstu et turbine umbra desiderabili protegeret. B. Am. Hom. 8.

Unfortunate are those souls who withdraw from this shelter, neglect their devotion to Mary, and fail to recommend themselves to her in trial. If the sun should no more rise upon the world, says St. Bernard, what would the world become but a chaos of darkness and horror?[39] If a soul loses her devotion to Mary, she will immediately be full of darkness, and that darkness of which the Holy Ghost says: "Thou hast appointed darkness, and it is night; in it shall the beasts of the woods go about."[40] When the divine light does not shine in a soul it is night, and it will become a den of all sins and demons. Woe to those, as St. Anselm says, who turn away from the light of this sun;[41] that is, who neglect devotion to Mary. St. Francis Borgia, with reason, feared for the perseverance of those in whom he did not find a special devotion to the blessed Virgin. When once he asked some novices to what saint they had the most devotion, and found that some of them were not especially devoted to Mary, he warned the master to watch more carefully these unfortunate persons; and it happened that they all lost their vocation and quitted religion.

St. Germanus justly called the most holy Virgin the breath of Christians; because, as the body cannot live without breathing, so the soul cannot live without having recourse and commending itself to Mary, through whose means the life of divine grace is obtained for us and preserved in us.[42] As respiration is not only the sign, but also the cause of life, so is the name of Mary, when it is spoken by the servants of God, not only proves that they are living, but procures and maintains this life, and obtains for them every aid. The blessed Alanus, when once assailed by a strong temptation, was on the point of being lost because he omitted to recommend himself to Mary; but the blessed Virgin appeared to him, and, to warn him against such neglect in future, gave him a blow on the ear, and said to him: "If thou hadst commended thyself to me, thou wouldst not have been exposed to this peril."

On the other hand: "Blessed is the man," says Mary, "that heareth me, and that watcheth daily at my gates, and waiteth at the posts of my doors."[43] Mary will certainly be ready to obtain light and strength for those faithful

---

39. Tolle corpus hoc solare, ubi dies? Tolle Mariam, quid, nisi tenebræ relinquentur? Serm. de Aquæd.
40. Posuisti tenebras, et facta est nox; in ipsa pertransibunt omnes bestiæ sylvæ. Psal. ciii. 20.
41. Væ væ eis qui solem istum aversantur!
42. Sicut respiratio non solum est signum vitæ, sed etiam causa; sic Mariæ nomen, quod in servorum Dei ore versatur, simul argumentum est quod vere vivant, simul etiam hanc vitam efficit et conservat; omnemque eis opem impertitur. Orat. de Deip.
43. Beatus homo qui audit me, qui vigilat ad fores meas quotidie, et observat ad postes ostii mei. Prov. viii. 34. In Festo Conc. B.V.M.

servants, that they may abandon their vices and walk in the paths of virtue. Hence is she, as Innocent III beautifully expresses it: The moon by night, the dawn of the morning, and the sun by day.[44] The moon, to him who is groping in the night of sin, to give him light to see his wretched state of condemnation; the dawn, the forerunner of the sun, to him who is enlightened, that he may come forth from sin and return to divine grace; and the sun, to him who is in grace, that he may not again fall into any precipice.

Theologians apply to Mary these words of Ecclesiasticus: "Her bands are a healthful binding."[45] Wherefore are they called bands, asks St. Lawrence Justinian, unless because she binds her servants, that they may not wander in forbidden fields?[46] St. Bonaventure explains in a similar manner the words of the office of Mary: "My abode is in the full assembly of saints."[47] He says that Mary is not only established in the fullness of the saints, but that she also upholds the saints, that they may not fall away; she sustains their virtue that it may not waver, and prevents the demons from doing them harm.[48]

It is said that "all her domestics are clothed with double garments."[49] Cornelius à Lapide thus describes this double garment: It is a double garment, because she clothes her servants with the virtues of her Son, as well as with her own;[50] and, thus clothed, they will preserve holy perseverance. For this reason, St. Philip Neri always admonished his penitents by saying to them: My children, if you desire perseverance, be devout to Mary. The venerable brother John Berchmans, of the Company of Jesus, also said: He who loves Mary, shall have perseverance. The reflection which Rupert the abbot makes upon the prodigal son is very beautiful. If the mother of this prodigal son had been living, he would either never have left his father's house or would have returned much sooner.[51] And by this he wished to say, that he who is a child of Mary, either never departs from God, or if for his misfortune he departs, by means of Mary he quickly returns.

Oh, if all men loved this most kind and loving Lady, and in temptations

44. Luna in nocte, aurora in diluculo, sol in die. Serm. 2, de Assump.
45. Vincula illius alligatura salutaris. Eccli. vi. 31.
46. Quare vinculæ? nisi quia servos ligat, ne discurrant per campos licentiæ.
47. In plenitudine sanctorum detentio mea. Eccli. xxiv. 16.
48. Ipsa quoque non solum in plenitudine sanctorum detinetur, sed etiam in plenitudine sanctos detinet, ne eorum plenitudo minuatur detinet nimirum virtutes, ne fugiant; detinet dæmones ne noceant. In spec.
49. Omnes domestici ejus vestiti sunt duplicibus. Prov. xxxi. 21.
50. Duplici veste ipsa ornat sibi devotos, quia tam Christi quam suis virtutibus eos induit.
51. Si prodigus filius viventem matrem habuisset, vel a paterna domo nunquam discessisset, vel forte citius rediisset.

always and immediately had recourse to her, who would fall? Who would be lost? He falls and is lost who does not flee to Mary. St. Lawrence Justinian applies to Mary these words of Ecclesiasticus: "I have walked in the waves of the sea;"[52] and makes her to say: I walked with my servants in the midst of the tempests to which they are exposed, to assist them, and prevent them from falling into the precipice of sin.[53]

Father Bernardine de Bustis relates that a hawk darted upon a bird which had been taught to say *Ave Maria*; the bird said *Ave Maria*, and the hawk fell dead. By this our Lord wished to show us, that if an irrational bird was saved from destruction by invoking Mary, how much more surely will he be prevented from falling into the power of evil spirits, who is mindful to invoke Mary in his temptations. Nothing remains to be done, says St. Thomas of Villanova, when the devil comes to tempt us, but, like the chickens when the kite appears, to run quickly under the shelter of the wings of our mother. Let us, then, at the approach of the temptations which assail us, without stopping to parley with them, place ourselves at once under the protection of Mary.[54] And then, the saint goes on to say, our Lady and mother must defend us; for, after God, we have no refuge but thee, who art our only hope, and the only protectress in whom we may confide.[55]

Let us, then, conclude with the words of St. Bernard:[56] Oh man, whoever thou art, thou knowest that in this miserable life thou art rather tossing on the tempestuous waves, among dangers and tempests, than walking upon the earth; if thou wouldst not sink, keep thy eye fixed on this star, namely, Mary. Look at the star, invoke Mary. When in danger of sinning, when tormented by temptations, when doubts disturb thee, remember that Mary can aid thee, and instantly call upon her. May her powerful name never depart from the confidence of thy heart, nor from the invocation of thy lips. If thou wilt follow Mary, thou shalt never wander from the path of safety. Commend thyself always to her, and thou shalt not despair. If she

---

52. In fluctibus maris ambulavi. C. xxiv. 8.
53. Scilicet cum familiaribus meis, ut ipsos eruerem a naufragio peccatorum.
54. Sicut pulli, volitantibus desuper milvis, ad gallinæ alas occurrunt, ita nos sub velamento alarum tuarum abscondimur. Serm. 3, de Nat. Virg.
55. Nescimus aliud refugium nisi te, tu sola es unica spes nostra, tu sola patrona nostra, ad quem omnes aspicimus.
56. O quisquis te intelligis in hujus sæculi pro fluvio magis inter procellas et tempestates fluctuare, quam per terram ambulare; ne avertas oculos a fulgore hujus sideris, si non vis obrui procellis; respice stellam, voca Mariam. In periculis, in angustiis, in rebus dubiis Mariam cogita, Mariam invoca. Non recedat ab ore, non recedat a corde. Ipsam sequens, non devias. Ipsam rogans, non desperas. Ipsa tenente, non corruis. Ipsa protegente, non metuis. Ipsa duce, non fatigaris. Ipsa propitia, pervenis. Sic fac, et vives. Hom. 2, super Missus.

upholds thee, thou shalt not fall. If she protects thee, thou need not fear ruin. If she guides thee, thou shalt be saved without difficulty. In a word, if Mary undertakes to defend thee, thou shalt certainly arrive at the kingdom of the blessed. Thus do, and thou shalt live.

EXAMPLE

In the celebrated history of St. Mary of Egypt, which we find in the first volume of the Lives of the Fathers, we read that, at twelve years of age she fled from her parents, and went to Alexandria, where she led an infamous life, and became the scandal of the city. After sixteen years spent in sin, she wandered off to Jerusalem; where, on the festival of the Holy Cross, she was led to enter the church, more from curiosity than devotion. On the threshold she was thrust back, as if by some invisible power; she attempted a second time to enter, and again was repelled, and a third and a fourth time the same thing happened. The wretched creature withdrew then into a corner of the portico, and there she was interiorly enlightened, and saw that God had refused her entrance into the church on account of her wicked life. By chance she raised her eyes, and saw a picture of Mary which was painted in the vestibule. She turned to it, weeping, and said: "Oh mother of God, have pity on this poor sinner! I know that, on account of my sins, I do not deserve that thou shouldst regard me; but thou art the refuge of sinners: for the love of Jesus, thy Son, help me. Obtain for me that I may enter the church, for I desire to change my life, and go and do penance wherever thou shalt direct." Then she heard an interior voice, as if the blessed Virgin answered her: "Come, since thou hast invoked me, and wishest to change thy life, enter the church, for the door will no longer be closed against thee." The sinner entered, adored the cross, and wept. She returned to the picture: "Oh Lady," she said, "I am ready; where shall I retire to do penance?" "Go," said the Virgin, "beyond the Jordan, and thou wilt find the place of thy repose." She made her confession, received holy communion, passed the river, reached the desert, and understood that there was her place of penance. During the first seventeen years that she lived in the desert, the evil spirits fiercely assailed her, to make her fall again. What did she then do? She recommended herself to Mary, and Mary obtained for her strength to resist for seventeen years, after which the conflict ceased. Finally, after fifty-seven years spent in the desert, in the eighty-seventh of her age, through Divine Providence, she was found by the abbot St. Zosimus. To him she related the story of her whole life, and begged him to return there the following year, and bring her holy communion. The holy abbot returned, and gave her communion. Then she implored him again to do the same thing. He returned the second time, and found her dead, her body surrounded with light, and at her head these words written in the sand: "Bury in this place the body of me, a miserable sinner, and pray God for me." A lion came and dug her grave, the abbot buried her, and, returning to the monastery, he related the wonders of divine mercy towards this happy penitent.

PRAYER

Oh mother of mercy! holy Virgin! behold at thy feet the traitor, who, returning ingratitude for the favors received through thee from God has betrayed thee and God. But, oh my Lady! know that my misery does not destroy, but increases my confidence in thee, because I see that my misery increases thy compassion for me. Show, oh Mary! that thou art the same to me as thou art to all those who invoke thee, full of grace and mercy. It is enough for me that thou regardest me with compassion. If in thy heart thou hast pity for me, thou wilt not cease to protect me; and if thou dost protect me, what should I fear? No, I fear nothing; I fear not my sins, for thou canst remedy their evil consequences; nor the demons, for thou art more powerful than hell; nor thy Son who is justly angry with me, for at one word of thine he will be appeased. I only fear that through negligence I may fail to implore thy protection in my temptations, and that this may cause my ruin. But I promise thee to-day, I will always have recourse to thee. Help me to keep this resolution. Behold the opportunity thou hast of satisfying thy desire to relieve so miserable a creature as I am.

Oh mother of God, I have great confidence in thee. From thee I expect the grace to do just penance for my sins, and from thee I hope the strength never more to fall back into them. If I am sick, thou canst heal me, oh heavenly physician. If my sins have made me weak, thy help can make me strong. Oh Mary, I hope every thing from thee, for thou hast all power with God.

SECTION 3
Mary renders death sweet to her servants

"He that is a friend loveth at all times; and a brother is proved in distress."[57] *True* friends and relatives are not known in times of prosperity, but in the season of adversity and misery. Worldly friends do not desert their friend when he is in prosperity; but if any misfortune overtakes him, particularly in the hour of death, immediately his friends abandon him. Not so does Mary desert her devoted servants. In their distresses, and especially at the trying hour of death, when our sufferings are the greatest that can be endured on earth, she our good Lady and mother cannot abandon her faithful servants; and as she is our life in the time of our exile, so is she also our sweetness in the hour of death, by obtaining for us that it may be sweet and blessed. For since that great day in which it was the lot and the grief of Mary to be present at the death of Jesus, her Son, who was the head of the elect, she obtained the grace of aiding at death all the elect. Hence the holy Church requires us to pray the blessed Virgin, that she would especially aid us in the hour of our death: "Pray for us sinners, now and at the hour of our death."[58]

The sufferings of the dying are very great, on account of their remorse for sins committed, their dread of approaching judgment, and the uncertainty of eternal salvation. At that moment especially, the devil puts forth all his power to gain the soul that is passing into eternity; knowing that the time is short in which he may win her, and that if he loses her, he has lost her forever. "The devil is come down unto you, having great wrath, knowing that he hath but a short time."[59] And therefore the devil, who has always tempted her in life, will not be satisfied to tempt her alone in

---

57. Omni tempore diligit qui amicus est, et frater in angustiis comprobatur. Prov. xvii. 17.
58. Ora pro nobis peccatoribus, nunc et in hora mortis nostræ.
59. Descendit Diabolus ad vos, habens iram magnam, sciens quod modicum tempus habet. Apoc. xii. 12.

death, but calls companions to his aid: "Their houses shall be filled with serpents."[60] When any one is at the point of death, his house is filled with demons, who unite to accomplish his ruin.

It is related of St. Andrew Avellino, that at the time of his death, ten thousand devils came to tempt him; and we read in his life, that at the time of his agony he had so fierce a struggle with hell, that it caused all his good religious who were present to tremble. They saw the face of the saint swell from agitation, so that it became black; they saw all his limbs trembling, and greatly agitated, rivers of tears flowed from his eyes, and his head shook violently; all these were signs of the horrible assault he was suffering from the powers of hell. All the religious wept in compassion, redoubled their prayers, and trembled with fear when they saw that a saint died thus. Yet they were consoled by seeing that the saint often turned his eyes, as if seeking help, towards a devout image of Mary, for they remembered that he had often said in life, that in the hour of his death, Mary must be his refuge. It finally pleased God to terminate this struggle by a glorious victory, for the agitation of his body ceased, his countenance gained its natural shape and color, and fixing his eyes tranquilly on that image, he devoutly bowed his head to Mary, who, it is believed, then appeared to him, as if to thank her, and quietly breathed forth in her arms his blessed soul, with heavenly peace depicted on his countenance. At the same time a Capuchin nun, in her agony, turned to the religious who were with her and said: "Say an Ave Maria, for a saint has just died."

Ah, how these rebels flee before the presence of their queen! If, in the hour of death, we have Mary on our side, what fear can we have of all the powers of hell? David, in dread of the agony of death, comforted himself with confidence in the death of his future Redeemer, and in the intercession of the Virgin mother: "For though I should walk in the midst of the shadow of death, I fear no evils, for thou art with me; thy rod and thy staff they have comforted me."[61] Cardinal Hugo understands the *staff* to signify the tree of the Cross, and the *rod* the intercession of Mary, who was the rod foretold by Isaias: "And there shall come forth a rod out of the root of Jesse, and a flower shall rise up out of his root."[62] This divine mother, says St. Peter Damian, is that powerful rod by which the fury of the infernal enemies is conquered.[63]

---

60. Implebuntur domus eorum draconibus. Isa. xiii. 21.
61. Et si ambulavero in medio umbræ mortis, virga tua, et baculus tuus ipsa me consolata sunt. Psal. xxii. 4.
62. Egredietur virga de radice Jesse, et flos de radice ejus ascendet. Isa. xi. 1.
63. Hæc est illa virga, qua retunduntur impetus adversantium dæmonum. Serm. de Assump. B. V.

Hence St. Antoninus encourages us, saying: If Mary is for us, who is against us?[64] Father Manuel Padial, of the Society of Jesus, being at the point of death, Mary appeared to him, and said, to comfort him: "The hour has at length come when the angels, rejoicing, say to thee, Oh happy labors! oh mortifications well recompensed!" At which words an army of devils was seen taking flight in despair, crying: "Alas! we have no power, for she who is without stain defends him."[65] In like manner, the devils assailed Father Jasper Haywood, when he was dying, with great temptations against faith; he immediately commended himself to the most holy Virgin, and then was heard to exclaim: "I thank thee, oh Mary, that thou hast come to my aid."[66]

St. Bonaventure says that Mary sends the archangel Michael, with all the angels, to the defense of her dying servants, to protect them from the assaults of evil spirits, and to receive the souls of all those who have especially and constantly recommended themselves to her.[67] When a man leaves this life, Isaias says that hell is in uproar, and sends its most terrible demons to tempt that soul before it leaves the body, and then afterwards to accuse it when it is presented at the tribunal of Jesus Christ to be judged: "Hell below was in an uproar to meet thee; at thy coming it stirred up the giants for thee."[68] But Richard says that the demons, when that soul is defended by Mary, will not even dare to accuse it; knowing that a soul protected by this great mother is never, and will never, be condemned.[69] St. Jerome wrote to the virgin Eustochium, that Mary not only assists her dear servants in their death, but also comes to meet them in their passage to the other life, to encourage them and accompany them to the divine tribunal.[70] And this agrees with what the blessed Virgin said to St. Bridget, speaking of her servants when they are at the point of death: "Then I, their most loving Lady and mother, hasten to them in death, that they may have consolation and comfort."[71] St. Vincent Ferrer adds: The blessed Virgin receives the souls of the dying. The loving queen receives their souls under her protection, and

---

64. Si Maria pro nobis, quis contra nos.
65. Patrig. Menol. alli. 28 Apr.
66. Patrig. Menol. etc.
67. Michael dux et princeps militiæ cœlestis cum omnibus administratoriis spiritibus, tuis, virgo, paret præceptis, in defendendis, et suscipiendis de corpore animabus Fidelium, specialiater tibi, Domina, die, ac nocte se commendantium. In Spec. B. V. c. 3.
68. Infernus subter te conturbatus est in occursum adventus tui, suscitabit sibi gigantes. Isa. xiv. 9.
69. Quis apud judicem accusare audeat, cui viderit matrem patrocinantem? Ricc. ap. Pep. to. 5, Lez. 244.
70. Morientibus beata virgo, non tantum succurrit, sed etiam occurrit. Epist. 2.
71. Tunc ego carissima eorum domina et mater occurram eis in morte, ut ipsi consolationem et refrigerium habeant. Rev. lib. 1, c. 20.

she herself presents them to the judge her Son, and thus certainly procures their salvation.[72] This happened to Charles, son of St. Bridget, who, dying in the perilous profession of a soldier, and far from his mother, the saint feared for his salvation; but the blessed Virgin revealed to her that Charles was saved for the love he bore her, in recompense of which she had assisted him in death, and had suggested to him the Christian acts necessary to be made at that moment. The saint saw at the same time Jesus upon a throne, and the devil bringing two accusations against the most holy Virgin: the first, that Mary had prevented him from tempting Charles at the moment of death; the second, that Mary herself had presented his soul to its judge, and thus had saved without even giving him an opportunity to expose the reasons why he claimed it as his own. She then saw him driven from the presence of the judge, and the soul of Charles taken to heaven.

"Her bands are a healthful binding; in the latter end thou shalt find rest in her."[73] Blessed art thou, oh brother, if in death thou shalt find thyself bound by the sweet chains of love for the mother of God! These chains are chains of salvation, which will secure to thee eternal salvation, and give thee in death that blessed peace which will be the commencement of thy eternal peace and rest. Father Binetti, in his book "On the Perfections of our Lord," relates that having been present at the death of a devoted servant of Mary, he heard from him these words before he breathed his last: "Oh, my Father, if you knew what happiness I find in having served the most holy mother of God! I could not describe to you the joy I feel at this moment."[74] Father Suarez, because he was all his life very devoted to Mary, used to say, that he would willingly exchange all his knowledge for the merit of one Hail Mary, and died with so much joy, that he exclaimed at his last moment, "I never imagined it would be so sweet to die,—non putabam tam dulce esse mori."[75] You too, devout reader, will doubtless feel the same peace and joy, if at death you can remember having loved this good mother, who cannot but be faithful to her children, when they are faithful to her service, paying her their offerings of visits, rosaries, and fasting, and especially thanking her, praising her, and often commending themselves to her powerful protection.

---

72. Beata virgo animas morientium suscipit. Serm. de Assump.
73. Vincula illius alligatura salutaris, in novissimis invenies requiem in ea. Eccli. vi. 29, 31.
74. C. 31.
75. Opusc. 33, c. 4.

Courtesy of Felipe Barandiarán

***Virgin of Mercy.* 19th century fresco. Chapel of Oldenburg Castle, Germany.**

Neither will you be deprived of this consolation on account of your sins if from henceforth you will be careful to live well, and to serve this very grateful and gracious Lady. In the trials and temptations with which the devil will assail you, that he may throw you into despair, she will comfort you, and even come herself to assist you in death. Martin, brother of St. Peter Damian, as the saint himself relates, finding that he had offended God, went one day before an altar of Mary to dedicate himself to her service, putting his girdle around his neck in token of his servitude, and thus said: "My Lady, mirror of purity, I, a poor sinner, have offended God and thee by violating chastity: I have no other remedy than to offer myself as thy servant; to thy service I dedicate myself to-day; receive this rebel, do not despise me." He then laid on the altar

a certain sum of money, promising to pay the same every year as a trib-
ute of his devotion to Mary. After some time Martin died; but before his
death he was heard one morning to say: "Arise, arise, pay homage to my
Lady;" and afterwards: "What a favor is this, oh queen of heaven, that
thou shouldst condescend to visit this thy poor servant. Bless me, oh
Lady, and permit me not to be lost after thou hast honored me with thy
presence." At this moment his brother Peter entered. Martin related to
him the visit of Mary, and how she had blessed him, lamenting that the
persons present had not arisen at her entrance; and shortly after quietly
passed away to our Lord. Such will be your death also, oh my reader, if
you are faithful to Mary, even if in your past life you have offended God.
She will give you a sweet and happy death.

And if then you are greatly alarmed and lose courage in view of the
sins you have committed, she will come to comfort you as she came to
Adolphus, Count of Alsace, who, having quitted the world and become
a Franciscan, as the chronicles relate, was very devoted to the mother of
God. His last days arrived, and at the remembrance of the life he had led
in the world, and the rigor of divine justice, he began to fear death and
doubt of his salvation. Then Mary, who never sleeps when her faithful servants are in trouble, accompanied by many saints, appeared to him, and
encouraged him with these tender words of consolation: "My dear Adolphus, thou art mine, thou hast given thyself to me, then why dost thou so
greatly fear death?"[76] The servant of Mary was consoled by these words,
every fear disappeared, and he died in great peace and contentment.

Let us, too, although we are sinners, take courage and have the confidence that Mary will come to assist us in death, and console us by her
presence, if we serve and love her during the remainder of our life on this
earth. Our queen, speaking one day to St. Matilda, promised that she
would be present at the death of all those devoted children who had faithfully served her in life.[77] Oh my God, what a consolation must it be in that
last hour of life, when our lot for eternity is to be decided, to find close by
our side the queen of heaven, who sustains and comforts us by promising
us her protection! Besides the examples already cited of the assistance
afforded by Mary to her faithful servants, there are innumerable others

---

76. Adolphe mi carissime, mori cur times, meus cum sis?
77. Ego omnibus qui mihi pie deserviunt, volo in morte fidelissime tamquam mater piissima adesse
eosque consolari ac protegere. Ap. Blos. p. 2, Concl. an. fid. cap. 12.

to be found in various books. This favor was granted to St. Clare, to St. Felix, a Capuchin, to the blessed Clara of Montefalco, to St. Theresa, and St. Peter of Alcantara. But for our common consolation, I will mention the few following examples. Father Crasset relates[78] that St. Mary of Oignies saw the blessed Virgin by the pillow of a devout widow of Villembroe, who was tormented by a burning fever. The most holy Mary was standing by her side consoling her, and cooling her with a fan. St. John of God, at death, expected a visit from Mary, to whom he was greatly devoted; but finding she did not come, he was afflicted, and perhaps complained a little. But at length the holy mother appeared to him, and as if reproaching him for his want of confidence, said to him these tender words, which should encourage all the servants of Mary: "John, it is not in my heart, at this hour, to desert my children."[79] As if she had said to him: My John, of what were you thinking? that I had abandoned you? Do you not know that I cannot abandon my devoted children at the hour of death? I did not come before, because it was not yet time; but now I come ready to take you, let us go to paradise. And soon after the saint expired, and flew to heaven to give thanks eternally to his most loving queen.[80]

EXAMPLE

I will now relate another example by way of conclusion to the subject of which I have been just speaking, and for the sake of showing how great is the tenderness of this good mother towards her children when they are dying.

The pastor of a certain place went to assist at the death-bed of a rich man. He was dying in a splendid house, and a multitude of relations, friends, and servants, surrounded his bed. But among these, the priest saw a number of devils in the shape of hounds, who waited to seize upon his soul, and who actually did so; for he died in sin. At the same time he was sent for by a poor woman, who was dying, and desired the holy

---

78. Div. alla verg. tom. 1, tr. 1, q. 11.
79. Joannes non est meum, in hac hora meos devotos derelinquere.
80. Bolland. 8 Martii.

sacraments; not being able to leave the dying rich man, whose soul was so much in need of his assistance, he sent another priest to her, who accordingly went, carrying with him the holy sacrament. He found in the dwelling of that good woman no servants, no retinue, no splendid furniture, for she was very poor, and we may suppose had only a little straw to lie upon. But what does he see? He sees in that apartment a great light, and near the bed of the dying person was Mary the mother of God, who was consoling her, and with a cloth was wiping the sweat from her brow. The priest seeing Mary, had not the courage to enter, but she made a motion to him to approach. He entered, Mary pointed to a seat, that he might sit down and hear the confession of her servant. The poor woman then made her confession, received the holy sacrament with much devotion, and at last expired happily in the arms of Mary.[81]

PRAYER

Oh my sweetest mother, what will be the death of me, a poor sinner? Even now, when thinking of that great moment, in which I must die, and be presented at the divine tribunal, and remembering how often, by my wicked consent, I myself have written my own sentence of condemnation, I tremble, am confounded, and fear greatly for my eternal salvation. Oh Mary, my hopes are in the blood of Jesus, and in thy intercession. Thou art the Queen of heaven! the Lady of the universe! it is sufficient to say that thou art the mother of God. Thou art great, but thy greatness does not separate thee from us; it even inclines thee to have more compassion on our miseries. When our earthly friends are raised to any dignity, they seclude themselves from those whom they have left in a low estate, and will not condescend even to look at them. But it is not so with thy loving and noble heart. Where thou dost behold the greatest misery, there thou art most intent on giving relief. When invoked, thou dost immediately come to our aid, and even anticipate our supplications; thou dost console us in our afflictions, dissipate all

---

81. Crisog. Mond. Mar. p. 3, d. 38.

tempests, put down our enemies; in a word, thou dost never omit an opportunity of doing us good. Ever blessed be that divine hand which has united in thee so much majesty and so much tenderness, so much greatness and so much love! I always thank our Lord, and congratulate myself that I can regard thy happiness and mine, thy fate and mine as one. Oh consoler of the afflicted, console in his affliction one who recommends himself to thee. I am tortured with remorse for my many sins; I am uncertain whether I have repented of them as I ought to have done; I see how corrupt and imperfect are all my works. The devil is awaiting my death in order to accuse me. Divine justice violated must be satisfied. Oh my mother, what will become of me? If thou dost not aid me, I am lost. Answer me, wilt thou aid me? Oh merciful Virgin, console me; obtain for me strength to amend, and to be faithful to God during what remains to me of life. And when I shall find myself in the last agony of death, oh Mary! my hope, do not abandon me; then more than ever assist me, and save me from despair at the sight of my sins, of which the devils will accuse me. Oh Lady, pardon my boldness; come, then, thyself to console me by thy presence. Grant me this favor which thou hast bestowed on so many; I also desire it. If my boldness is great, greater still is thy goodness, which seeks the most miserable to console them. In this, thy goodness, I trust. May it be to thy eternal glory that thou hast saved from hell a miserable wretch, and brought him to thy kingdom, where I hope to console myself by being always at thy feet to thank, bless, and love thee throughout eternity. Oh Mary, I wait for thee, do not leave me then disconsolate. Come, come. Amen, amen.

The Virgin intercedes with Christ on behalf of the souls in Purgatory. **Philippe de Champaigne. 1655. Musée des Augustins, Toulouse, France.**

CHAPTER 3

Spes nostra, salve
Hail, our hope

SECTION 1
Mary is the hope of all

Modern heretics cannot endure that we should salute Mary in this manner by calling her our hope. Hail, our hope, "spes nostra salve." They say that God alone is our hope, and that he who places his hope in a creature is accursed of God.[1] Mary, they exclaim, is a creature, and, as a creature, how can she be our hope? Thus say the heretics, but notwithstanding this, the Church requires all the clergy, and all religious daily to raise their voices, and in the name of all the faithful, invoke and call Mary by the sweet name of our hope, the hope of all: "Hail, our hope!"

In two ways, says the angelic St. Thomas, can we place our hope in a person: as the principal cause, and as the intermediate cause. Those who hope for some favor from the king, hope for it from the king as sovereign, and hope for it from his minister or favorite as intercessor. If the favor is granted, it comes in the first place from the king, but it comes through the medium of his favorite; wherefore, he who asks a favor justly calls that intercessor his hope. The king of heaven, because he is infinite goodness, greatly desires to enrich us with his graces; but, because confidence is necessary on our part, in order to increase our confidence, he has given his own mother for our mother and advocate, and has given her all power to aid us; and hence he wishes us to place in her all our hopes of salvation, and of every blessing. Those who place all their hope on creatures, without dependence upon God, as sinners do, who to obtain the friendship and favor of man, are willing to displease God, are certainly cursed by God, as Isaias says. But those who hope in Mary, as mother of God, powerful to obtain for them graces and life eternal, are blessed, and please the heart of God, who wishes to see that noble creature honored, who, more than all men and angels, loved and honored him in this world.

---

1. Maledictus homo qui confidit in homine. Jer. xvii. 5.

Hence we justly call the Virgin our hope hoping, as Cardinal Bellarmine says, to obtain, by her intercession what we could not obtain by our prayers alone.[2] We pray to her, says St. Anselm, in order that the dignity of the intercessor may supply our deficiencies.[3] Therefore, the saint adds, to supplicate the Virgin with such hope, is not to distrust the mercy of God, but to fear our own unworthiness.[4]

With reason does the Church, then, apply to Mary the words of Ecclesiasticus, with which he salutes her: "Mother of holy hope;"[5] that mother who inspires us not with the vain hope of the miserable and transitory advantages of this life, but with the holy hope of the immense and eternal good of the blessed life to come. St. Ephrem thus salutes the divine mother: "Hail, hope of the soul! hail, secure salvation of Christians! hail, helper of sinners! hail, defense of the faithful, and salvation of the world!"[6] St. Basil teaches us that, next to God, we have no other hope than Mary, and for this reason he calls her: After God our only hope, "Post Deum sola spes nostra;" and St. Ephrem, reflecting on the order of Providence in this life, by which God has ordained (as St. Bernard says, and we shall hereafter prove at length) that all those who are saved must be saved by means of Mary, says to her: Oh Lady, do not cease to receive and shelter us under the mantle of thy protection, since, after God, we have no hope but thee.[7] St. Thomas of Villanova says the same thing, calling her our only refuge, help, and protection.[8] St. Bernard assigns the reason for this by saying: Behold, oh man, the design of God, a design arranged for our benefit, that he may be able to bestow upon us more abundantly his compassion; for, wishing to redeem the human race, he has placed the price of our redemption in the hands of Mary, that she may dispense it at her pleasure.[9]

God ordered Moses to make a propitiatory of the purest gold, telling him that from it he would speak to him: "Thou shalt make a propitiatory of the purest gold. Thence will I give orders, and will speak to thee."[10] A certain

---

2. D. Beat. SS. lib. 2 cap. 2.
3. Ut dignitas intercessoris suppleat inopiam nostram. De Exc. V. c. 6.
4. Unde Virginem interpellare, non est de divina misericordia diffidere, sed de propria indignitate formidare. Loc. cit.
5. Mater sanctæ spei. Cap. xxiv. 24.
6. Ave animæ spes; ave Christianorum firma salus; ave peccatorum adjutrix; ave vallum fidelium; et mundi salus. De Laud. Virg.
7. Nobis non est alia quam a te fiducia, O Virgo sincerissima; sub alis tuæ pietatis protege et custodi nos. De Laud. Virg.
8. Tu unicum nostrum, refugium subsidium, et asylum. Con. 3, de Conc. Virg.
9. Intuere, homo, consilium Dei, consilium pietatis; redempturus humanum genus, universum præstium contulit in Maria. Serm. de Nat.
10. Facies et propitiatorium de auro mundissimo ... Inde præcipiam et loquar ad te. Exod. c. xxv. v. 17, 22.

author explains this propitiatory to be Mary, through whom the Lord speaks to men, and dispenses to them pardon, graces, and favors.[11] And therefore St. Irenæus says that the divine Word, before incarnating himself in the womb of Mary, sent the archangel to obtain her consent, because he would have the world indebted to Mary for the mystery of the incarnation.[12] Also the Idiot remarks, that every blessing, every help, every grace that men have received or will receive from God, to the end of the world, has come to them, and will come to them, through the intercession and by means of Mary.[13] Rightly, then did the devout Blosius exclaim: Oh Mary, who art so amiable, and so grateful to him who loves thee, who will be so stupid and unhappy as not to love thee! In doubt and perplexity thou dost enlighten the minds of those who have recourse to thee in their troubles. Thou art the comfort of those who trust in thee, in time of danger. Thou dost help those who invoke thee. Thou art, continues Blosius, next to thy divine Son, the secure salvation of thy servants. Hail then, oh hope of the despairing. Hail helper of the destitute! Oh Mary, thou art omnipotent, since thy Son would honor thee by immediately doing all that thou desirest.[14]

St. Germanus, recognizing Mary to be the source of every blessing, and the deliverance from every evil, thus invokes her: Oh my Lady thou alone art my help, given me by God; thou art the guide of my pilgrimage, the support of my weakness, my riches in poverty, my deliverer from bondage, the hope of my salvation: graciously listen, I pray thee to my supplications, take compassion on my sighs, thou my queen, my refuge, my life, my help, my hope, my strength.[15]

Justly, then, does St. Antoninus apply to Mary that passage of wisdom: "Now all good things came to me together with her."[16] Since Mary is the mother of God and the dispenser of all good, the world may truly say, and especially those in the world who are devoted to this queen, that, together

---

11. Te universus mundus continet commune propitiatorium. Inde pientissimus Dominus loquitur ad cor; inde responsa dat benignitatis et veniæ; inde munera largitur; inde nobis omne bonum emanat.
12. Quid est quod sine Mariæ consensu non perficitur incarnationis mysterium? quia nempe vult illam Deus omnium bonorum esse principium. Lib. 3, contr. Valent. c. 33.
13. Per ipsam habet mundus, et habiturus est omne bonum. In Præf. Contempl. B. M.
14. O Maria quis te non amet? Tu in dubiis es lumen, in mœroribus solatium, in periculis refugium. Tu post unigenitum tuum certa fidelium salus. Ave desperantium spes, ave destitutorum adjutrix. Cujus honori tantum tribuit Filius, ut quod vis, mox fiat. Cimeliarch, Embol. 1, ad Mar.
15. O Domina mea, sola mihi ex Deo solatium, itineris mei directio, debilitatis meæ potentia, mendicitatis meæ divitiæ, vulnerum meorum medicina, dolorum meorum relevatio, vinculorum meorum solutio, salutis meæ spes; exaudi orationes meas, miserere suspiriorum meorum, Domina mea, refugium, vita, auxilium, spes et robur meum. In Encom. Deip.
16. Venerunt autem mihi omnia bona pariter cum illa. Cap. vii. v. 11.

with devotion to Mary, they have obtained every good thing.[17] Wherefore the Abbot of Celles said positively: He who has found Mary finds every good thing.[18] He finds all graces and all virtues; since she by her powerful intercession obtains for him in abundance all that he needs to make him rich in divine grace. She gives us to know that she has with her all the riches of God, that is, the divine mercies, that she may dispense them for the benefit of those who love her. "With me are riches and glory, that I may enrich them that love me."[19] Hence St. Bonaventure says: We should all keep our eyes fixed on the hands of Mary, that through her we may receive the blessings we desire.[20]

Oh! how many of the proud have found humility through devotion to Mary; how many of the violent, meekness; how many blind, the light; how many despairing, confidence; how many lost, salvation! And precisely this she herself predicted when she pronounced in the house of Elizabeth that sublime canticle: "Behold, from henceforth all generations shall call me blessed."[21] Which words St. Bernard repeats, and says: All nations will call thee blessed, for to all nations thou hast given life and glory; in thee sinners find pardon, and the just find perseverance in divine grace.[22] Whence the devout Lanspergius represents the Lord thus speaking to the world: Venerate my mother with especial veneration. Oh men, he says, poor children of Adam, who live in the midst of so many enemies and so much misery, strive to honor with particular affection my mother and yours. I have given her to the world as an example of purity, a refuge and asylum for the afflicted.[23] That is, I have given Mary to the world for your example, that from her you may learn to live as you ought; and for your refuge, that you may have recourse to her, in your tribulations. This my child, says God, I have created such that no one can fear her, or be unwilling to have recourse to her, for I have created her with so benign and compassionate a nature, that she will

---

17. Omnium bonorum mater est; et venerunt mihi omnia bona cum illa, scilicet virgine, potest dicere mundus. S. Anton. Part. 4. tit. 17, c. 20.
18. Inventa Maria, invenitur omne bonum.
19. Mecum sunt divitiæ et opes superbæ ... ut ditem diligentes me. Prov. viii. 18-21.
20. Oculi omnium nostrum ad manus Mariæ semper debent respicere, ut per manus ejus aliquid boni accipiamus. In Spec.
21. Ecce enim ex hoc beatam me dicent omnes generationes. Luc. i. 48.
22. Ex hoc beatam te dicent omnes generationes, quæ omnibus generationibus vitam et gloriam genuisti. In te peccatores veniam, justi gratiam inveniunt in æternum. Serm. 2, in Pentec.
23. Matrem meam venerationem præcipua venerare; ego enim mundo dedi in puritatis exemplum, in præsidium tutissimum, ut sit tribulatis asylum, quam nemo formidet; nemo ad eam accedere trepidet. Propterea namque adeo feci eam mitem, adeo misericordem ut neminem aspernat, nulli se neget; omnibus pietatis sinum apertum teneat, neminem a se redire tristem sinat. Lib. 4. Min. Op

not despise any who seek her protection, and she will deny no favor to any who ask it. She spreads the mantle of her compassion over all, and never permits any one to go from her feet unconsoled. May the great goodness of our God, then, be ever blessed, who has given us this great mother and advocate, so loving and tender. Oh! how tender are the sentiments of confidence which filled the heart of the most loving St. Bonaventure for his dear Redeemer Jesus, and for our loving intercessor Mary! Let the Lord chastise me as much as seemeth to him good, I know that he will not refuse himself to those who love him and who seek him with an upright heart. I will embrace him with my love, and I will not let him go till he has blessed me, and he will not depart without me. If I can do nothing else, at least I will hide myself in his wounds; there I will remain, and out of himself he shall not be able to find me.[24] Finally, he adds, if my Redeemer, for my sins, drives me from his feet, I will cast myself at the feet of his mother Mary, and, prostrate there, I will not depart until she has obtained my pardon; for this mother of mercy has never failed to take pity on misery and console the wretched who seek her aid; and therefore, if not from obligation, at least from compassion, she will not fail to induce her Son to pardon me.[25]

Look upon us, then, we will conclude with the words of Euthymius, look upon us, then, with thine eyes of compassion, oh our most merciful mother, for we are thy servants, and in thee we have placed all our hope.[26]

EXAMPLE

It is related in the Fourth Part of the Treasure of the Rosary, miracle eighty-fifth, that a gentleman who was most devoted to the divine mother, had set apart in his palace an oratory where, before a beautiful statue of Mary, he was accustomed often to remain praying, not only by day, but also by night, inter-

24. Quantumcumque me Deus præsciverat, scio quod seipsum negare non potest. Eum amplexabor, et si mihi non benedixerit, eum non demittam; et sine me recedere non valebit. In cavernis vulnerum suorum me abscondam, ibique extra se me invenire non poterit.
25. Ad matris suæ pedes provulutus stabo, et mihi veniam impetret; ipsa enim non misereri ignorat; et miseris non satisfacere nunquam scivit. Ideoque ex compassione mihi ad indulgentiam Filium inclinabit. P. 3, Stim. Div. Am. c. 13
26. Respice, O mater misericordiosissima, respice servos tuos, in te enim omnem spem nostram collocavimus. Orat. de Deip.

rupting his rest to go and honor his beloved Lady; but his wife, for he was married, though she was a very devout person, observing that her husband in the deepest silence of the night left his bed, and going from his apartment did not return for a long time, became jealous, and was suspicious of evil; wherefore, one day, to free herself from this thorn which tormented her, she ventured to ask him if he ever loved any other woman but herself. Smiling, he answered her: "I assure you that I love the most amiable lady in the world; to her I have given my whole heart and rather would I die than cease to love her; if you knew her, you would say that I ought to love her more than I do." He meant the most holy Virgin whom he loved so tenderly. But his wife, conceiving a greater suspicion than before, in order to ascertain the truth better, interrogated him anew, and asked him if he arose from his bed and left the room every night to meet that lady. The gentleman, who did not perceive the great trouble of his wife, answered "Yes." The wife was completely deceived, and, blinded by passion, one night when her husband according to his custom, had left the chamber, seized a knife in despair, cut her throat, and very soon died. Her husband having finished his devotions, returned to his apartment, but on going to bed, found it wet. He called his wife; she did not answer: he tried to arouse her; she was immovable. At length he took a light, found the bed full of blood, and his wife dead, with her throat cut. Then he perceived that she had destroyed herself through jealousy. What does he do? He locks the door of his apartment, returns to the chapel, prostrates himself before the most blessed Virgin, and shedding a torrent of tears, said to her: "Oh my mother, behold my affliction: if thou dost not console me, to whom shall I go? Remember I am so unfortunate as to see my wife dead and lost because I have come hither to pay thee honor, oh my mother, who dost help us in all our troubles, help me now." How surely does every one obtain what he wishes if he supplicates with confidence this mother of mercy! No sooner did he offer this prayer than he heard a servant-maid calling him: "My lord, come to your apartment, for your lady calls you." The gentleman could hardly believe these words for joy. Return, he said to the servant, and see if she really calls me. She returned, entreating him to go quickly, for her mistress was waiting for him. He went, opened the door, and found his wife living; she threw herself at his feet in tears and begged him to pardon her, saying: "Oh, my husband, the mother of God, through thy prayer, has delivered me from hell." Weeping for joy, they went to their oratory to thank the blessed Virgin. The next day the husband made a feast for all their relations, to whom the wife herself related the facts, at the same time showing the marks of the wound, and all were more deeply inflamed with the love of the divine mother.

PRAYER

Oh mother of holy love, oh our life, our refuge, and our hope, thou knowest that thy Son Jesus Christ, not content with making himself our perpetual intercessor with the eternal Father, would have thee also engaged in obtaining for us, by thy prayers, the divine mercy. He has ordained that thy prayers should aid in our salvation, and has given such power to them that they obtain whatever they ask; I, a miserable sinner, turn to thee then, oh hope of the wretched. I hope, oh Lady, through the merits of Jesus Christ and thy intercession to secure my salvation. In these I trust; and so entirely do I trust in thee, that if my eternal salvation were in my own hands, I would wish to place it in thine; for in thy mercy and protection I would trust far more than in my own works. My mother and my hope, do not abandon me, as I deserve. Behold my misery, pity me, help me, save me. I confess that I have often, by my sins, shut out the light and aid which thou hast obtained for me from the Lord. But thy compassion for the wretched and thy power with God are far greater than the number and malignity of my sins. It is known in heaven and on earth that he who is protected by thee will certainly not perish. Let all forget me, but do not thou forget me, oh mother of the omnipotent God. Say unto God that I am thy servant, tell him that I am defended by thee, and I shall be saved. Oh Mary, I trust in thee: in this hope I live, and in this hope I wish to die, repeating always: "Jesus is my only hope, and after Jesus, Mary."[27]

SECTION 2
Mary, the hope of sinners

After God had created the earth he created two lights, the greater and the less: the sun to give light by day, and the moon to give light by night.[28] The sun, says Cardinal Hugo, was the type of Jesus Christ, in whose light

---

27. Unica spes mea Jesus, et post Jesum Virgo Maria.
28. Fecitque Deus duo luminaria magna; luminare majus ut præesset diei, luminare minus ut præesset nocti. Gen. i. 16.

the just rejoice who live in the daylight of divine grace; but the moon was the type of Mary, by whom sinners are enlightened, who are living in the night of sin.[29] Mary, then, being the moon, so propitious to miserable sinners, if any unhappy person, says Innocent III finds that he has fallen into this night of sin, what must he do? Since he has lost the light of the sun, by losing divine grace, let him turn to the moon, let him pray to Mary, and she will give him light to know the misery of his condition, and strength to come forth from it.[30] St. Methodius says that by the prayers of Mary innumerable sinners are continually converted.[31]

One of the titles by which the holy Church teaches us to invoke the divine mother, and which most encourages poor sinners, is the title of "Refuge of Sinners," with which we invoke her in the Litanies. There were anciently, in Judea, cities of refuge; and criminals, who sought protection in them, were free from the penalty of their offenses. Now, there are not so many cities of refuge, but instead of these there is one only, Mary; of whom it was spoken: Glorious things are said of thee, oh city of God—Gloriosa dicta sunt de te civitas Dei.[32] But with this difference, that not all criminals could find refuge in those ancient cities, nor for all sorts of crime; but under the mantle of Mary all offenders may find protection, whatever crimes they have committed. It is sufficient for any one to have recourse to her for protection. "I am the city of refuge for all those who flee to me,"[33] as St. John of Damascus says, speaking in her name.

It is enough that we have recourse to her. He who has been so happy as to enter this city need not speak in order to secure his safety. "Assemble yourselves and let us enter into the fenced city, and let us be silent there."[34] This fenced city, as the blessed Albertus Magnus explains it, is the holy Virgin, whose defense is grace and glory. "Let us be silent there, since we may not dare to supplicate the Lord for pardon, it is enough that we enter into the city and are silent, for then Mary will speak and will pray for us."[35] Whence a devout writer exhorts all sinners to seek shelter under the mantle of Mary, saying: Fly, oh Adam, oh Eve, and ye their children, who

29. Luminare majus Christus, qui præest justis; luminare minus, idest Maria, quæ præest peccatoribus.
30. Qui jacet in nocte culpæ, respiciat lunam, deprecetur Mariam. Serm. 2. de Assump. B. V.
31. Mariæ virtute et precibus pene innumeræ peccatorum conversiones fiunt.
32. Psal. lxxxvi. 3.
33. Ego civitas refugii omnium ad me confugientium. Or. 2. de Dorm.
34. Convenite celeriter et ingrediamur civitatem munitam, et sileamus ibi. Jerem. viii. 14.
35. Et sileamus ibi. Quia non audemus deprecari Dominum quem offendimus, ipsa, deprecetur et roget.

have offended God; fly and take refuge in the bosom of this good mother. Do you not know that she is the only city of refuge, and the only hope of sinners?[36] As St. Augustine has called her, The only hope of sinners: "Unica spes peccatorum."[37]

Hence St. Ephrem says: Thou art the only advocate of sinners, and of those who are deprived of every help; and he thus salutes her: Hail! refuge and retreat of sinners, to whom alone they can flee with confidence.[38] And this is what David intended to express, says a certain author, when he said: "He hath protected me in the secret place of his tabernacle."[39] And what is this tabernacle, if not Mary? As St. Germanus calls her, a tabernacle made by God, in which none but God has entered, in order to complete the great mysteries of human redemption.[40] On this subject the great Father St. Basil says: The Lord has given us Mary as a public hospital where all the infirm, who are poor and destitute of every other help, may assemble: "Aperuit nobis Deus publicum valetudinarium." Now, in hospitals established expressly for the reception of the poor, I would ask, who have the first claim to be received, if not the poorest and most infirm?

Wherefore, let him who finds himself most miserable, because most destitute of merit, and most afflicted by the maladies of the soul, namely, sins, say to Mary: Oh Lady, thou art the refuge of the infirm; do not reject me, for, because I am the poorest and most infirm of all, I have the greater claim upon thee to receive me. Let us say with St. Thomas of Villanova: Oh Mary, we poor sinners know no refuge but thee. Thou art our only hope; to thee we entrust our salvation. Thou art the only advocate with Jesus Christ; to thee we all have recourse.[41]

In the Revelations of St. Bridget, Mary is called the star going before the sun: "Sidus vadens ante solem."[42] By which we are to understand, that when devotion to the divine mother first dawns in a sinful soul, it is a certain sign that God will soon come to enrich her with his grace. The glorious St.

---

36. Fugite O Adam, O Eva, fugite eorum liberi intra sinum matris Mariæ. Ipsa est civitas refugii, spes unica peccatorum. B. Fernandez, in c. iv. Gen.
37. Serm. 18, de Sanct.
38. Ave peccatorum refugium et hospitium: ad quam nimirum confugere possunt peccatores. De. Laud. Virg.
39. Protexit me in abscondito tabernaculi sui. Psal. xxvi. 5.
40. Tabernaculum a Deo fabricatum, in quo solus Deus ingressus est sacris mysteriis operaturus in te pro salute omnium hominum.
41. Nescimus aliud refugium nisi te. Tu sola es unica spes nostra in qua confidimus. Tu sola patrona nostra, ad quam omnes aspicimus. Serm. 3. de Nat. B.V.
42. Rev. entr. c. 50.

Bonaventure, in order to revive in the hearts of sinners confidence in the protection of Mary, represents to us the sea in a tempest, in which sinners who have fallen from the bark of divine grace, tossed about by remorse of conscience, and by the fear of divine justice, without light and without a guide, have almost lost the breath of hope, and are nearly sinking in despair; at this critical moment the saint, pointing to Mary, who is commonly called "The star of the sea," raises his voice and exclaims: Oh poor, lost sinners, do not despair, lift your eyes to that beautiful star, take courage and trust, for she will guide you out of the tempest, and bring you to the port of safety.[43]

St. Bernard has said the same thing: If you would not be overwhelmed in the tempest, turn to this star, and call Mary to thy aid.[44] The devout Blosius also says that she is the only refuge for those who have offended God: the asylum of all those who are tempted and afflicted.[45] This mother of mercy is all kindness and all sweetness, not only with the just, but also with sinners and those who are in despair; so that when she beholds them turning towards her, and sees that they are with sincerity seeking her help, she at once welcomes them, aids them, and obtains their pardon from her Son.[46] She neglects none, however unworthy they may be, and refuses to none her protection; she consoles all; and no sooner do they call upon her, than she hastens to their help.[47] With her gentleness she often wins their devotion, and raises those sinners who are most averse to God, and who are the most deeply plunged in the lethargy of their vices that she may dispose them to receive divine grace, and at last render themselves worthy of eternal glory.[48] God has created this his beloved daughter with a disposition so kind and compassionate, that no one can hesitate to have recourse to her intercession.[49] The devout writer concludes with saying: It is not possible that any one can be lost, who with exactness and humility practices devotion to this divine mother.[50]

She is called a plane-tree: As a plane-tree was I exalted: "Quasi platanus exaltata sum."[51] Sinners may understand by this, that as the plane-tree

---

43. Respirate ad illam perditi peccatores, et perducet vos ad portum. In Psal. viii.
44. Si non vis obrui procellis, respice stellam, voca Mariam. Hom. 2. sup. Miss.
45. Ipsa peccantium singulare refugium; ipsa omnium quos tentatio urget, aut calamitas, aut persecutio, tutissimum asylum.
46. Tota mitis est et suavis, non solum justis, verum etiam peccatoribus, et desperatis. Quos, ut ad se ex corde clamare conspexerit, statim adjuvat, suscipit et Judici reconciliat.
47. Nullum aspernens, nulli se negat; omnes consolatur, et tenuiter invocata, præsto adest.
48. Sua bonitate sæpe eos, qui Deo minus afficiuntur ad sui cultum blande allicit; potenterque excitat, ut per hujusmodi studium præparentur ad gratiam, et tandem apti reddantur regno cœlorum.
49. Talis a Deo facta est, ut nemo ad eam accedere trepidet.
50. Fieri non potest, ut pereat, qui Mariæ sedulus et humilis cultor extiterit. In can. Vit. Spir. cap. 18.
51. Eccli. xxiv. 19.

gives a shelter to travelers, where they may take refuge from the heat of the sun, thus Mary, when she sees the anger of divine justice kindled against them, invites them to resort to the shelter of her protection. St. Bonaventure remarks that Isaias, in his day lamented, and said, "Behold, thou art angry and we have sinned. . . . there is none that riseth up and taketh hold of thee;"[52] because Mary was not yet born into the world.[53] But now, if God is offended with any sinner, and Mary undertakes to protect him, she restrains the Son from punishing him, and saves him.[54] Also, continues St. Bonaventure, no one can be found more fit than Mary to place her hand upon the sword of divine justice, that it may not descend upon the head of the sinner.[55] Richard of St. Laurence expresses the same thought, when he says: God lamented, before the birth of Mary, that there was no one to restrain him from punishing the sinner; but Mary being born, she appeases him.[56]

St. Basil encourages sinners with the same thought, and says: Oh sinner, be not timid, but in all thy necessities flee to Mary, invoke her aid, and thou wilt always find her ready to assist thee, for it is the divine will that she should aid all men in all their necessities.[57] This mother of mercy has such a desire to save the most abandoned sinners, that she even goes to seek them; and if they have recourse to her, she will surely find a method of rendering them dear to God.

Isaac being desirous to eat the flesh of some venison, promised to give his benediction in exchange for it to Esau; but Rebecca wishing that her other son Jacob should receive this benediction, ordered him to bring her two kids, for she would prepare the food that Isaac loved. "Go thy way to the flock, bring me two kids."[58] St. Antoninus says that Rebecca was the type of Mary, who says to the angels, Bring me sinners (who are typified by the kids), that I may prepare them in such a manner (by obtaining for them sorrow and good resolutions) as to render them dear and acceptable to my Lord.[59] The Abbot Francone, pursuing the same thought, says, that

---

52. Ecce tu iratus es, et peccavimus ... non est qui consurgat et teneat te. Isa. lxiv. 5, 7.
53. Ante Mariam non fuit qui sic Deum detinere auderet.
54. Detinet Filium ne peccatoribus percutiat.
55. Nemo tam idoneus, qui gladio Domini manus objiciat.
56. Querebatur Dominus ante Mariam: Non est qui consurgat, et teneat me. Ezech. xxii. Donec inventa est Maria, quæ tenuit eum, donec emolliret. De Laud. Virg.
57. Ne diffidas, peccator, sed in cunctis Mariam sequere et invoca, quam voluit Deus in cunctis subvenire. De Annunc. B. Virg.
58. Pergens ad gregem, affer mihi duos hædos. Gen. xxvii. 9.
59. Part. 4, tit. 15, c. 2.

Mary so well understands how to prepare these kids, that they not only equal, but sometimes even surpass the flavor of venison.[60]

The blessed Virgin herself revealed to St. Bridget, that no sinner in the world is so great an enemy to God, that if he has recourse to her and invokes her aid, does not return to God and is not restored to his favor.[61] And the same St. Bridget heard one day Jesus Christ saying to his mother, that she could obtain the divine favor even for Lucifer, if he would humble himself so far as to ask her help.[62] That proud spirit would never stoop to implore the protection of Mary, but if such a thing could happen, Mary would take pity upon him, and the power of her prayers would obtain from God his pardon and salvation. But what cannot happen to the devil may well happen to sinners who seek the help of this mother of mercy.

Noah's ark also prefigured Mary; because as in that all the animal creation found refuge, so under the mantle of Mary all sinners find protection, who have made themselves like the brutes by their vices and sensuality. With this difference, however, says a certain author: The brutes entered into the ark and remained brutes still; the wolf remained a wolf, the tiger a tiger.[63] But under the mantle of Mary the wolf becomes a lamb, the tiger a dove. St. Gertrude once saw Mary with her mantle outspread, and under it wild beasts of various kinds, leopards, lions, and bears; and the Virgin not only did not drive them from her but with her gentle hand kindly received them and caressed them. The saint understood that these wild beasts were miserable sinners who when they take refuge with Mary are received by her with sweetness and love.[64]

Justly, then, did St. Bernard say to the Virgin: Oh Lady, thou dost abhor no sinner, however abandoned and vile he may be, when he has recourse to thee; if he asks thy help thou wilt condescend to extend thy kind hand to draw him from the depths of despair.[65] Oh ever blessed and thanked be our God, oh most amiable Mary, who made thee so merciful and kind towards the most miserable sinners. Oh, wretched are those who do not love thee, and who, having it in their power to seek help of thee, do not trust in thee!

---

60. Vere sapiens mulier, quæ novit sic hædos condire, ut gratiam cervorum coæquent, aut etiam superent. Tom. 3, de Grat.
61. Nullus ita abjectus a Deo, qui si me invocaverit, non reveriatur ad Deum.
62. Etiam diabolo misericordiam exhiberes si humiliter peteret. Rev. 1. 1. c. 6.
63. Quod arca animalia suscepit, animalia servavit. Paciucch., de B. V.
64. Ap. Blosius in Cant. Vit. Spir. cap. 1.
65. Tu peccatorem quantumcumque fœtidum non horres, si ad te suspiraverit, tu illum a desperationis barathro pia manu retrahis. Orat. Paneg. ad B. V.

He who does not implore the aid of Mary is lost; but who has ever been lost that had recourse to her?

It is related in Scripture that Booz permitted the woman named Ruth to glean the ears that the reapers dropped and left behind them: "Colligebat spicas post terga metentium."[66] St. Bonaventure adds that as Ruth found favor in the eyes of Booz, so Mary has found favor in the eyes of the Lord, and is permitted to glean after the reapers.[67] The reapers are the apostolic laborers, missionaries, preachers, and confessors, who toil through the day to gather and win souls to God. But there are some rebellious and obdurate souls who are left behind even by these reapers, and it is granted to Mary alone by her powerful intercession to save these abandoned ears. But unhappy are those who do not yield themselves to this sweet Lady! for they will be entirely lost and accursed! Blessed, on the other hand, are those who have recourse to this good mother! There is no sinner in the world, says the devout Blosius, so lost and sunk in sin, that Mary would abhor him and reject him. Ah, if such would seek her aid, this good mother could and would reconcile them to her Son, and obtain for them pardon.[68]

With reason, then, oh my sweetest queen, does St. John of Damascus salute thee and call thee: "The hope of the despairing."[69] Justly does St. Laurence Justinian name thee: "The hope of evil-doers."[70] St. Augustine: "The only refuge of sinners."[71] St. Ephrem: "The secure haven for the shipwrecked."[72] The same saint calls thee even by another appellation: "The protectress of the condemned."[73] Finally, St. Bernard, with reason, exhorts the desperate not to despair; whence, full of joy and tenderness towards this his most dear mother, he asks her lovingly: Oh Lady, who would not trust in thee, if thou dost thus relieve even the despairing? I do not doubt in the least, he adds, that if we always applied to thee we should obtain what we wish. In thee, then, let the despairing hope.[74] St. Antoninus relates

---

66. Ruth, ii, 3.
67. Ruth in oculis Booz, Maria in oculis Domini hanc gratiam invenit, ut ipsa spicas, idest animas a messoribus derelictas, colligere ad veniam possit. In Spe. cap. 8.
68. Nullum tam execrabilem peccatorem orbis habet, quem ipsa abominetur, et a se repellat; quemque dilectissimo nato suo (modo suam precetur opem) non possit, sciat et velit reconciliare. Blos. de dictis, P. P. c. 5.
69. Salve spes desperatorum.
70. Spes delinquentium. P. P. cap. 5.
71. Unica spes peccatorum.
72. Naufragorum portus tutissimus.
73. Protectrix damnatorum.
74. Quis non sperabit in te, quæ etiam adjuvas desperatos! Non dubito, quod si ad te venerimus; habebimus quod volemus. In te ergo speret qui desperat. Sup. Salv. Reg.

that a sinner finding himself in disgrace before God, imagined himself standing before the tribunal of Jesus Christ: the devil was accusing him and Mary defending him. The enemy presented against this poor criminal the catalogue of his offenses, which, placed in the balance of divine justice far outweighed his good works; but what then did his great advocate do? She extended her kind hand and placed it in the other scale; it descended in favor of her suppliant, and thus it was given him to understand, that she would obtain his pardon if he would change his life; and, indeed, after that vision he was converted and changed his life.

EXAMPLE

The blessed John Erolto, who, through humility, called himself *the disciple*, relates,[75] that there was once a married man who lived in disgrace in the sight of God. His wife, a virtuous woman, not being able to induce him to abandon his vicious courses, entreated him that at least, while he was in so miserable a condition, he would offer this devotion to the mother of God, namely, to say a "Hail Mary" every time he passed before her altar. He accordingly began to practice this devotion. One night, when he was about to commit a sin, he saw a light, and, on closer observation, perceived that it was a lamp burning before a holy image of the blessed Virgin, who held the infant Jesus in her arms. He said a "Hail Mary," as usual; but what did he see? He saw the infant covered with wounds, and fresh blood flowing from them. Both terrified and moved in his feelings, he remembered that he himself too had wounded his Redeemer by his sins, and began to weep, but he observed that the child turned away from him. In deep confusion, he had recourse to the most holy Virgin, saying: "Mother of mercy, thy Son rejects me; I can find no advocate more kind and more powerful than thou, who art his mother; my queen, aid me, and pray to him in my behalf." The divine mother answered him from that image: "You sinners call me mother of mercy,

---

75. In Promptuar.

but yet you do not cease to make me mother of misery, renewing the passion of my Son, and my dolors." But because Mary never sends away disconsolate those who cast themselves at her feet, she began to entreat her Son that he would pardon that miserable sinner. Jesus continued to show himself unwilling to grant such a pardon, but the holy Virgin, placing the infant in the niche, prostrated herself before him, saying: "My Son, I will not leave thy feet until thou hast pardoned this sinner." "My Mother," answered Jesus, "I can deny thee nothing; dost thou wish for his pardon? for love of thee I will pardon him. Let him come and kiss my wounds." The sinner approached, weeping bitterly, and as he kissed the wounds of the infant, they were healed. Then Jesus embraced him as a sign of pardon. He changed his conduct, led a holy life, and was ever full of love to the blessed Virgin, who had obtained for him so great a favor.

PRAYER

I venerate, oh most pure Virgin Mary, thy most sacred heart, which was the delight and repose of God; a heart filled with humility, purity, and divine love. I, an unhappy sinner, come to thee with a heart filled with uncleanness and wounds. Oh mother of mercy, do not on this account despise me, but let it excite thee to a greater compassion, and come to my help. Do not look for virtue or merits in me before thou grantest me thy aid; I am lost, and only merit hell. Look at nothing, I pray thee, but the confidence I have in thee, and the desire I cherish of amending my life. Look at what Jesus has done and suffered for me, and then abandon me if thou canst. I offer to thee all the afflictions of his life, the cold that he suffered in the stable, his journey to Egypt, the blood that he shed, his poverty, toil, sweat, and sadness, the death he endured in thy presence, for love of me; and, for the love of Jesus, promise to save me. Ah, my mother, I will not and I cannot fear that thou wilt cast me from thee, when I flee to thee and implore thy help. To fear this, would be unjust to thy mercy, which seeks the miserable to relieve them. Oh Lady, do not refuse thy compassion to him to whom Jesus has not refused his blood; but the merits of this blood will not be applied to me, if thou dost not recommend me to God. From thee I hope salvation. I do not ask of thee riches, honors, or the other goods of earth; I only ask of thee the grace of God, love for thy Son, the fulfillment of his will, and paradise, where I may love him eternally. Is it possible that thou wilt not hear me? No, already thou dost hear me, as I hope; already thou art praying for me, already thou art procuring me the favors I ask, already thou art receiving me under thy protection. My mother, do not leave me; continue, continue to pray for me, until thou seest me safe in heaven at thy feet, to bless and thank thee through all eternity. Amen.

CHAPTER 4

Ad te clamamus exules filii Evæ
To thee do we cry, poor banished children of Eve

SECTION 1
How ready Mary is to succor those who call upon her

We poor children of the unhappy Eve, guilty before God of her sin, and condemned to the same punishment, go wandering through this valley of tears, exiles from our country, weeping and afflicted by innumerable pains of body and soul! But blessed is he who in the midst of so many miseries turns to the consoler of the world, to the refuge of the unhappy, to the great mother of God, and devoutly invokes her and supplicates her! "Blessed is the man that heareth me, and that watcheth daily at my gates."[1] Blessed, says Mary, is he who listens to my counsels, and incessantly watches at the door of my mercy, invoking my help and intercession! The holy Church instructs us her children with how great attention and confidence we should have continually recourse to this our loving protectress; ordaining special devotions to her, that during the year many festivals should be celebrated in her honor; that one day of the week should be especially consecrated to her; that every day, in the divine office, all ecclesiastics and members of religious orders should invoke her in behalf of the whole Christian people, and that three times a day all the faithful, at the sound of the bell, should salute her. This will suffice to show how, in all seasons of public calamity, the holy Church always directs her children to have recourse to the divine mother with novenas, prayers, processions, visits to her churches and altars. This, Mary herself wishes us to do, namely, always to invoke and supplicate her, not to ask our homage and praise, which are too poor in comparison with her merit, but that our confidence and devotion to her thus increasing, she may aid and console us more. She seeks such as approach her devoutly and reverently, says St. Bonaventure; these she cherishes, loves, and adopts as her children.[2]

The same St. Bonaventure says, that Mary was prefigured by Ruth, whose name, being interpreted, signifies *seeing, hastening*,[3] for Mary, seeing our miseries, hastens to aid us by her compassion.[4] To which Novarino adds,

---

1. Beatus homo qui audit me, et vigilat ad fores meas quotidie! Proverbs viii. 34.
2. Ipsa tales quærit qui ad eam devote et reverenter accedant; hos enim diligit, hos nutrit, hos in filios suscipit. P. 3. Stim. Div. Am. c. 16.
3. Videns et festinans. In Spec.
4. Videns enim nostram miseriam, est et festinans ad impendendam suam misericordiam.

Immaculate Heart of Mary. **Anonymous. Church of St. Peter, Vienna, Austria.**

that Mary is so desirous to do us good, that she can bear no delay; and not being a miserly keeper of her favors, but the mother of mercy, she cannot restrain herself from dispensing, as soon as possible among her servants, the treasures of her liberality.[5]

Oh, how ready is this good mother to aid him who invokes her! "Thy two breasts are like two young roes."[6] Richard of St. Laurence, explaining this passage, says that the breasts of Mary readily, like the roe's, give the milk of mercy to those who ask it.[7] The same author assures us that the mercy of Mary is bestowed on all who ask it, though they offer no prayer but a "Hail Mary." Hence, Novarino affirms, that the blessed Virgin not only hastens, but flies to aid those who have recourse to her. She, says this author, in exercising mercy, cannot but resemble God; for, as the Lord hastens to succor those who ask help from him, being very faithful to observe the promise which he has made to us—Ask, and you shall receive[8]—so Mary, when she is invoked, immediately hastens to help those who call upon her.[9] And by this is explained who was the woman of the Apocalypse, with two wings of a great eagle, that she might fly into the desert.[10] Ribeira explains these two wings to signify the love with which Mary always hastens to God.[11] But the blessed Amadeus says, remarking on this passage, that the wings of an eagle signify the velocity with which Mary, surpassing in swiftness the seraphs, always comes to the help of her children.[12]

We read in the Gospel of St. Luke, that when Mary went to visit St. Elizabeth, and bestow blessings on all her family, she was not slow, but travelled that whole journey with haste.[13] But we do not read that it was so on her return. For the same reason, it is said in the sacred Canticles, that the hands of Mary are turned.[14] For, as Richard of St. Laurence explains it, The art of turning is easier and quicker than other arts, so Mary is more ready than any other of the saints to aid her suppliants.[15] She has the greatest desire to console all, and she scarcely hears herself invoked before she

---

5. Nescit nectere moras benefaciendi cupida, nec gratiarum avara custos est; tardare nescit molimina misericordiæ mater beneficentiæ suæ thesauros in suos effusura. Nov. Umbr. Virg. c. 10, Exc. 75.
6. Duo ubera tua sicut duo hinnulli capreæ. Cant. iv. 5.
7. Compressione levissima angelicæ salutationis larga stillabunt stillicidiæ.
8. Petite et accipietis.
9. Alis utitur Dens; ut suis opituletur, statim advolat; alas sumit et Virgo, in nostri auxilium advolatura. Nov. c. 10, Excurs. 73.
10. Et datæ sunt mulieri alæ duæ aquilæ magnæ ut volaret in desertum. Apoc. xii. 14.
11. Pennas habet aquilæ, quia amore Dei volat.
12. Motu celerrimo seraphin alas excedens, ubique suis ut mater occurrit. Hom. 8, de Laud. Virg.
13. Exurgens Maria abiit in montana cum festinatione. Luc. ii. 1-39.
14. Manus illius tornatiles. Cant. v. 14.
15. Sicut ars tornandi promptior est aliis artibus, sic Maria ad benefaciendum promptior est aliis sanctis. De Laud. Virg. i. 5.

graciously receives the petition and comes to our aid.[16] Justly, then, St. Bonaventure calls Mary, The salvation of those who invoke her: "O salus te invocantium!" signifying, that to be saved it is sufficient to appeal to this divine mother, who, according to Richard of St. Laurence, is always ready to aid those who pray to her.[17] For, as Bernardine de Bustis says: This great Lady is more desirous to confer favors upon us than we are to receive them.[18]

Neither should the multitude of our sins diminish our confidence that we shall be graciously heard by Mary, if we cast ourselves at her feet. She is the mother of mercy, and there would be no occasion for mercy, if there were no wretchedness to be relieved. Therefore, as a good mother does not hesitate to apply a remedy to her child, however loathsome its disease, although the cure may be troublesome and disgusting; thus our good mother does not abandon us, when we recur to her however great may be the filth of our sins, which she comes to cure.[19] This sentiment is taken from Richard of St. Laurence. And Mary intended to signify the same when she appeared to St. Gertrude, spreading her mantle to receive all who had recourse to her: at the same time it was given the saint to understand, that the angels are waiting to defend the devout suppliants of Mary from the assaults of hell.[20]

So great is the love and pity which this good mother has for us, that she does not wait for our prayers before giving us her aid. "She preventeth them that covet her, so that she first showeth herself unto them."[21] These words of wisdom St. Anselm applies to Mary, and says that she anticipates those who desire her protection. By this we are to understand that she obtains many graces from God for us before we ask them from her. Therefore Richard of St. Victor says: Mary is called the moon: Pulchra ut luna;[22] not only because she hastens as the moon to shine on those who seek her light,[23] but because she so earnestly desires our welfare that in our necessities she anticipates our prayers, and in her compassion she is more prompt to help us than we are to have recourse to her.[24] For, adds the

16. Omnes consolatur, et tenuiter invocata præsto adest. Blosius in Cant. Vit. Spir. c. 18.
17. Inveniens semper paratam auxiliari.
18. Plus vult illa facere tibi bonum, quam tu accipere concupiscas. Mar. 1, Serm. 5, de Nom. Mar.
19. Non enim mater hæc dedignatur peccatorem sicut nec bona mater filium scabiosum. Quia propter hoc factam se recolit misericordiæ genitricem. Ubi enim non est miseria, misericordia non habet locum. De Laud. Virg. lib. 4.
20. Rev. lib. 4, cap. 49.
21. Præoccupat, qui se concupiscunt, ut illis se prius ostendat. C. vi. 4.
22. In Cant. c. 23.
23. Velocitate præstat.
24. Velocius occurrit ejus pietas, quam invocatur, et causas miserorum anticipat. Loc. cit.

same Richard, the breast of Mary is so full of pity that she scarcely knows our miseries before she offers us the milk of her mercy, neither can this gracious queen perceive the necessities of any soul without relieving it.[25]

And truly, Mary manifested to us while she was on earth, in the nuptials of Cana,[26] her great compassion for our sufferings, which prompts her to relieve them before we pray to her. This kind mother saw the trouble of that pair who were mortified to find that their wine had failed at the wedding banquet; and without being requested, moved only by her compassionate heart, which cannot look upon the afflictions of others without pity, prayed her Son, to console them by merely mentioning to him the necessities of the family: They have no wine: "Vinum non habent."[27] After which, her Son, to comfort that family, and still more to satisfy the compassionate heart of his mother, performed, as she desired, the well-known miracle of changing the water contained in vases into wine. Novarino here remarks, that if Mary, though unasked, is so ready to aid us in our necessities, how much more so will she be when we invoke her and implore her aid![28]

If any one doubts that he shall be assisted by Mary when he has recourse to her, let him listen to the words of Innocent III: Who has ever invoked this sweet Lady, and has not been heard by her?[29] Who, oh holy Virgin, exclaims the blessed Eutychian, has ever sought thy powerful protection, which can relieve the most miserable and rescue the most degraded, and has been abandoned by thee? No, this has never happened, and never will happen.[30] Let him be silent concerning thy mercy, oh blessed Virgin, whose necessities have been neglected by thee after he has implored thy aid.[31]

Sooner will heaven and earth be destroyed, says the devout Blosius, than Mary fail to aid those who, with a pure intention, recommend themselves to her and put their confidence in her.[32] And to increase our confidence, St. Anselm adds that when we have recourse to this divine mother, we may not only be sure of her protection, but that sometimes we shall be sooner heard and saved by invoking her holy name than that of Jesus

25. Adeo replentur ubera tua misericordia, ut alterius miseriæ notitia tacta, lac fundant misericordiæ. Nec possis miserias scire, et non subvenire. In Cant. c. 23.
26. Luc. ii.
27. Joan. ii. 3.
28. Si tam prompta ad auxilium currit non quæsita, quid quæsita præstitura est. C. 10, Ex. 27.
29. Quis invocavit eam et non est auditus ab ipsa? Serm. 2, de Assump. B. V.
30. Quis unquam, O Beata, fideliter omnipotentem tuam rogavit opem, et fuit derelictus? Revera nullus unquam. In vita S. Theoph.
31. Sileat misericordiam tuam, Virgo beata, qui in necessitatibus te invocatam meminerit defuisse. Serm. 1, de Assump.
32. Citius cœlum cum terra perierint, quam Maria aliquem serio se implorantem sua ope destituat. In Spec. c. 12.

our Savior.[33] And he gives this reason: Because it belongs to Christ, as our judge, to punish, but to Mary, as our advocate, to pity.[34] By this he would give us to understand, that we sooner find salvation by recurring to the mother than the Son; not because Mary is more powerful than her Son to save us, for we know that Jesus is our only Savior, and that by his merits alone he has obtained and does obtain for us salvation; but because when we have recourse to Jesus, considering him also as the judge to whom it belongs to punish the ungrateful, we may lose the confidence necessary to be heard; but going to Mary, who holds no other office than that of exercising compassion towards us as mother of mercy, and defending us as our advocate, our confidence will be more secure and greater. We ask many things of God and do not obtain them; we ask them from Mary and obtain them; how is this? Nicephorus answers: This does not happen because Mary is more powerful than God, but because God has seen fit thus to honor his mother.[35]

How consoling is the promise that our Lord himself made on this subject to St. Bridget. We read in her revelations, that one day this saint heard Jesus speaking with his mother, and that he said to her: "Mother, ask of me whatever thou wilt, for I will refuse nothing that thou dost ask;[36] and be assured," he added, "that all those who for love of thee seek any favor, although they are sinners, if they desire to amend, I promise to hear them."[37] The same thing was revealed to St. Gertrude, who heard our Redeemer himself say to Mary, that he had in his omnipotence permitted her to exercise mercy towards sinners who invoke her, in whatever manner it should please her.[38]

Every one invoking this mother of mercy may then say, with St. Augustine: "Remember, oh most compassionate Lady! that since the beginning of the world there never has been any one abandoned by thee. Therefore pardon me if I say that I do not wish to be the first sinner who has sought thy aid in vain."[39]

---

33. Velocior nonnunquam est nostra salus, invocato nomine Mariæ, quam invocato nomine Jesu. De Exc. V. c. 6.
34. Quia ad Christum, tanquam judicem, pertinet etiam punire; ad Virginem tanquam patronam nonnisi misereri. Loc. cit.
35. Multa petuntur a Deo, et non obtinentur; multa petuntur a Maria et obtinentur; non quia potentior sed quia Deus eam decrevit sic honorare. Ap. P. Pep. Grandez, etc.
36. Nulla erit petitio tua in me, quæ non audiatur. Lib. 1, 80.
37. Et per te omnes, qui per te petunt misericordiam, cum voluntate se emendandi, gratiam habebunt. Loc. cit.
38. Ex omnipotentia mea, Mater, tibi concessi propitiationem omnium peccatorum, qui devote invocant tuæ pietatis auxilium, qualicumque modo placeat tibi. Ap. Pep. loc. cit
39. Memorare piissima Maria, a sæculo non esse auditum, quamquam ad tua præsidia confugientem esse derelictum.

EXAMPLE

St. Francis of Sales, as we read in his life, efficaciously experienced the power of this prayer. At seventeen years of age he was living in Paris, engaged in study, and at the same time wholly devoted to pious exercises and holy love of God, which gave him a perpetual foretaste of heavenly joy. At this time the Lord, to try his faith, and attach him more strongly to his love, permitted the devil to represent to him that his efforts were in vain, because he was already condemned by the divine decree. The darkness and dryness in which it pleased God to leave him at the time, for he was insensible to all consoling thoughts of the divine goodness, caused this temptation to have more power over the heart of the holy youth; so that through great fear and desolation he lost his appetite, sleep, color, and cheerfulness, and excited the compassion of all those who looked upon him.

Whilst this horrible conflict lasted, the saint could conceive no other thoughts and utter no other words but those of sorrow and distrust. "Shall I, then," he said, as it is related in his life, "be deprived of the favor of my God, who hitherto has shown himself so gracious and so kind to me? Oh love! oh beauty! to which I have consecrated all my affections, shall I never more enjoy your consolations? Oh Virgin mother of God, the most beautiful of all the daughters of Jerusalem, am I then never to see thee in paradise? Ah, my Lady! if I am never to see thy lovely face, do not permit me to be forced to blaspheme and curse thee in hell." These were the tender sentiments of that afflicted heart, still so enamored of God and the Virgin. This temptation lasted for a month, but at length the Lord was pleased to deliver him from it by means of the consoler of the world, most holy Mary, to whom the saint had before made a vow of chastity, and upon whom he used to say he had placed all his hopes. One evening, on returning home, he entered a church, where he saw a small tablet suspended from the wall; he found written on it the prayer of St. Augustine above mentioned: "Remember, oh most merciful Mary! that no one, in any age, was ever known to have fled to thee for help and found himself abandoned." He prostrated himself before the altar of the divine mother, and recited with deep feeling this prayer; he renewed his vow of chastity, promised to recite daily the rosary, and then added: "Oh my queen, be my advocate with thy Son, whom I dare not approach. My mother, if in the other world I should be so unhappy as not to be able to love my Lord, whom I know is so worthy to be loved, at least obtain for me that I may love him as much as I can in this world. This is the grace that I ask of thee, and from thee I hope for it." Thus he supplicated the Virgin, and then abandoned himself to the divine mercy, resigning himself entirely to the will of God. But hardly had he finished his prayer, when by his most sweet mother he was suddenly freed from temptation; he immediately recovered his interior peace, and with it health of body, and from that time continued to live a most devout servant of Mary, whose praises and mercies he never ceased to proclaim in his preaching and his writings to the end of his life.

PRAYER

Oh mother of God! oh queen of angels! oh hope of men! listen to him who invokes thee and has recourse to thee. Behold me to-day prostrate at thy feet; I, a miserable slave of hell, consecrate myself to thee as thy servant forever, offering myself to serve and honor thee to the utmost of my power all the days of my life. I know that thy honor is not increased by the service of so vile and wretched a slave as I am, who have so grievously offended thy Son and my Redeemer Jesus. But if thou wilt accept one so unworthy as I for thy servant, and changing him by thy intercession, wilt render him worthy, thy own compassion will confer upon thee that honor which I, vile as I am, cannot render thee. Accept me, then, and do not reject me, oh my mother! The eternal Word came from heaven upon earth to seek the lost sheep, and to save them, became thy Son. And wilt thou despise a poor sheep, who comes to thee to help him find Jesus? The price has already been paid for my salvation; my Savior has shed his blood, which is enough to save infinite worlds. It only remains this blood should be applied to me; and to thee it belongs, oh blessed Virgin! to thee it belongs, as St. Bernard says, to bestow the merits of this blood on whomsoever it may please thee. To thee it belongs, as St. Bonaventure also says, to save whom thou wilt.[40]

---

40. Quem ipsa vis salvus erit.

Oh my queen, help me, then! my queen, save me! To you this day I commit my soul; and do thou secure its safety. Oh, salvation of those who invoke thee! I will exclaim with the same saint, save me.[41]

SECTION 2
How powerful Mary is in protecting those who invoke her in temptations of the devil

Not only is most holy Mary queen of heaven and of the saints, but also of hell and the devils, for she has bravely triumphed over them by her virtues. From the beginning of the world God predicted to the infernal serpent the victory and the empire which our queen would obtain over him, when he announced to him that a woman would come into the world who should conquer him. "I will put enmities between thee and the woman; she shall crush thy head."[42] And what woman was this enemy if not Mary, who, with her beautiful humility and holy life, always conquered him and destroyed his forces? St. Cyprian affirms that the mother of our Lord Jesus Christ was promised in that woman:[43] and hence he remarks, that God did not use the words I put, but I will put, lest the prophecy should seem to appertain to Eve.[44] He said, I will put enmity between thee and the woman, to signify that this his vanquisher was not the living Eve, but must be another woman descending from her, who was to bring to our first parents greater blessings, as St. Vincent Ferrer says, than those they had lost by their sin.[45] Mary, then, is this great and strong woman who has conquered the devil, and has crushed his head by subduing his pride, as the Lord added: "She shall crush thy head."[46] Some of the commentators doubt whether these words refer to Mary or to Jesus Christ, because in the Septuagint version we read: "He shall crush thy head."[47] But in our Vulgate, which is the only version approved by the Council of Trent, it is She, and not He. And thus St. Ambrose, St. Jerome, St. Augustine, St. John Chrysostom, and many others have understood it. However this may be, it is certain that the Son by means of the mother, or the mother by means of the Son, has van-

---

41. O salus te invocantium.
42. Inimicitias ponam inter te et mulierem; ipsa conteret caput tuum. Gen. iii. 15.
43. Mater Domini Jesu Christi in illa muliere promissa est.
44. Non pono, sed ponam ne ad Evam pertinere videatur.
45. Parentibus primis Virginem ab ipsis processuram; quæ afferret majus bonum quam ipsi perdiderunt. Serm. 2, de Nat. Virg.
46. Ipsa conteret caput tuum.
47. Ipse conteret caput tuum.

quished Lucifer; so that this proud spirit, as St. Bernard tells us, has been ignominiously overpowered and crushed by this blessed Virgin.[48] Hence as a slave conquered in war, he is forced always to obey the commands of this queen. St. Bruno says, that Eve, by yielding to the serpent, brought into the world death and darkness; but that the blessed Virgin, by conquering the devil brought us life and light: and she has bound him so that he cannot move to do the least harm to her servants.[49]

Richard of St. Laurence gives a beautiful explanation to these words of Proverbs: "The heart of her husband trusteth in her, and he shall have no need of spoils."[50] Richard says: The heart of her husband, that is, Christ, trusts in her, and he shall have no need of spoils, for she will endow him with the spoils which she has taken from the devil.[51] God has intrusted the heart of Jesus, as à Lapide expresses it, to the care of Mary, that she may procure for it the love of men; and thus he will not be in need of spoils, that is, of the conquest of souls, for she will enrich him with those souls of which she despoils hell, and which she has rescued from the demons by her powerful aid.

It is well known that the palm is the emblem of victory, and for this reason our queen has been placed on a high throne in the sight of all potentates, as a palm, the sign of certain victory, which all can promise themselves who have recourse to her. "I was exalted like a palm-tree in Cades."[52] That is, for a defense[53] as blessed Albertus Magnus says: Oh, my children, Mary seems to say to us with these words, when the enemy assails you, lift your eyes to me, behold me and take courage; for in me, who defends you, you will behold, at the same time, your victory. So that recourse to Mary is the most certain means of overcoming all the assaults of hell; for she, as St. Bernardine of Sienna says, is queen over hell, and ruler of the spirits of evil, for she controls and conquers them.[54] And therefore Mary is called terrible against the power of hell, as an army set in array. "Terrible as an army set in array."[55] Set in array, because she knows how to array her powers, that is, her compassion and her prayers, to the

---

48. Sub Mariæ pedibus conculcatus et contritus miseram patitur servitutem. Serm. in Sign. Magn.
49. Et Eva mors, et caligo; in Maria, vita consistit, et lux. Illa a diabolo victa est; hæc diabolum vicit et ligavit. Ap; Scala Franc. p. 4, c. 10.
50. Confidit in ea cor viri sui, et spoliis non indigebit. Prov. xxxi. 11.
51. Confidit in ea cor viri sui, scilicet Christi. Et spoliis non indigebit; ipsa enim quasi ditat sponsum suum, quibus spoliat diabolum.
52. Quasi palma exaltata sum in Cades. Eccli. xxiv. 18.
53. Scilicet ad defendendum.
54. Beata Virgo dominatur in regno inferni. Dicitur igitur domina dæmonum, quasi domans dæmones. Serm. 3, de Glor. Nom. Mar.
55. Terribilis ut castrorum acies ordinata. Cant. vi. 3.

confusion of the enemy and the benefit of her servants, who, in their temptations, invoke her powerful aid.

"As the vine I have brought forth a pleasant odor."[56] "I, like the vine, as the Holy Spirit puts it in her mouth to say, have given fruit of sweet odor." "It is said," adds St. Bernard, on this passage, "that every venomous reptile shuns the flowering vines."[57] As from vines all poisonous serpents flee, thus the demons flee from those fortunate souls in whom they perceive the odor of devotion to Mary. On this account she also is called a cedar: "I was exalted like a cedar in Lebanon,"[58] not only because as the cedar is free from corruption, so Mary is free from sin, but also because, as Cardinal Hugo remarks upon this passage, as the cedar with its perfume puts serpents to flight, so Mary with her sanctity puts to flight the devils.[59]

Victories were gained in Judea by means of the ark. Thus Moses conquered his enemies. "When the ark was lifted up, Moses said, Arise, oh Lord, and let thy enemies be scattered."[60] Thus Jericho was conquered; thus were the Philistines conquered; "for the ark of God was there."[61] It is well known that this ark was the type of Mary. As the ark contained the manna, thus Mary contained Jesus, whom the manna also prefigured, and by means of this ark, victories were gained over the enemies of earth and over hell.[62] Wherefore St. Bernardine of Sienna says that when Mary, the ark of the New Testament, was crowned queen of heaven, the power of hell over men was weakened and overthrown.[63]

"Oh, how the devils in hell," says St. Bonaventure, "tremble at Mary and her great name!"[64] The saint compares these enemies to those of whom Job makes mention and says: "He diggeth through houses in the dark. . . . If the morning suddenly appear, it is to them the shadow of death."[65] Thieves enter houses in the dark to rob them, but when the dawn comes they flee, as if the image of death appeared to them. In the same manner, as St. Bonaventure expresses it, the demons enter into the soul in times of darkness, that is,

---

56. Ego quasi vitis fructificavi suavitatem odoris. Eccli. xxiv. 23.
57. Aiunt de florescentibus vitibus omne reptile venantium excedere loco. Serm. 60, in Cant.
58. Quasi cedrus exaltata sum in Libano. Eccli. xxiv. 17.
59. Cedrus odore suo fugat serpentes, et beata Virgo dæmones.
60. Cum elevaretur arca, dicebat Moyses; Surge Domine, et dissipentur inimici tui. Num. x. 33.
61. Erat enim ibi arca Dei. 1, Reg. xiv. 18.
62. Arca continens manna, idest Christum, est B. Virgo, quæ victoriam contra homines et dæmones largitur. Cornel. à Lap.
63. Quando elevata fuit Virgo gloriosa a celestia regna, dæmonis potentia imminuta est et dissipata. Tom. 3, de B. V. Serm. 11.
64. O quam tremenda est Maria dæmonibus. Spec. Virg. c. 3.
65. Perfodit in tenebris domos ... Si subito apparuerit aurora; arbitrantur umbram mortis. Job xxiv. 16, 17.

when the soul is obscured by ignorance; they dig through the houses of our minds in the darkness of ignorance; but then, he adds, as soon as the grace and the mercy of Mary enter the soul, this beautiful aurora dissipates the darkness, and the infernal enemies flee as at the approach of death.[66] Oh, blessed is he who always, in his conflicts with hell, invokes the beautiful name of Mary!

In confirmation of this it was revealed to St. Bridget that God has given Mary such power over all evil spirits, that whenever they assail any of her servants who implore her aid, at the slightest sign from her they flee far away in terror, preferring that their pains should be redoubled rather than that Mary should domineer over them in this manner.[67]

À Lapide remarks upon the words with which the divine spouse praises his beloved bride, when he calls her the lily, and says that as the lily is among thorns, so is his beloved among the other daughters;[68] that, as the lily is a remedy against serpents and poisons, so the invocation of Mary is a special remedy for overcoming all temptations, particularly those of impurity, as they who have tried it have universally experienced.[69]

St. John of Damascus said, and every one may say the same who is so happy as to be devoted to this great queen: Oh, mother of God, if I trust in thee, I shall surely not be vanquished; for, defended by thee, I will pursue my enemies, and opposing to them thy protection and thy powerful support as a shield, I shall surely conquer them.[70] James the Monk, reputed a doctor among the Greek fathers, discoursing of Mary to our Lord, says: Thou, oh my Lord, hast given us this mother for a powerful defense against all our enemies.[71]

It is related in the Old Testament that the Lord guided his people from Egypt to the promised land, by day in a pillar of clouds, by night in a pillar of fire.[72] This pillar, now of clouds, now of fire, says Richard of St. Laurence, was a type of Mary and her double office, which she exercises continually in our behalf; as a cloud she protects us from the heat of divine justice,

---

66. Perfodiunt in tenebris ignorantiæ domos mentium nostrarum. Si subito supervenerit aurora, idest Mariæ gratia, et misericordia, sic fugiunt, sicut omnes fugiunt mortem. In Spec. Virg.
67. Super omnes etiam malignos spiritus ipsam sic potentem effecit, quod quotiescumque ipsi hominem Virginis auxilium implorantem impugnaverint, ad ipsius Virginis nutum illico pavidi procul diffugiunt; volentes potius suas pœnas multiplicari, quam ejusdem Virginis potentiam super se taliter dominari. Serm. Ang. c. 20.
68. Sicut lilium inter spinas, sic amica mea inter filias. Cant. ii. 2.
69. Sicut lilium valet inter serpentes et venena, sic beatæ Virginis invocatio singulare est remedium in omni tentatione, præsertim libidinis, ut experientia constat.
70. Insuperabilem spem tuam habens, O Deipara, servabor. Persequar inimicos meos, solam habens ut thoracem protectionem tuam, et omnipotens auxilium tuum. In Annunc. Dei Gen.
71. Tu arma omni vi belli potentiora, trophæumque invictum præstitisti.
72. Per diem in columna nubis, et per noctem in columna ignis. Exod. xiii. 21.

and as fire she protects us from demons.[73] Fire, as St. Bonaventure adds, for as wax melts at the approach of fire, thus the evil spirits lose all power in the presence of those souls who often call upon the name of Mary, and devoutly invoke her, and more than all, strive to imitate her.[74]

Oh, how the devils tremble, exclaims St. Bernard, if they only hear the name of Mary uttered![75] As men, says Thomas à Kempis, fall to the earth through fear, when a thunderbolt strikes near them, so fall prostrate the devils when but the name of Mary is heard.[76] How many noble victories have the servants of Mary not gained over these enemies by the power of her most holy name! Thus St. Anthony of Padua conquered them, thus the blessed Henry Suso, thus many other lovers of Mary. It is related in the accounts of the missions to Japan that a great number of demons appeared in the form of ferocious animals to a certain Christian of that country, to alarm him and threaten him, but he spoke to them in these words: "I have no arms with which to terrify you; if the Most High permits it, do with me according to your pleasure. Meanwhile I use as my defense the most sweet names of Jesus and Mary." Hardly had he uttered these words, when behold, at the sound of those fearful names, the earth opened and those proud spirits were swallowed up. St. Anselm also asserts that he had seen and heard many persons who at the mention of the name of Mary were delivered from their dangers.[77]

Very glorious, oh Mary, and wonderful, exclaims St. Bonaventure, is thy great name. Those who art mindful to utter it at the hour of death, have nothing to fear from hell, for the devils at once abandon the soul when they hear the name of Mary.[78] And the saint adds, that an earthly enemy does not so greatly fear a great army, as the powers of hell fear the name and protection of Mary.[79] Thou, oh Lady, says St. Germanus, by the invocation alone of thy most powerful name, dost render thy servants secure from all the assaults of the enemy.[80] Oh, if Christians were mindful in temptations

73. Ecce duo officia, ad quæ data est nobis Maria, scilicet, ut nos protegat a calore solis justitiæ, tamquam nubes, et tamquam ignis; ut omnes nos protegat contra diabolum. Lib. 7, de Laud. Virg.
74. Fluunt sicut cera a facie ignis, ubi inveniunt crebram hujus nominis recordationem, devotam invocationem, solicitam imitationem. In Spec.
75. In nomine Mariæ omne genuflectitur, et dæmones non solum pertimescunt, sed, audita hac voce, contremiscunt. Serm. sup. Miss.
76. Expavescunt cœli reginam spiritus maligni et diffugiunt, audito nomine ejus velut ab igne, tamquam tonitru de cœlo factum sit, prosternuntur ad sanctæ Mariæ vocabulum. L. 4, ad Nov.
77. Sæpe vidimus et audivimus plurimos homines in suis periculis nominis recordari Mariæ, et illico omnis periculi malum evasisse. S. Ans. de Exc. Virg. c. 6.
78. Gloriosum et admirabile est nomen tuum O Maria; qui illud retinent non expavescunt in puncto mortis; nam dæmones audientes hoc nomen Mariæ statim relinquunt animam. In Psalt. B. V.
79. Non sic timent hostes visibiles castrorum multitudinem copiosam, sicut æreæ potestates Mariæ vocabulum, et patrocinium. Loc. cit.

to invoke with confidence the name of Mary, it is certain that they would never fall; for, as blessed Alanus remarks, at the thunder of that great name, the devil flees and hell trembles.[81] This heavenly queen herself revealed to St. Bridget, that even from the most abandoned sinners, who had wandered the farthest from God, and were most fully possessed by the devil, the enemy departs as soon as he hears her most powerful name invoked by them, if they do it with a true intention of amending.[82] But the Virgin added, that if the soul does not amend, and with contrition quit its sins, the demons immediately return to it and hold it in their possession.[83]

EXAMPLE

In Reisberg there lived a Canon regular named Arnold, who was very devoted to the blessed Virgin. Being at the point of death, he received the sacraments, and calling his religious to him, begged them not to leave him at the last moment. Scarcely had he said this, when he began to tremble violently and roll his eyes; cold sweat fell from him, and with an agitated voice he exclaimed: "Do you not see those demons who would seize me and carry me to hell?" Then he cried: "My brothers, invoke for me the help of Mary; I trust in her that she will give me the victory." They immediately began to recite the Litany of our Lady, and at the words, Holy Mary, pray for him, "Sancta Maria, ora pro eo," the dying man cried: "Repeat, repeat the name of Mary, for I am even now at the tribunal of God." He stopped for a moment, and then added: "It is true that I did it, but I have done penance for it." Then turning to the Virgin, he said: "Oh Mary, I shall be delivered if thou wilt help me." The demons soon after made another attack, but he defended himself by blessing himself with the crucifix, and invoking Mary. Thus he passed the whole night, but when morning dawned, Arnold, restored to serenity, joyfully said: "Mary, my Lady, and my refuge, has obtained for me pardon and salvation." Then beholding

---

80. Tu servos tuos contra hostis invasiones, sola tui nominis invocatione tutos servas. Serm. de Zona. Virg.
81. Satan fugit, infernus contremiscit, cum dico Ave Maria.
82. Omnes dæmones audientes hoc nomen, Maria, statim relinquunt animam quasi territi. L. 1, Rev. c. 9.
83. Et revertuntur ad eam, nisi aliqua emendatio subsequatur. Lib.1. Rev.. c. 9.

the Virgin, who summoned him to follow her, he said: "I come, oh Lady, I come." He made an effort to rise, but not being able to follow her with the body, gently expiring, he followed her with his soul, as we hope, to the blessed kingdom of glory.[84]

PRAYER

Behold at thy feet, oh Mary my hope, a poor sinner who many times, through his own fault, has been the slave of hell. I know that I have often been conquered by the devil, because I have neglected to recur to thee, oh my refuge. If I had always sought thy protection, if I had invoked thee, I should never have fallen. I hope, oh my Lady, most worthy of love, that by thy help I have escaped the powers of hell, and that God has pardoned me. But I tremble for the future, lest I again fall into their power. I know that these enemies of mine have not lost all hope of reconquering me, and at this moment they are preparing new assaults and temptations. Oh, my queen and refuge, aid me. Shelter me beneath thy mantle, let me not become again their slave. I know that thou wilt succor me and give me victory whenever I invoke thee. I fear only that in my temptations I may forget thee, and neglect to call upon thee. This, then, is the grace, oh most holy Virgin, that I seek and wish from thee, that I may always remember thee, and especially when I find myself in conflict with the enemy; let me not then fail to invoke thee often with the words: "Oh Mary, help me, help me, oh Mary." And when at length the day of my last conflict with hell, the day of my death arrives, oh, my queen, powerfully assist me then, and remind me thyself to invoke thee more frequently, with the voice or with the heart, that expiring with thy most sweet name, and that of thy son Jesus on my lips, I may go to bless and praise thee, and never leave thy feet in paradise through all eternity. Amen.

---

84. Father Auriemma, Affetti Scambiev. Tom. i. c. 7.

Our Lady Star of the Sea. Church of Stella Maris, Sliema, Malta.

CHAPTER 5

Ad te suspiramus gementes et flentes
in hac lacrymarum valle
To thee do we send up our sighs,
groaning and weeping in this valley of tears

SECTION 1
The need we have of the intercession of Mary for our salvation

To invoke and pray to the saints, especially to the queen of saints, most holy Mary, that they may obtain for us, by their intercession, the divine favor, is not only a lawful but a useful and holy practice, and this is of faith, being established by the Councils, against heretics, who condemn it as injurious to Jesus Christ, who is our only mediator; but if a Jeremias, after his death, prays for Jerusalem;[1] if the elders of the Apocalypse present to God the prayers of the saints; if a St. Peter promises his disciples to remember them after his death; if a St. Stephen prays for his persecutors; if a St. Paul prays for his companions; if, in a word, the saints pray for us, why may we not implore the saints to intercede for us? St. Paul commends himself to the prayers of his disciples: Pray for us: "Orate pro nobis."[2] St. James exhorts the Christians to pray for each other: "Pray for one another, that ye may be saved."[3] We may then do likewise.

No one will deny that Jesus Christ is the only mediator of justice, and that by his merits he has obtained for us reconciliation with God. But, on the other hand, it is impious to deny that God is pleased to grant favors at the intercession of the saints, and especially of Mary his mother, whom Jesus desires so much to see loved and honored by us. Every one knows that honor paid to a mother redounds to her children.[4] Hence St. Bernard says, let not any one think that by greatly praising the mother he will throw into the shade the glories of the Son; for the more he honors the mother, so much more he honors the Son.[5] St. Ildephonsus says, that all the honor which is paid to the mother and the queen, is rendered to the Son and king.[6] And there is no doubt that on account of the merits of Jesus,

---

1. Mach. xv. 14.
2. Thess. 1, c. v. 25.
3. Orate pro invicem ut salvemini. C. v. 16.
4. Gloria filiorum Patres eorum. Prov. xvii. 6.
5. Non est dubium, quidquid in laudibus matris profermius, ad filium pertinere. Hom. 4, Sup. Miss.
6. Refunditur in filium quod impenditur matri, transfunditur honor in regem, qui defertur in famulatum reginæ.

the great privilege has been granted to Mary to be the mediatrix of our salvation; not, indeed, mediatrix of justice, but of grace and intercession, as she is called by St. Bonaventure.[7] St. Lawrence Justinian also says: Can she be otherwise than full of grace, who has been made the ladder of paradise, the gate of heaven, the most true mediatrix between God and man?[8]

Wherefore St. Anselm well remarks, that when we implore the holy Virgin to obtain graces for us, it is not that we distrust the divine mercy, but rather that we distrust our own unworthiness, and commend ourselves to Mary that her merits may compensate for our unworthiness.[9]

It cannot be doubted, therefore, except by those who are deficient in faith, that it is a useful and holy thing to have recourse to the intercession of Mary. But the point that we here propose to prove is, that the intercession of Mary is even necessary for our salvation: necessary, to speak properly, not indeed absolutely, but morally. And we affirm that this necessity arises from the will of God itself, who has ordained that all the favors which he dispenses should pass through the hands of Mary, according to the opinion of St. Bernard, which may well be considered at the present day the common opinion of doctors and divines, as the author of "The Kingdom of Mary" has already called it. It is embraced by Vega, Mendoza, Paciucchelli, Segneri, Poiré, Crasset, and innumerable other learned authors. Even Father Noel Alexander, an author usually very reserved in his assertions, declares it to be the will of God that we receive all favors through the intercession of Mary.[10] In confirmation of this, he quotes the celebrated passage of St. Bernard: This is the will of him who would have us receive all things through Mary.[11] The same opinion is held by Father Contensone who, explaining the words of Jesus Christ on the cross to John, behold thy mother, "Ecce mater tua," says: It is as if he said, no one shall partake of my blood except by the intercession of my mother. My wounds are fountains of grace, but to none can their streams be conveyed except by the channel of Mary. Oh John, my disciple, even as thou lovest my mother, so shalt thou be loved by me.[12]

---

7. Maria fidelissima mediatrix nostræ salutis.
8. Quomodo non est plena gratia, quæ effecta est paradisi scala, cœli janua, Dei atque hominum verissima mediatrix? Serm. de Annunc.
9. Ut dignitas intercessoris suppleat inopiam nostram. Unde Virginem interpellare, non est de divina misericordia diffidere, sed de propria indignitate formidare. De Exc. V. c. 6.
10. Qui vult ut omnia bona ab ipso expectemus, potentissima Virginis matris intercessione impetranda, cum eam, ut par est, invocamus. Epist. 76, in calce tom. 4, Moral.
11. Sic est voluntas ejus, qui totum nos habere voluit per Mariam.
12. Quasi diceret, nullus sanguinis mei particeps erit, nisi intercessione matris meæ. Vulnera gratiarum fontes sunt, sed ad nullos derivabuntur rivi, nisi per Mariæ canalem. Joannes discipule, tantum a me amaberis, quantum eam amaveris. Theol. Mentis, et cord. tom. 2, l. 10, D. 4, c. 1.

The statement that whatsoever we receive from the Lord comes to us by means of Mary, does not find favor with a certain modern author, who, although he treats with much piety and learning of true and false devotion, yet speaking of the devotion towards the divine mother, has shown himself very sparing in granting her the glory that a St. Germanus, a St. Anselm, a St. John of Damascus, a St. Bonaventure, a St. Antoninus, a St. Bernardine of Sienna, the venerable Abbot of Celles, and so many other doctors, have not hesitated to attribute to her, who have not scrupled to declare that for the above-mentioned reason the intercession of Mary is not only useful, but necessary. The above-named author says that this proposition, namely, that God grants no favor except through Mary, is an hyperbole and an exaggeration which has escaped from the mouth of some saints in a moment of fervor, and properly speaking, is to be understood only in the sense that through Mary we have received Jesus Christ, by whose merits we receive all graces. Otherwise, he continues, it would be an error to believe that God could not grant graces, without the intercession of Mary, since the apostle says: "There is one God and one Mediator of God and men, the man Christ Jesus."[13] So much for the above-named author.

But with his leave I will suggest to him what he himself in his book teaches me, that the mediation of justice by means of merit, and the mediation of grace by means of prayer, are very different things. Thus it is also one thing to say that God cannot, another to say he will not grant favors without the intercession of Mary. We willingly acknowledge that God is the fountain of every good, and absolute Lord of all graces and that Mary is only a pure creature who, through grace, receives whatever she obtains from God. But who can deny it to be reasonable and proper to assert that God, in order to exalt this noble creature, who, more than all other creatures, has loved and honored him in her life, having chosen her for the mother of his Son the Redeemer of the world, has also seen fit to dispense through her hands all the graces which are to be granted to redeemed souls? We acknowledge that Jesus Christ is the only mediator of justice, as we have stated above, who by his merits obtains for us grace and salvation; but we affirm that Mary is the mediatrix of grace, and although whatever she obtains, she obtains through the merits of Jesus Christ, and because she prays and asks for it in the name of Jesus Christ, yet whatever favors

13. 1 Tim. ii. 5.

American TFP Archive / Michael Gorre

Mary Help of Christians. **America Needs Fatima headquarters, Pennsylvania.**

we ask are all obtained through her intercession.

In this there is certainly nothing opposed to the sacred doctrines; on the contrary, it is entirely conformed to the sentiments of the Church, who, in the public prayers, by her approved, teaches us to appeal constantly to his divine mother, and invoke her as the Health of the weak: "Salus infirmorum." The Refuge of sinners: "Refugium peccatorem." The Help of Christians: "Auxilium christianorum." Our life and our hope: "Vita et spes nostra." The same holy Church, in the office which she requires to be recited on the Festivals of Mary, applying to her the words of Wisdom, gives us to understand that in Mary we shall find every hope: "In me is all hope of life and virtue."[14] That in Mary we shall find every grace: "In me is all grace of the way and of the truth."[15] In a word, that we shall find in Mary life and eternal salvation: "He that shall find me shall find life, and shall

---

14. In me omnis spes vitæ et virtutis.
15. In me omnis gratia viæ et veritatis.

have salvation from the Lord."[16] And again: "They that work by me shall not sin. They that explain me shall have life everlasting."[17] All which passages signify the need we have of the intercession of Mary.

This then is the sentiment in which so many theologians and holy fathers concur, of whom we cannot with justice say, as the author quoted above has asserted, that to exalt Mary they have uttered *hyperboles*, and that *excessive exaggerations* have fallen from their lips. To exaggerate and utter hyperboles is to exceed the limits of truth, which cannot be said of the saints who have spoken, enlightened by the Spirit of God, who is the Spirit of truth. And here, if I may make a brief digression, let me express a sentiment of mine, namely: when an opinion is in any way honorable to the most holy Virgin, and has some foundation, and is not repugnant to the faith and the decrees of the Church, and to the truth, the rejection of it, and opposition to it, because the contrary may also be true, indicates little devotion to the mother of God. I would not be one of the number of these, nor would I see you, my reader, one of them, but rather of the number of those who fully and firmly believe all that can be believed, without error, concerning the greatness of Mary, as the Abbot Rupert says, who places among the offerings of devotion most pleasing to this mother, that of a firm belief in her great privileges.[18] If no one else, St. Augustine at least might remove from us all fear of exaggeration in the praise of Mary, who asserts that all we may say in her praise is little in comparison with what she merits on account of her dignity as mother of God. The holy Church also, in the Mass of the blessed Virgin, requires these words to be read: "For thou art happy, oh sacred Virgin Mary, and most worthy of all praise."[19]

But let us return to our subject, and hear what the saints say of the opinion in question. St. Bernard says that God had bestowed all graces on Mary, that men, through her as through a channel, may receive whatever good is in store for them.[20] Moreover, the saint here makes an important reflection, and says that before the birth of the most holy Virgin there flowed no such current of grace for all, since this desired channel did not yet exist.[21] But for this end, he adds, Mary has been given to the world,

---

16. Qui me invenerit, inveniet vitam, et hauriet salutem a Domino.
17. Qui operantur in me, non peccabunt. Qui elucidant me, vitam æternam habebunt.
18. Ejus magnalia firmiter credere. Laud. Virg.
19. Felix namque es, sacra Virgo Maria, et omni laude dignissima.
20. Plenus aquæductus, ut accipiant cæteri de plenitudine. Serm. de Aquæd.
21. Propterea tempore humano generi fluenta gratiæ defuerunt, quod necdum intercederet is de quo loquimur, tam desiderabilis aquæductus. Serm. de Aquæd.

that through this channel the divine graces might continually flow down upon us.[22]

As Holofernes, in order to gain the city of Bethulia, directed the aqueducts to be broken, so the devil makes every effort to deprive souls of their devotion to the mother of God; for, if this channel of grace were closed, he could easily succeed in gaining them to himself. The same holy father continues, and says: Observe, then, oh souls, with what affection and devotion the Lord would have us honor this our queen, by always seeking and confiding in her protection; for in her he has placed the fullness of all good, that henceforth we may recognize as coming from Mary whatever of hope, grace, or salvation we receive.[23] St. Antoninus says the same thing: All the mercies ever bestowed upon men have all come through Mary.[24]

For this reason she is called the moon, because, as St. Bonaventure remarks, as the moon is between the sun and the earth, and reflects upon the latter what she receives from the former, so Mary receives the celestial influences of grace from the divine Son, to transfuse them into us who are upon the earth.[25]

For this reason, too, she is called the gate of heaven by the holy Church: "Felix cœli porta;" because, St. Bernard again observes, as every rescript of grace sent by the king comes through the palace gate, so it is given to Mary, that through her thou shouldst receive whatever thou hast.[26] St. Bonaventure, moreover, says that Mary is called the gate of heaven, because, no one can enter heaven if he does not pass through Mary, who is the door of it.[27]

St. Jerome confirms us in the same sentiment (or, as some persons think, another ancient author of a sermon upon the Assumption which is inserted among the works of St. Jerome), when he says, that in Jesus Christ was the fullness of grace as in the head, whence descend to the members, which we are, all the vital spirits, that is, the divine aids for attaining eternal salvation: in Mary likewise was fullness as in the neck, through

22. Descendit per aquæductum vena illa cœlestis stillicidia gratiæ arentibus cordibus nostris infundens. Loc. cit.
23. Intueamini quanto devotionis affectu a nobis eam voluit honorari, qui totius boni plenitudinem posuit in Maria; ut proinde si quid spei nobis est, si quid gratiæ, si quid salutis, ab ea noverimus redundare. Serm. de Nat. Virg.
24. Per eam de cœlis exivit quidquid gratiæ venit in mundum. P. 4. tit. 15, c. 20.
25. Quia sicut luna inter corpora cœlestia et terrena est media, et quod ab illis accipit ad inferiora refundit; sic et Virgo regina inter nos et Deum est media, et gratiam ipsa nobis refundit. Serm. 74, de Nat. Dom.
26. Datum est Mariæ, ut per illam acciperes quicquid haberes. Serm. 3, in Virg. Nat.
27. Nullus potest cœlum intrare, nisi per Mariam transeat tamquam per portam.

which those vital spirits pass to the members.[28] This is confirmed by St. Bernardine of Sienna, who more clearly unfolded this thought, saying that through Mary are transmitted to the faithful, who are the mystic body of Jesus Christ, all the graces of the spiritual life, which descend upon them from Jesus their head.[29]

St. Bonaventure also attempts to assign the reason for this when he says: God being pleased to dwell in the womb of this holy Virgin, she has acquired thereby, in a certain sense, a kind of jurisdiction over all graces; since Jesus came from her sacred womb, together with him proceed from her, as from a celestial ocean, all the streams of divine gifts.[30] St. Bernardine of Sienna expresses this in even clearer terms. From the time, he asserts, that this mother conceived in her womb the Divine Word, she acquired, if we may thus express it, a special right to the gifts which proceed to us from the Holy Spirit, so that no creature has received any grace from God except by the intervention and hand of Mary.[31]

And thus is explained by a certain author[32] that passage of Jeremias where the prophet, speaking of the incarnation of the Word and of Mary his mother, says, that "a woman shall compass a man."[33] The author above named explains this to mean that, as no line proceeds from the centre of a circle which does not pass through its circumference, thus no grace comes to us from Jesus, who is the centre of every good, that does not pass through Mary, who encompassed him after she had received him in her womb.

Hence, says St. Bernardine, all gifts, all virtues, and all graces, are dispensed by Mary to whom she will, when she will, and in the manner she will.[34] Richard likewise says, that God wishes all the good he bestows on creatures to pass through the hands of Mary.[35] Hence the venerable Abbot of Celles exhorts every one to have recourse to this treasurer of graces, as

---

28. In Christo fuit plenitudo gratiæ sicut in capite influente, in Maria sicut in collo transfundente. Serm. de Assump. B. V.
29. Per Virginem a capite Christi vitales gratiæ in ejus corpus mysticum transfunduntur. Serm. 61, de Nat. Virg. c. 8.
30. Cum tota natura divina intra Virginis uterum extiterit; non timeo dicere quod in omnes gratiarum effluxus quamdam jurisdictionem habuerit hæc Virgo, de cujus utero quasi de quodam divinitatis oceano flumina emanabant omnium gratiarum. In Spec. cap. 3.
31. A tempore quo virgo mater concepit in utero verbum Dei, quamdam, ut sic dicam, jurisdictionem obtinuit, in omni spiritus sancti processione temporali; ita ut nulla creatura aliquam a Deo obtinuit gratiam, nisi secundum ipsius piæ matris dispensationem. Serm. 61, tract. 1, art. 8.
32. Crasset, Div. della Verg.
33. Fœmina circumdabit virum. Jerem. xxxi. 22.
34. Ideo omnia dona, virtutes, et gratiæ, quibus vult, quando vult, et quomodo vult, per ipsius manus dispensantur. Serm. 61, ut sup.
35. Deus quicquid boni dat creaturis suis, per manus matris Virginis vult transire.

he calls her: "Thesaurariam gratiarum;" for only by her means the world and men are to receive all the good they may hope for.[36] By which it is evident that the saints and authors above quoted, in saying that all graces come to us through Mary, have not intended to say this only because we have received from Mary, Jesus Christ, who is the fountain of every good, as the author named above would imply; but they assure us that God, after having given us Jesus Christ, has decreed that all the graces which have been dispensed, are dispensed, and shall be dispensed to men, even to the end of the world, through the merits of Jesus, shall be dispensed through the hands and by the intercession of Mary.

Hence Father Suarez concludes it to be the universal sentiment of the Church at the present day, that the intercession of Mary is not only useful, but necessary.[37] Necessary, as we said before, not in the sense of absolute necessity, because only the mediation of Jesus Christ is absolutely necessary for us, but in the sense of moral necessity; for the Church holds the opinion, with St. Bernard, that God has chosen to bestow no grace upon us but by the hands of Mary.[38] St. Ildephonsus affirmed this before St. Bernard, when, addressing the Virgin, he says: Oh Mary, God has decreed to commit to thee all the favors that he would confer upon men; hence he has confided to thee all the treasures and riches of grace.[39] And therefore St. Peter Damian says,[40] that God would not become man without the consent of Mary, that, in the first place, we might remain greatly indebted to her; and secondly, that we might understand the salvation of all men to be made dependent upon her good pleasure.

St. Bonaventure, contemplating the words of Isaias, where the prophet says: From the race of Jesse there shall come forth a rod—that is, Mary; and from that the flower—that is, the Word incarnate,[41] utters these beautiful words: Let him who would obtain the grace of the Holy Spirit, seek the flower in the rod, Jesus in Mary; since by the rod we obtain the flower, and by the flower we find God.[42] And he afterwards adds: If thou wouldst have this flower, strive, with prayers, to incline the stem of the flower in

---

36. Accede ad Virginem, quia per ipsam mundus habiturus est omne bonum. De contempl. V. In Prol.
37. Sentit Ecclesia intercessionem B. Virginis esse sibi utilem, et necessariam. Tom. 2, in 3, par. disp. 23, sect. 3.
38. Nihil Deus habere nos voluit, quod per manus Mariæ non transiret. Serm. 3, in Vigil. Nat.
39. Omnia bona quæ illis summa majestas decrevit facere, tuis manibus decrevit commendare; commissi quippe sunt thesauri, et ornamenta gratiarum. In Cor. Virg. c. 15.
40. De Nat. Virg. ap. Pac. Exc. 1, n. 15.
41. Egredietur virga de radice Jesse, et flos de radice ejus ascendet, et requiescet super eum spiritus Domini. Isa. xi. 1, 2.
42. Quicumque Spiritus Sancti gratiam adipisci desiderat, florem, in virga quærat; per virgam enim ad florem, per florem ad spiritum pervenimus. In Spec. c. 6.

thy favor, and thou wilt obtain it.[43] The seraphic Doctor, also commenting on the words: "They found the child with Mary his mother,"[44] says: Jesus is never found but with and through Mary;[45] and concludes with these words: He seeks Jesus in vain who does not look for him with Mary.[46] Hence St. Ildephonsus says: I would be a servant of the Son, and as he can never be a servant of the Son who is not the servant of the mother, my ambition is to be a servant of Mary.[47]

EXAMPLE

It is related by Belluacensis[48] and Cesarius,[49] that a noble youth having lost by his vices the wealth left him by his father, became so poor that he was obliged to beg. He quitted his native land, that he might live with less shame in a distant country where he was unknown. On this journey he met one day an old servant of his father, who, seeing him so cast down by the poverty he was suffering, told him to cheer up, for he would take him to a prince who was so liberal that he would provide him with everything he needed. Now this wretch was an impious sorcerer. One day he took the youth with him to a wood on the borders of a moor, where he began to address some invisible person. The youth asked to whom he was speaking. "To the devil," he answered; and seeing the youth terrified, bade him not to fear. Continuing to speak with the devil, he said: "This youth, oh my master, is reduced to extreme necessity, and wishes to be restored to his former condition." "If he will obey me," said the enemy, "I will make him richer than before; but in the first place, he must renounce God." At this the youth shuddered, but urged on by that cursed magician, he yielded, and renounced God. "But this is not sufficient," said the demon; "he must also renounce Mary; for it is to her that we attribute our greatest losses. Oh, how many souls she has snatched from us, and led back to God and

---

43. Si hunc florem habere desideras, virgam floris precibus flectas. Loc. cit.
44. Invenerunt puerum cum Maria matre ejus. Matth. ii. 11.
45. Nunquam invenitur Christus, nisi cum Maria, nisi per Mariam. Serm. 25, In Epiph.
46. Frustra igitur quærit qui cum Maria invenire non quærit.
47. Ut sim servus filii, servitutem appeto genitricis. De Virg. Mar. c. 12.
48. Spec. Hist 1. 7, c. 105.
49. Dist. 2, c. 2.

saved!" "Oh, this I will not do," exclaimed the youth; "deny Mary! Why she is my only hope. I would rather be a beggar all my life." With these words he left the place. On his way he happened to pass a church dedicated to Mary. The unhappy youth entered it, and kneeling before her altar, began to weep and implore the most holy Virgin that she would obtain the pardon of his sins. Mary immediately began to intercede with the Son for that miserable being. Jesus at first said: "But that ungrateful youth, my mother, has denied me." But seeing that his mother still continued to entreat him, he at last said: "Oh, my mother, I have never refused thee any thing; he shall be pardoned, since thou dost ask it." The citizen who had purchased the inheritance of that prodigal was secretly present at this scene, and beholding the mercy of Mary towards that sinner, he gave him his only daughter in marriage, and made him heir of all his possessions. Thus that youth recovered, through the intercession of Mary, the favor of God and even his temporal possessions.

PRAYER

Oh my soul! behold the beautiful hope of salvation, and of life eternal, which the Lord has granted thee, by giving thee, in his mercy, confidence in the protection of his mother, when thou hast by thy sins so often merited his displeasure and the pains of hell. Give thanks, then, to God, and to thy protectress, Mary, who hath deigned to shelter thee beneath her mantle, as already thou certainly knowest, by the many graces that thou hast received through her. Yes, I thank thee, oh my loving mother! for the good thou hast done me, a miserable sinner, deserving of hell. From how many dangers hast thou delivered me, oh my queen! How much light and how many mercies hast thou obtained for me, from God, by thy intercession! What great advantage, or what great honor hast thou received from me, that thou art thus intent on doing me good?

Thy goodness alone, then, hath moved thee in my behalf. Ah! if I were to give my blood, my life for thee, it would be little compared to what I owe thee, for thou hast delivered me from eternal death; thou, who hast enabled me to recover, as I hope, the divine favor, and from thee finally I acknowledge all my blessings to proceed. Oh my Lady! most worthy of love, I a miserable creature can make thee no return but always to praise and love thee. Ah! do not disdain to accept the affection of a poor sinner, who is enamored of thy goodness. If my heart is not worthy to love thee, because it is evil and full of earthly affections, do thou change it. Ah! unite me to my God, and unite me so that I can never be separated from his love. This thou desirest of me, that I may love thy God, and this I wish from thee. Obtain for me that I may love him, and love him always, and I ask nothing more. Amen.

SECTION 2
The same subject continued. . .

St. Bernard says that as a man and a woman have co-operated for our ruin, so it was fit that another man and another woman should co-operate for our restoration; and these were Jesus and his mother Mary. Doubtless, says the saint, Jesus Christ alone was all-sufficient for our redemption: yet it was more fitting that each sex should take part in our redemption, when both took part in our corruption.[50] For this reason blessed Albertus Magnus calls Mary the co-operatrix with Christ in our redemption: "Adjutrix Redemptionis." And she herself revealed to St. Bridget, that as Adam and Eve sold the world for one apple, so her Son and herself with one heart redeemed the world.[51] God could, indeed, as St. Anselm asserts, create the world from nothing; but when it was lost by sin, he would not redeem it without the co-operation of Mary.[52]

In three ways, says Father Suarez, the divine mother shared in the work of our salvation: first, by having merited, that is, with merit of congruity, the Incarnation of the Word. Secondly, by praying much for us while she lived on the earth. Thirdly, by willingly sacrificing to God the life of her Son for our salvation; and therefore the Lord has justly ordained that as Mary has, with so much love for man, aided in the salvation of all, and thereby so greatly promoted the glory of God, all through her intercession shall obtain salvation.

Mary is called the co-operatrix with her Son in our justification, because

---

50. Congruum magis fuit ut adesset nostræ reparationi sexus uterque, quorum corruptioni neuter defuissit. Serm. in Sig Magn.
51. Adam et Eva vendiderunt mundum pro uno pomo; filius meus et ego redemimus mundum uno corde. Lib. 5, c. 35.
52. Qui potuit omnia de nihilo facere, noluit ea violata sine Maria reficere. In Alloq. cœl. n. 37.

God has committed to her keeping all the graces that he has destined for us.[53] Wherefore St. Bernard affirms, that all men, past, present, and to come, should regard her as the medium and negotiator of the salvation of all ages.[54]

Jesus Christ has said that no one could find him unless his Eternal Father drew him by his divine grace.[55] Thus, also, according to Richard, Jesus said of his mother: No one comes to me unless my mother draw him with her prayers.[56]

Jesus was the fruit of Mary, as Elizabeth expressed it: "Blessed art thou among women, and blessed is the fruit of thy womb."[57] Whoever, then, wishes for the fruit, must go to the tree; whoever wishes for Jesus must go to Mary; and he who finds Mary, certainly also finds Jesus. St. Elizabeth, when the most holy Virgin came to visit her in her house, not knowing how to thank her, in deep humility exclaimed: "How have I merited that the mother of my God should come to visit me?"[58] But why! we may ask: did not Elizabeth already know that not Mary only, but Jesus also, had entered her dwelling? And why, then, does she call herself unworthy to receive the mother, and not rather unworthy of receiving a visit from the Son. Ah, well did the saint understand that when Mary comes she brings Jesus also; and hence it was sufficient for her to thank the mother, without naming the Son.

"She is like the merchant's ship, she bringeth her bread from afar."[59] Mary is that blessed ship, which brought to us from heaven Jesus Christ, the living bread that came from heaven to give us life eternal, as he has said: "I am the living bread which came down from heaven: if any man eat of this bread, he shall live forever."[60] Hence Richard of St. Laurence says, that all those will be lost in the sea of this world who are not received into this ship, that is, protected by Mary.[61] He also adds, that whenever we find ourselves in danger of destruction from the temptations or passions of the present life, we ought to flee to Mary, crying quickly, Oh Lady, help us; save us, if thou wouldst not see us lost.[62] And let it be remarked here, in passing,

---

53. Auxiliatrix nostræ justificationis, quia Deus omnes gratias faciendas Mariæ commisit.
54. Ad illam sicut ad medium, sicut ad negotium omnium sæculorum respiciant, et qui præcesserunt, et nos qui sumus, et qui sequentur. Serm. 2, in Pentec.
55. Nemo venit ad me, nisi Pater meus traxerit eum.
56. Nemo venit ad me, nisi Mater mea suis precibus traxerit eum. In Cant. c. 2, v. 3.
57. Benedicta tu inter mulieres, et benedictus fructus ventris tui. Luc. i. 42.
58. Et unde hoc mihi ut veniat mater Domini mei ad me? Lec. 2. 42.
59. Facta est quasi navis institoris, de longo portans panem suum. Prov. xxxi. 14.
60. Ego sum panis vivus, qui de cœlo descendi, si quis manducaverit ex hoc pane vivet in æternum. Joan. vi. 51.
61. In mare mundi submergentur omnes illi, quos non suscepit navis ista. De Laud.Virg.
62. Ideo quoties videmus insurgentes fluctus hujus maris, clamare debemus ad Mariam; Domina, salva nos, perimus. Loc. cit.

that this writer does not hesitate to say to Mary: Save us, we perish—"Salva nos, perimus;" as the author mentioned several times in the previous section does, who denies that we can ask the Virgin to save us, because, as he says it belongs only to God to save us. But if a person condemned to death may ask some favorite of the king to save him by interceding for him with his prince, why cannot we implore the mother of God to save us by obtaining for us through her prayers the grace of eternal life? St. John of Damascus did not hesitate to say to the Virgin: Oh pure and immaculate queen, save me, deliver me from eternal damnation.[63] St. Bonaventure called Mary the salvation of those invoking her.[64] The Church allows us to invoke her: Health of the weak—"Salus infirmorum;" and shall we hesitate to ask her to save us, when, according to a certain author, to no one is the door of salvation open except through her?[65] And before him St. Germanus, speaking of Mary, said: No one can be saved except through thee.[66]

But let us see what more the saints say of the need we have of the intercession of the divine mother. The glorious St. Cajetan said that we could ask for graces, but we could never obtain them without the intercession of Mary. And St. Antoninus confirms this, expressing himself thus beautifully: Whoever asks and wishes to obtain graces without the intercession of Mary, attempts to fly without wings;[67] for, as Pharaoh said to Joseph, "The land of Egypt is in thy hand;"[68] and as he sent all those to Joseph who applied to him for assistance, saying: Go to Joseph—"Ite ad Joseph;" so God, when we supplicate him for favors, sends us to Mary: Go to Mary— "Ite ad Mariam;" for he has decreed, says St. Bernard, that he will grant no favors except through the hands of Mary.[69] Hence Richard of St. Laurence says: Our salvation is in the hands of Mary, and we Christians can more justly say to her than the Egyptians to Joseph, our salvation is in thy hand.[70] The venerable Idiot says the same thing: Our salvation is in her hands—"Salus nostra in manu illius est."[71] Cassian asserts the same thing, but in stronger language. He absolutely affirms that the salvation of the whole world depends upon the favor and protection of Mary.[72] St. Bernar-

---

63. Regina immaculata et pura, salva me, libera ab eterna damnatione. Orat. Paneg.
64. O salus te invocantium.
65. Nemini nisi per eam patet aditus ad salutem. Paciucch. de B. Virg.
66. Nemo qui salvus fiat nisi per te. Serm. de Zona. Virg.
67. Qui petit sine ipsa, sine alis tentat volare. P. 3, tit. 15, c. 22, n. 9.
68. Terra Egypti in manu tua est.
69. Decrevit nihil dare, nisi per Mariam. Serm. de Nat. Virg.
70. Salus nostra in manu Mariæ est, ut ei dicere multo melius valeamus nos Christiani, quam Egyptii dixerunt Joseph salus nostra im manu illius est. L. 2, de Laud. Virg. p. 1.
71. In Præf. Cant. 5.

dine of Sienna thus addresses her: Oh Lady, since thou art the dispenser of all graces, and we must receive the grace of salvation through thy hand alone, then our salvation depends on thee.[73]

Richard says rightly then, that as a stone falls so soon as the earth is removed from beneath it, in like manner a soul, if the support of Mary is taken away, will fall first into sin and then into hell.[74] St. Bonaventure adds, that God will not save us without the intercession of Mary,[75] and goes on to say, that as an infant cannot live without its nurse, so no one without the protection of Mary can be saved.[76] Therefore he exhorts us in this way: Let thy soul thirst for devotion to Mary; preserve it always, never abandon it until you arrive in heaven and receive her maternal benediction.[77] Who, says St. Germanus, would ever know God, if it were not through thee, oh most holy Mary? Who would be saved? Who would be free from peril? Who would receive any favor if it were not through thee, oh mother of God? Oh Virgin mother, oh full of grace![78] And in another place he says: If thou didst not open the way, no one would be free from the sting of the flesh and of sin.[79]

As we have access to the eternal Father only through Jesus Christ, so, says St. Bernard, we have access to Jesus Christ only through Mary.[80] And St. Bernard gives us the reason why the Lord decreed that all men should be saved by the intercession of Mary, namely that through Mary we might be received by that Savior who, through Mary, has been given to us; and therefore the saint calls her the mother of grace and of our salvation. Then, resumes St. Germanus, what would become of us? what hope of salvation would remain to us if thou, oh Mary, didst abandon us, thou who art the life of Christians?[81]

But, the modern author above quoted remarks: If all graces pass through Mary, when we implore the intercession of the saints, they must

---

72. Tota salus mundi consistit in multitudine favoris Mariæ.
73. Tu dispensatrix omnium gratiarum; salus nostra in manu tua est. Serm. 1, de Nat. B. Virg.
74. Sicut lapis, subtracta terra, delabitur in profundum; ita subtracto Mariæ adjutorio, homo delabitur in peccatum, et inde in infernum. L. 8, de Laud. Virg. c. 11.
75. Ipse sine ea non salvabit te.
76. Quemadmodum infans sine nutrice non potest vivere, ita sine domina nostra non potes habere salutem. In Cant. B. V. pro Sabb.
77. Sitiat ergo anima tua ad ipsam; tene, nec dimitte, donec benedixerit tibi.
78. Nemo est, o sanctissima, qui ad Dei notitiam venit, nisi per te; nemo qui salvus fiat, nisi per te, Dei parens; nemo liber a periculis nisi per te, Virgo mater. Nemo donum Dei suscepit, nisi per te, gratia plena. Serm. de Zona. Virg.
79. Nisi enim tu iter aperieres, nemo spiritualis evaderet. Orat. de Dorm. Deip.
80. Per te accessum habemus ad filium, o inventrix gratiæ, mater salutis, ut per te nos suscipiat, qui per te datus est nobis.
81. Si nos deserueris, quid erit de nobis, Vita Christianorum? Serm. de Zona Virg.

have recourse to the meditation of Mary to obtain for us these graces. This, however, says he, no one believes, or has ever thought of. I reply, that there can be no error or difficulty in believing this. What difficulty is there in saying that God, to honor his mother, having crowned her queen of the saints, and having ordained that all graces should be dispensed by her hands would have the saints also invoke her to obtain favors for their clients? As to saying that no one has ever thought of it, I find that St. Bernard, St. Anselm, St. Bonaventure, Father Suarez[82] also, and others expressly assert it. In vain, says St. Bernard, would one pray to the other saints for a desired favor, if Mary did not intercede to obtain it for them.[83] Thus also a certain author explains, in this connection, that passage of David: "All the rich among the people shall entreat thy countenance."[84] The rich of that great people of God are the saints, who, when they wish to obtain a favor for one of their clients, all recommend themselves to Mary, that she may obtain it for them. Justly, then, says Father Suarez, we implore the saints to be our intercessors with Mary, who is their lady and queen.[85]

It is precisely this which St. Benedict promised to St. Frances of Rome, as we learn from Father Marchese.[86] The above-named saint appeared to her one day, and taking her under his protection, promised to be her advocate with the divine mother. St. Anselm adds, in confirmation of this, addressing the blessed Virgin: Oh Lady, what the prayers of all these saints can obtain, in union with thine, thou canst obtain, by thy intercession alone without their aid.[87] But wherefore hast thou such power? "quare hoc potes?" continues the saint. Because thou alone art the mother of our common Savior, thou art the spouse of God, the universal queen of heaven and earth.[88] If thou dost not speak for us, no saint will pray for us and aid us.[89] But if thou art moved to pray for us, all the saints will engage to intercede for us and help us.[90] So says Father Segneri,[91] applying to Mary, as the holy Church does, these words of Wisdom: "I alone have

---

82. Tom. 2, in 3, p. D. 28, sect. 3.
83. Frustra alios sanctos oraret, quem ista non adjuvaret.
84. Vultum tuum deprecabuntur omnes divites plebis. Psal. xliv. 13.
85. Inter sanctos non solemus uti uno tamquam intercessore ad alium, cum omnes sint ejusdem ordinis, ad virginem autem tamquam ad Dominam ac Reginam alii sancti adhibentur intercessores.
86. Nel Diario di Maria alli 21 di Marzo.
87. Quid possunt omnes isti tecum, tu sola potes sine illis omnibus. Orat. 45, ad S. Virg. Mar.
88. Quia mater es salvatoris nostri, sponsa Dei, regina cœli et terræ. Lib. Or. Exc. v. ap. Pac. Exc. 20, in sal. Ang. 2, 7.
89. Te tacente, nullus juvabit, nullus orabit.
90. Te, domina orante, omnes juvabunt et orabunt.
91. In his book, *Divoto di Maria.*

compassed the circuit of heaven."[92] As with its motion the first sphere puts in motion all the others, so when Mary is moved to pray for a soul, she moves all heaven to pray with her. St. Bonaventure says, that when she commands, as being their queen, all the saints and angels accompany her and unite their prayers to hers.[93]

So we see, finally, why the holy Church requires us to invoke and salute the divine mother with the great name of our hope: Hail our hope, "Spes nostra salve." The impious Luther could not endure that the holy Roman Church should call Mary, our hope;[94] because, as he said, God only and Jesus Christ as our mediator are our hope; but that God curses those who place their hope in any creature, as we find in Jeremias: "Cursed be the man that trusteth in man."[95] But the Church teaches us everywhere to invoke Mary, and call her our hope: "Spes nostra salve." Whoever places his hope in a creature, independently of God, is certainly accursed of God, since God is the only fountain and the dispenser of every good, and the creature, without God, has nothing and can do nothing. But if the Lord has ordained, as we have proved, that all graces shall pass through Mary, as a channel of mercy, we can, and ought even to assert that Mary is our hope, by whose intercession we receive divine graces, and therefore it is St. Bernard called her the whole cause of his hope.[96] St. John of Damascus expresses the same thing when, addressing the blessed Virgin, he says to her: Oh Lady, in thee I have placed all my hope, and with firm confidence I look to thee for my salvation.[97] St. Thomas says that Mary is all the hope of our salvation.[98] St. Ephrem explains: Oh most holy Virgin, receive us under thy protection, if thou wilt see us saved, since we have no other hope of being saved but through thee.[99]

We will then conclude in the words of St. Bernard: Let us strive, with all the affections of our heart, to reverence this divine mother, Mary, since this is the will of that Lord who would have us receive all good from her

---

92. Gyrum cœli circuivi sola. Eccli. xxiv. 8.
93. Quando virgo sanctissima procedit ad Deum pro nobis deprecandum imperat angelis et sanctis, ut eam comitentur, et simul cum ipsa altissimum pro nobis exorent. In Spec. V. c. 3.
94. Ferre nequeo ut Maria dicatur spes et vita mea. In Post Maj. Evang. in Nat. Mar.
95. Maledictus homo qui confidit in homine. xvii. 5.
96. Filioli, hæc maxima mea fiducia, hæc tota ratio spei meæ. Or. Pan. ad B. V.
97. In te spem meam collocavi ex animo et intentis oculis, abs te pendeo. Ap. Auriem. to. 1, c. 7.
98. Omnes spes vitæ. Opusc. 7.
99. Nobis non est alia quam a te fiducia, o virgo sincerissima. Sub alis tuæ pietatis protege et custodi nos. De Laud. Virg.

hands.[100] And the saint exhorts us, whenever we desire and ask any favor, to recommend ourselves to Mary, and trust that we shall obtain it through her intercession.[101] For, says the saint, if you do not deserve from God the favor you ask, Mary, who asks it in your behalf, merits to obtain it.[102] Hence the same Bernard exhorts us each and all, that, whatever we offer to God, whether works or prayers, we recommend all to Mary, if we wish our Lord to accept them.[103]

EXAMPLE

Eutychian, Patriarch of Constantinople, relates the following well-known story of Theophilus. The Patriarch was an eye-witness of the fact which we here relate, and which is confirmed by St. Peter Damian, St. Bernard, St. Bonaventure, St. Antoninus, and others.[104] Theophilus was archdeacon of the Church of Adanas, a city of Cilicia; and was so much esteemed, that the people wished him to become their bishop, but his humility prevented his consent. Some malicious persons afterwards accused him, and he was deposed from his office. This afflicted him so much, that, blinded by passion, he went to a Jewish magician, who induced him to apply to Satan for help in his misfortunes. The devil answered that if he wished his assistance, he must renounce Jesus, and Mary his mother, and hand over to him the act of renunciation, written with his own hand. Theophilus executed the vile document. On the following day the bishop having heard of the wrong done him by his calumniators, asked his forgiveness, and restored him to his office. But Theophilus began then to feel so tortured by remorse of conscience on account of the great crime he had committed, that he wept continually. What does he do? He enters a church, prostrates himself in tears before an altar of the blessed Virgin,

---

100. Totis medullis cordium hanc Mariam veneremur, quia sic est voluntas ejus, qui totum nos habere voluit per Mariam. Serm. de Nat. B. V.
101. Quæramus gratiam, et per Mariam quæramus. Serm. de Aquæd.
102 .Quia indignus eras, cui donaret, datum est Mariæ ut per illam acciperes quidquid haberes. Serm. 3, in Virg. Nativ.
103. Quidquid Deo offerre potes, Mariæ commendare memento, si non vis sustinere repulsum. Serm. de Aquæd.
104. Crasset Div. alla B. V. tom. 1, tr. 1, q. 10.

and exclaims: "Oh mother of God, I will not despair having thee, who art so merciful, to aid me." He persevered forty days in weeping and praying thus to the holy Virgin; when behold, one night the mother of mercy appeared to him and said: "Oh Theophilus, what have you done? you have renounced my friendship and that of my Son; and for whom? for your own and my enemy." "Oh Lady," answered Theophilus, "it belongs to thee to pardon me, and to obtain my pardon from thy Son." Then Mary, seeing his confidence, answered, "Take courage, and I will pray for thee." Theophilus, encouraged by these words, redoubled his tears, his penance, and his prayers, remaining constantly at the foot of the altar. And, behold, Mary appeared to him again, and with a joyful countenance said to him: "Theophilus, rejoice, I have presented thy tears and thy prayers to God; he hath accepted them, and hath already pardoned thee; henceforth be grateful and faithful." "Oh Lady," replied Theophilus, "this is not sufficient to console me; the enemy still holds that impious deed, by which I have renounced thee and thy Son; thou canst obtain it for me." After three days Theophilus awoke one night, and found the paper on his breast. The next day, when the bishop with a large assembly were present in the church, Theophilus cast himself at his feet, related the whole story, weeping bitterly, and gave him the infamous writing, which the bishop immediately ordered to be burned in presence of all the people, who wept for joy, praising the goodness of God, and the mercy of Mary towards that miserable sinner. Theophilus returned to the church of the Virgin, and there, three days afterwards, he died happily, with thanksgivings to Jesus and his holy mother on his lips.

PRAYER

Oh Queen and Mother of mercy! who dost dispense graces to all those who have recourse to thee, so liberally because thou art queen, and with so much love because thou art our most loving mother; to thee I commend myself to-day, destitute of merits and virtues as I am, and laden with debts to the divine justice. Oh Mary, thou hast the keys of all the divine mercies, do not forget my miseries, and do not leave me in my great poverty. Thou who art so liberal with all, and who givest more than is asked of thee, do so with me, Oh Lady, protect me, this is all I ask. If thou dost protect me I fear nothing. I do not fear the demons, for thou art more powerful than all the spirits of hell; nor my sins, for one word of thine in my behalf can obtain pardon of them all from God. If I have thy favor I do not fear even the anger of God, for he is appeased by one prayer of thine. In a word, if thou dost protect me I hope all things, because all things are possible with thee. Oh mother of mercy, I know that thou takest pleasure and pride in giving succor to the most miserable, for thou canst aid them, if not prevented by their obstinacy. I am a sinner, but I am not obstinate; I wish to change my life. Thou canst, then, help me; do help and save me. To-day I place myself entirely in thy hands. Teach me what I must do to please God, and I will do it; and I hope to do so with thy aid, oh Mary, Mary, my mother, my light, my consolation, my refuge, and my hope. Amen, amen, amen.

Our Lady of the Forsaken. **Patroness of Valencia, Spain.**

CHAPTER 6

Eja ergo, advocata nostra
Ah, then, our advocate

SECTION 1
Mary is an advocate, powerful to save all

So great is the authority of mothers over their children that although they may be monarchs, having absolute dominion over all the persons in their kingdom, yet their mothers can never become subject to them. It is true that Jesus is now in heaven, for he is seated there at the right hand of the Father even as man, as St. Thomas explains it; by reason of the hypostatic union with the person of the Word, and has supreme dominion over all, and even over Mary; yet it will always be true, that at the time when our Redeemer lived on this earth, he was pleased to humble himself and make himself subject to Mary, as St. Luke teaches us: And he was subject to them: "Erat subditus illis."[1] St. Ambrose even says, that Jesus Christ having deigned to make Mary his mother, was obliged as her son to obey her. And therefore, observes Richard of St. Laurence, it is said of the other saints, that they are with God; but of Mary alone can it be said, that not only was it her lot to be subject to the will of God, but that God was also subject to her will.[2] And as it is said of the other holy virgins, as the same author remarks, that they follow the divine lamb wherever he goes: "sequuntur agnum quocumque ierit;"[3] of the Virgin Mary it may be said, that the divine Lamb followed her on this earth, having become subject to her.[4]

Hence we may say, that though Mary is in heaven, and can no longer command her Son, yet her prayers will ever be the prayers of a mother, and therefore most powerful to obtain whatever she asks. Mary, says St. Bonaventure, has this privilege with her Son that she is most powerful to obtain by her prayers whatsoever she will.[5] And wherefore? Precisely for the

---

1. C. ii. v. 51.
2. Cum de ceteris sanctis dicatur, eos esse cum Deo, Maria majus aliquid sortita est, ut non solum ipsa subjiceretur voluntati Dei, sed etiam Dominus voluntati ipsius. L. I, de Laud. Virg. c. 5.
3. Ap. 14.
4. De virgine autem Maria secure dici potest, quod agnus sequebater eam, quocumque ivit; ex illo Lucæ: Erat subditus illis. Loc. cit.
5. Grande privilegium Mariæ, quod apud filium sit potentissima. In Spec. c. 8.

reason which we have before mentioned, and which we will now examine more fully, namely, because the prayers of Mary are the prayers of a mother. And therefore, says St. Peter Damian, the Virgin has all power in heaven as on earth, being able to raise to the hope of salvation even the most despairing.[6] And then he adds, that when the mother asks any favor for us of Jesus Christ (called by the saint the altar of mercy where sinners obtain pardon from God), the Son has so great regard for the prayers of Mary, and so great a desire to please her, that when she prays, she seems to command rather than request, and to be a mistress rather than a handmaid.[7] Thus Jesus would honor this his dear mother, who has honored him so much in her life, by granting her immediately whatever she asks and desires. St. Germanus beautifully confirms this by saying to the Virgin: Thou art mother of God, omnipotent to save sinners, and needest no other recommendation with God, since thou art the mother of true life.[8]

St. Bernardine of Sienna does not hesitate to say that all obey the commands of Mary, even God himself;[9] signifying by these words, that God listens to her prayers as though they were commands. Hence St. Anselm thus addresses Mary: The Lord, oh holy Virgin, has so highly exalted thee, that by his favor thou canst obtain all possible graces for thy servants, for thy protection is omnipotent.[10] Thy help is omnipotent, oh Mary: "Omnipotens auxilium tuum, O Maria;" as Cosmas of Jerusalem exclaims. Yes, Mary is omnipotent, adds Richard of St. Laurence, since the queen, by every law, must enjoy the same privileges as the king. For as the power of the Son and mother are the same, the mother by the omnipotent Son is made omnipotent.[11] As St. Antoninus says: God has placed the whole Church, not only under the patronage, but also under the dominion of Mary.[12]

As the mother, then, must have the same power as the Son, justly was Mary made omnipotent by Jesus, who is omnipotent; it being, however, always true, that whereas the Son is omnipotent by nature, the mother is so by grace. And her omnipotence consists in this, that the Son denies

6. Data est tibi omnis potestas in cœlo et in terra; et nihil tibi impossibile, cui possibile est etiam desperatos in spem salutis relevare. Serm. 1, de Nat. B. V.
7. Accedis enim ad illud humanæ reconciliationis altare, non solum rogans, sed imperans; domina, non ancilla; nam filius nihil negans honorat. Loc. cit.
8. Serm. 3, in Dorm. B. V.
9. Imperio Virginis omnia famulantur, etiam Deus. Tom. 2, Serm. 61.
10. Te Deus, o virgo, sic exaltavi, ut omnia tibi secum possibilia esse donaris. Lib. de Conc. Virg.
11. Eisdem privilegiis secundum leges gaudet rex et regina. Cum autem eadem sit potestas filii et matris, ab omnipotente filio omnipotens mater facta est. L. 4, de Laud. Virg.
12. Ecclesia est, non tantum sub Virginis patrocinio, verum etiam sub dominatione ac potestate. P. 4, tit. 15, c. 20, 62.

nothing that the mother asks; as it was revealed to St. Bridget, who heard Jesus one day addressing Mary in these words: "Oh my mother, thou knowest how I love thee; ask from me, then, whatever thou dost desire, for there is no demand of thine that will not be graciously heard by me."[13] And the reason that he added was beautiful: "Mother, when thou wast on earth, there was nothing thou didst refuse to do for love of me; now that I am in heaven, it is just that I refuse nothing which thou dost ask of me."[14] Mary is, then, called omnipotent in the sense in which it can be understood of a creature, who is not capable of any divine attribute. She is omnipotent, because she obtains by her prayers whatever she wishes.

With reason, then, oh our great advocate! says St. Bernard, dost thou only wish, and it is done: "Velis tu et omnia fient." And St. Anselm: Whatever thou askest, oh Virgin! cannot but be done.[15] Wish, and it will be done; dost thou wish to raise the most abandoned sinner to an exalted sanctity, to thee it is given to do it. The blessed Albertus Magnus represents Mary speaking thus: I must be asked to wish, for if I wish it must be done.[16] Hence St. Peter Damian, contemplating this great power of Mary, and praying her to have pity on us, says: Oh Mary! oh our beloved advocate! since thou hast a heart so compassionate, that thou canst not behold the miserable without pity, and, at the same time, hast so great a power with God to save all those whom thou dost defend; deign to intercede in behalf of us miserable creatures, who place in thee all our hopes. If our prayers do not move thee, may thy merciful heart at least move thee; may thy power at least move thee, since God, for this end, has enriched thee with so much power, that the richer thou art in the power to aid us, so much more compassionate thou mayest be in thy desire to aid us.[17] Of this, St. Bernard assures us, saying, that Mary is abundant in mercy as well as in power; as her charity is most powerful, so also is it most merciful in our behalf, and this is manifested to us continually by its effects.[18]

Even when she was living on this earth, the only thought of Mary, after the glory of God, was to relieve the wretched. And we know that then she enjoyed already the privilege of obtaining whatever she asked. This we know

13. Pete quod vis a me, non enim potest esse inanis petitio tua. Rev. 1. c. 4.
14. Quia tu mihi nihil negasti in terris, ego nihil tibi negabo in cœlis.
15. Quicquid tu Virgo velis, nequaquam fieri non poterit. De Exc. Virg. c. 12.
16. Roganda sum, ut velim; quia, si volo, necesse est fieri. Ap. P. Pep. Grand, etc.
17. Moveat te natura; potentia moveat; quia quanto potentior tante misericordior esse debebis. Serm. 1, de N. B. V.
18. Potentissima, et piissima charitas matris Dei, et affectu compatiendi, et subveniendi abundat effectu; æque locuples in utroque. Serm. 4. de Assump.

from what took place at the nuptials of Cana of Galilee, when the wine failed, and the blessed Virgin, compassionating the distress and mortification of that family, asked the Son to relieve them by a miracle, making known to him this want: They have no wine: "Vinum non habent."[19] Jesus answered: "Woman, what is that to thee and to me? my hour is not yet come."[20] Observe, that although the Lord appeared to refuse this favor to his mother, by saying: Of what importance is it, oh woman, to me and to thee that the wine has failed? It does not become me now to perform any miracle, as the time has not arrived, the time of my preaching, when with signs I must confirm my doctrine; yet notwithstanding this, Mary, as if the Son had already granted her the favor, said to the attendants, fill the water-pots with water: "Imple hydrias aqua."[21] Come fill the water-pots, and you will be consoled; and Jesus Christ, indeed to please his mother, changed that water into the best wine. But how is this? If the time appointed for miracles was the time of preaching, how could it be anticipated by the miracle of the wine, contrary to the divine decree? Nothing, it may be answered, was done contrary to the divine decree; for although, generally speaking, the time for signs had not come, yet from eternity God had established by another general decree, that nothing the divine mother could ask should be denied her; and therefore Mary, well acquainted with her privilege, although her Son seemed to have then set aside her petition, said notwithstanding, that the water-pots should be filled, as though the favor was already granted. This, St. John Chrysostom would express, when commenting on the passage of John above mentioned—"Oh woman, what is that to thee and to me?"—he says, that although Jesus had answered thus, yet, for the honor of his mother, he did not fail to comply with her demand.[22] St. Thomas confirms the same, when he observes, that by these words—"My hour has not yet come"—Jesus Christ wished to show that he would have deferred the miracle, if another had asked him to perform it; but because his mother asked it, he immediately performed it.[23] St. Cyril and St. Jerome confirm this, according to Barrada. And Jansenius of Ghent says, commenting on the same passage of St. John: That he might honor his mother, he anticipated the time of working miracles.[24]

---

19. Joan. ii. 3.
20. Quid mihi et tibi, mulier? nondum venit hora mea. Joan. ii. 4.
21. Joan. ii. 7.
22. Et licet ita responderit, maternis tamen precibus obtemperavit.
23. Per illa verba, nondum venit hora mea, ostendit se dilatucum fuisse miraculum, si alius rogasset; quia tamen rogabat mater, fecit. Apud. Defens. cultus Mariani, auctore R. D. Henr. de Cerf. p. 129.
24. Quo matrem honoraret, prævenit tempus miraculi faciendi.

In a word, it is certain that no creature can obtain for us miserable sinners so many mercies as this good advocate, who is honored by God with this privilege, not only as his beloved handmaid, but also as his true mother. William of Paris says this when addressing her.[25] It is enough that Mary speaks, and the Son does all she wishes. The Lord, speaking to the spouse of the Canticles, by whom is understood Mary, says: "Thou that dwellest in the gardens, the friends hearken, make me hear thy voice."[26] The friends are the saints, who, when they ask any favor for their clients, wait until their queen prays to God for it and obtains it; for, as was said before in Chapter 5, no favor is dispensed except by the intercession of Mary. And how does Mary obtain favors? It is enough that her Son hears her voice: Make me to hear thy voice: "Fac me audire vocem tuam;" it is enough that she speaks, and her Son immediately hears her. William of Paris, explaining in the same way the passage above named, introduces the Son, who thus addresses Mary: Oh thou who dwellest in the celestial gardens, intercede with confidence for whomsoever thou wilt, for I cannot forget that I am thy Son, or think of refusing any thing to my mother. It is enough for thee to speak, and thy Son will graciously hear and grant thy petition.[27] The Abbot Godfrey says that Mary, although she obtains favors by praying, yet prays with a kind of maternal authority; hence we may be sure that she will obtain whatever she desires and asks for us.[28]

It is related of Coriolanus, by Valerius Maximus,[29] that when he held Rome besieged, all the prayers of his friends and of the citizens could not induce him to withdraw his forces; but when his mother Veturia came to entreat him he could not resist, and immediately raised the siege. But the prayers of Mary are as much more powerful with Jesus than the prayers of Veturia with her son, as the love and gratitude of Jesus to Mary exceeds that of the son of Veturia for his mother. Father Justin Micoviensis writes: One sigh of Mary has more power than the prayers of all the saints united.[30] The devil himself confessed this same thing to St. Dominic, when, constrained by his commands, he spoke through the mouth of a possessed person, saying,

---

25. Nulla creatura tot et tanta impetrare posset apud filium tuum miseris, quam tu impetras eisdem; in quo procul dubio non tamquam ancillam, sed tamquam matrem verissimam te honorat.
26. Quæ habitas in hortis, amici auscultant, fac me audire vocem tuam. Cant. viii. 13.
27. Quæ habitas in hortis cœlestibus, fiducialiter pro quibus volueris intercede; non enim possum oblivisci me filium tuum, ut matri quidpiam denegandum putem. Tantum ut vocem proferat, quia a filio audiri, exaudiri est.
28. Virgo Maria ex eo quod ille homo est, et natus ex ea, quasi quodam matus imperio, apud ipsum impetrare quod voluerit pia fiducia non dubitatur. Serm. viii. de B.Virg.
29. Lib. 5, cap. 4.
30. Unum beatæ Mariæ suspirium plus posset, quam omnium sanctorum simul suffragia. In tit. B. V. verbo. Virg. pot.

as Father Paciucchelli narrates,[31] that one sigh of Mary availed more with God than the united prayers of all the saints. St. Antoninus says, that the prayers of the blessed Virgin being the prayers of a mother, have a certain kind of authority, hence it is impossible that she should not be heard when she prays.[32] On this account St. Germanus encourages sinners to recommend themselves to this advocate with these words: Thou, oh Mary, having the authority of a mother with God, dost obtain pardon for the vilest sinners; for the Lord, who in all things recognizes thee for his true mother, cannot refuse to grant thee whatever thou dost ask.[33] St. Bridget, too, heard the saints in heaven saying to the Virgin: What is there that thou canst not do? Whatever thou dost desire is done.[34] To which corresponds that celebrated verse: What God by a command, thou, oh Virgin, by a prayer canst effect.[35] Is it not, says St. Augustine, worthy of the goodness of the Lord thus to guard the honor of his mother? for he asserts that he has come on the earth, not to break, but to fulfill the law, which, among other things, commands us to honor our parents.[36]

St. George, Archbishop of Nicomedia, even adds, that Jesus Christ grants to his mother all her petitions, as if to satisfy the obligation that he is under to her for having caused, by her consent, that the human nature should be given him.[37] Wherefore, St. Methodius, the martyr exclaims: Rejoice, oh Mary, that a Son has fallen to thy lot as thy debtor, who gives to all and receives from none. We are all debtors to God for whatever we possess, since every thing is his gift; but God has wished to make himself a debtor to thee, taking from thee his body and becoming man.[38] So also St. Augustine says: Mary having merited to give flesh to the Divine Word, and by that to furnish the price of the divine redemption, that we might be delivered from eternal death; therefore is she, says the same doctor, more powerful than any other to help us and obtain for us eternal salvation.[39] Hence St. Theophilus, Bishop of Alexandria, who lived

---

31. De B. V.
32. Oratio Deiparæ habet rationem imperii; unde impossibile est, eam non exaudiri. P. 4. tit. 15, c. 17, n. 4.
33. Tu autem materna in Deum auctoritate pollens, etiam iis qui enormiter peccant, eximiam remissionis gratiam concilias; non enim potes non exaudiri, cum Deus tibi ut veræ et intemeratæ Matri in omnibus morem gerat. Van. Enc. Deip.
34. Domina benedicta, quid est quod non poteris? Quod enim vis, hoc factum est. L. 4, Rev. c. 74.
35. Quod Deus imperio, tu prece Virgo potes.
36. Nunquid non pertinet ad benignitatem Domini, matris honorem servare, qui legem non venit solvere; sed adimplere?
37. Filius quasi exsolvens debitum, implet petitiones tuas. Or. de Ex. Mar.
38. Euge euge, quæ debitorem habes filium, qui omnibus mutuatur. Deo enim universi debemus, tibi autem etiam ille debitor est. Orat. in Hyp. Dom.
39. Virgo quæ meruit pro liberandis proferre pretium, potest plus omnibus suffragium liberatis impendere. Orat. 2. de aff. B. V.

in the time of St. Jerome, thus wrote: The Son is pleased to be entreated by his mother, because he wishes to grant for her sake all that he does grant; and thus to recompense the favor he has received from her when she gave him flesh. Hence St. John Damascene addresses the Virgin in these words: Thou, then, oh Mary, being mother of God, canst save all men by thy prayers, which are enforced by a mother's authority.[40]

Let us conclude with the words of St. Bonaventure, who, considering the great benefit which the Lord has conferred on us in giving us Mary for our advocate, thus addresses her: Oh truly immense and admirable goodness of God, who to us miserable, guilty creatures, has granted thee, oh our Lady, for our advocate, that thou mightest, by thy powerful intercession, obtain for us whatever good thou wilt.[41] Oh, the great mercy of God, continues the saint, who, that we might not flee to hide ourselves from the sentence to be pronounced upon us, has destined his own mother and the treasurer of graces for our advocate.[42]

EXAMPLE

Father Razzi, of the order of Camaldoli, relates that a certain youth having lost his father, was sent by his mother to the court of a prince.[43] The mother, who had a great devotion to Mary, when she parted with him made him promise to recite every day a "Hail Mary," and add these words: *"Blessed Virgin, help me in the hour of my death."* The youth arrived at court, but soon began to lead so dissolute a life, that his master was obliged to send him away. In despair, without means of support, he went into the country and became a highway robber; but even then he did not omit to recommend himself to our Lady, as his mother had directed him. At length he fell into the hands of justice, and was condemned to death. Being in

---

40. Potes quidem omnes salvare, ut Dei Altissimi Mater, precibus materna auctoritate pollentibus. Ex. Men. 1, Jan. Ode. 4.
41. O certe Dei nostri mira benignitas, qui suis reis te Dominam tribuit advocatam, ut auxilio tuo, quod volueris, valeas impetrare. In Salv. Reg.
42. O mirabilis erga nos, misericordia Dei nostri, qui ne fugeremus pro sententia, voluit matrem ac dominam gratiæ instituero advocatam!
43. Mirac. di Maria, Mir. 47.

prison the evening before his execution, and thinking of his disgrace, the grief of his mother, and the death which awaited him, he fell to weeping bitterly. The devil seeing him so oppressed by melancholy, appeared to him in the form of a beautiful young man, and said to him that he would release him from death and prison, if he would follow his directions. The convict engaged to do all that he required. Then the pretended youth made known to him that he was the devil and had come to his assistance. In the first place, he ordered him to renounce Jesus Christ and the holy sacraments. The youth consented. He then required him to renounce the Virgin Mary and her protection. "This," exclaimed the young man, "I will never do," and turning to Mary, repeated the accustomed prayer that his mother had taught him: *Blessed Virgin, help me in the hour of my death*. At these words the devil disappeared. The youth remained in great affliction for the wickedness he had committed in denying Jesus Christ. He invoked the blessed Virgin, and she obtained for him, by her prayers, a great sorrow for all his sins, so that he made his confession with much weeping and contrition. On his way to the gallows, happening to pass before a statue of Mary, he saluted her with his usual prayer: *Blessed Virgin, help me in the hour of my death*, and the statue, in the presence of all, inclined its head and saluted him. Deeply moved, he begged to be allowed to kiss the feet of the image. The executioners refused, but afterwards consented on account of the clamor of the people. The youth stooped to kiss her feet, and Mary extended her arm from that statue, took him by the hand and held him so strongly that no power could move him. At this prodigy the multitude shouted "Pardon, pardon;" and pardon was granted. Having returned to his country, he led an exemplary life, and was always most devoted to Mary, who had delivered him from temporal and eternal death.

PRAYER

Oh great mother of God, I will say to thee with St. Bernard: Thy Son hears thee and will grant thee whatsoever thou dost ask.[44] Speak then, speak, oh Mary our advocate, in behalf of us miserable creatures.

---

44. Loquere, Domina, quia audit filius tuus et quæcumque petieris impetrabis.

Remember that thou hast received thy great power and dignity even for our benefit. A God has chosen to become thy debtor, by taking from thee the human nature to the end that thou mayest dispense to the miserable the riches of divine mercy. We are thy servants, in a special manner consecrated to thy service, and among these I hope to be one. We glory in living under thy protection. If thou doest good to all, even to those who do not know thee and do not honor thee, and who even insult and blaspheme thee; how much ought we to hope from thy kindness, who dost seek for the wretched that thou mayest relieve them! we who honor, love, and trust in thee! We are great sinners, but God has granted thee mercy and power greater than all our sins. Thou canst and wilt save us; and we will so much the more earnestly desire this, as we are unworthy of it, that we may glorify thee the more in heaven, when we shall have been received there by thy intercession. Oh, mother of mercy, we present to thee our souls once pure and washed with the blood of Jesus Christ, but since defiled with sin. To thee we present them, wilt thou purify them? Obtain for us sincere amendment, obtain for us the love of God, perseverance, paradise. We ask great things of thee, but canst thou not obtain them all for us? Are they greater than the love God has for thee? Thou hast only to open thy lips in prayer to thy Son, and he will grant thee all things. Pray, then, pray, oh Mary, for us; and surely thou wilt be heard graciously, and we shall be saved.

SECTION 2
Mary is a merciful advocate, who does not refuse to defend the cause of the most miserable sinners

There are so many reasons why we should love this our loving queen, that if all the earth should praise Mary, and all sermons treat of her alone, and all men should give their lives for Mary, it would yet be little compared to the homage and gratitude we owe her, for the very tender love she bears to all men, even to the most miserable sinners who preserve towards her any feeling of devotion. Raymond Jordan declares that Mary cannot but love those who love her. Nay she does not disdain even to serve those who serve

---

45. Maria diligit diligentes se; imo sibi servientibus servit. Ipsa benedicto filio suo irato potentissime reconciliat servos et amatores suos. Præf. in Cant.

her, using, if they are sinners, all the power of her intercession to obtain pardon for them from her blessed Son.[45] And so great, he goes on to say, is her kindness and compassion, that no one, however degraded he may be, should fear to cast himself at her feet, since she rejects no one who has recourse to her.[46] Mary, as our most loving advocate, offers herself to God the prayers of her servants, especially those which are offered to her; for as the Son intercedes for us with the Father, thus she intercedes for us with the Son, and never ceases to intercede with both for our salvation, and to obtain for us the favors that we ask.[47] Rightly, then, does the blessed Denis, the Carthusian, call the holy Virgin the peculiar refuge of the lost, the hope of the wretched and the advocate of all sinners who have recourse to her.[48]

But if there ever be any sinner who, indeed, does not doubt the power, but has no trust in the mercy of Mary, fearing that she may not be willing to aid him on account of the magnitude of his offenses, St. Bonaventure encourages him by saying: Great and peculiar is the privilege which Mary has with her Son, of obtaining by her prayers whatever she desires;[49] but what would this great power of Mary avail us, he adds, if she should be indifferent to our welfare?[50] No, let us not doubt, concludes the saint, let us be secure, and always thank the Lord and his divine mother for it; for, as she is the most powerful of all saints with God, so she is the most loving advocate, and the most desirous of our welfare.[51] And who, oh mother of sinners! joyfully exclaims St. Germanus, who, after thy Jesus, has so much care of us, and of our welfare, as thou?[52] Who doth defend us in the trials that afflict us, as thou dost defend us? Who take upon himself to protect sinners, as if combating in their behalf, as thou dost?[53] Wherefore, he adds, thy patronage, oh Mary! is more powerful and loving than we are able to comprehend.[54] Whilst, as the Idiot says, all the other saints can aid their own servants by their patronage more than others;

---

46. Tanta est ejus benignitas, quod nulli formidandum est ad eam accedere; tantaque misericordia ut nemo ab ea repellatur.
47. Ipsa preces servorum, maxime quæ sibi exhibentur, repræsentat in conspectu divinæ majestatis; quia ipsa est advocata nostra apud filium, sicut filius apud Patrem. Imo apud Patrem et Filium procurat negotia et preces nostras. In dict. Præf.
48. Singulare perditorum refugium, miserorum spem, advocatam omnium iniquorum ad se confugientium.
49. Grande privilegium Mariæ, quod apud filium sit potentissima. In Spec. lect. 6, 7.
50. Sed quid tanta Mariæ potentia prodesset nobis; si ipsa nihil curaret de nobis?
51. Carissimi sciamus indubitanter, et pro hoc gratias agamus incessanter, quia sicut ipsa apud eum omnibus sanctis est potentior, ita pro nobis omnibus est sollicitior.
52. Quis post filium tuum curam gerit generis humani, sicut tu? Serm. de Zona. Virg.
53. Quis ita nos defendit in nostris afflictionibus. Quis pugnat pro peccatoribus?
54. Propterea patrocinium tuum majus est quam apprehendi possit.

the divine mother, as she is the queen of all, so is she the advocate of all, and cares for the salvation of all.[55]

She cares for all, even for sinners, and glories especially in being called their advocate; as she herself declared to the venerable sister Mary Villani, saying: "Next to the title of mother of God, I glory most in being named the advocate of sinners." The blessed Amadeus says, that our queen is always before the divine Majesty, interceding for us with her powerful prayers.[56] And since in heaven she knows perfectly our miseries and necessities, she cannot but have pity on us; so, with the affection of a mother, moved by compassion for us, she kindly and mercifully endeavors to relieve and save us.[57] It is with good reason, then, that Richard of St. Laurence encourages every one, however degraded he may be, to appeal confidently to this sweet advocate, in the certain belief that he will always find her ready to help him.[58] It is also well said by Godfrey, that Mary is ever ready to pray for all.[59]

And oh, with how much efficacy and love, St. Bernard exclaims, this good advocate of ours conducts the cause of our salvation![60] St. Augustine, contemplating the affection and earnestness with which Mary is continually occupied in interceding with the divine Majesty for us, that the Lord may pardon our sins, assist us with his grace, free us from dangers, and relieve us from our miseries, thus addresses the holy Virgin:[61] Oh Lady! It is true that all the saints desire our salvation and pray for us; but the charity and tenderness which thou dost manifest for us in heaven, by obtaining with thy prayers so many mercies from God, obliges us to confess, that we have in heaven only one advocate, that is thyself, and that thou alone art the only true lover watchful of our welfare. And who can comprehend the solicitude with which Mary is always waiting on God in our behalf? St. Germanus says: She is never satisfied with defending us: "Non est satietas defensionis ejus." The expression is beautiful. So great is the pity which Mary has for our miseries, and so great is the love she bears us, that she

---

55. Cæteri sancti jure quodam patrocinii pro sibi specialiter commissis plus possunt prodesse, quam pro alienis; beatissima vero Virgo, sicut omnium est regina, sic est omnium patrona et advocata, et cura illi est de omnibus. De Contempl. B. V. in Prol.
56. Adstat beatissima Virgo vultui conditoris prece potentissima, semper interpellans pro nobis.
57. Videt enim nostra discrimina, nostrique clemens Domina materno affectu miseretur.
58. Inveniet semper paratam auxiliari.
59. Ipsa pro universe mundo paratissima est ad precandum.
60. Advocatam præmisit peregrinatio nostra; quæ tamquam judicis mater, et mater misericordiæ, suppliciter et efficaciter salutis nostræ negocia pertractabit. Serm. 1, de Assump.
61. Unam te ac solam pro nobis in cœlo fatemur esse sollicitam. Ap. In Spec. lect. 6.

prays always, and prays again and is never satisfied with praying for us, and defending us from evil with her prayers, and obtaining for us favors— she is never satisfied with defending us.

What poor sinners we should be if we had not this advocate, so powerful and so merciful, and at the same time so prudent and so wise, that the judge, her Son, cannot condemn the guilty, if she defends them, as Richard of St. Laurence says.[62] Well then, does St. John (the geometrician) salute her: Hail, authority which puts an end to strife.[63] For all the causes defended by this most wise advocate are gained. Hence Mary is called by St. Bonaventure, the wise Abigail "Abigail sapiens." This was the woman who, as we read in the First Book of Kings, knew so well how to appease King David, by her persuasive entreaties, when he was full of indignation against Nabal, that he himself blessed and thanked her for having with her sweet words, prevented him from revenging himself upon Nabal with his own hands.[64] Precisely the same thing does Mary continually in heaven, in behalf of innumerable sinners: she knows so well how to appease the divine justice with her tender and wise entreaties, that God himself blesses her for it, and as it were thanks her, that thus she restrains him from abandoning and punishing them as they deserve. For this end, says St. Bernard, the eternal Father, desirous to show all possible compassion towards us, besides Jesus Christ, our principal advocate with himself, has given us Mary for our advocate with Jesus Christ.

There is no doubt, says St. Bernard, that Jesus is the only mediator of justice between men and God, who in virtue of his merits can, and according to his promises will, obtain for us pardon and divine grace; but because men recognize and fear in Jesus Christ the divine majesty, which dwells in him as God, it was necessary that another advocate should be assigned to us, to whom we could have recourse with less fear and more confidence; and this is Mary, than whom we can find no advocate more powerful with the divine majesty and more compassionate towards us.[65] But he would greatly wrong the mercy of Mary, continues the saint, who should still fear to cast himself at the feet of this most sweet advocate, who is in nothing severe or terrible, but is in all things kind, lovely, and compassionate.[66]

---

62. Tam prudens et diserta est advocata Maria, quod non potest filius vindicare in eos, pro quibus ipsa allegat. De Laud. v. l. 2, p. 2.
63. Salve jus dirimens lites. Ap. Pep. Lez. to. 5.
64. Benedicta tu, quæ prohibuisti me hodie, ne ulciscerer me manu mea. C. xxv.
65. Fidelis et potens mediator Dei et hominum; sed divinam reverentur in eo homines majestatem, opus est enim mediatore ad mediatorem ipsum: nec alter nobis utilior quam Maria. Serm. in Sign. Magn.
66. Quid ad Mariam accedere trepidet humana fragilitas? Nihil austerum in ea, nihil terribile, tota suavis est.

Read and revolve as much as you will all the history found in the Gospel, and if you find any act of austerity in Mary, then fear to approach her. But you will never find any; go then joyfully to her, for she will save thee by her intercession.[67]

Exceedingly beautiful is the exclamation which William of Paris puts in the mouth of a sinner who has recourse to Mary: Oh mother of my God, I come to thee full of confidence, even in the miserable state to which I find myself reduced by my sins; if thou dost reject me, I will plead with thee, for in a certain sense thou art bound to help me since all the Church of the faithful calls thee and proclaims thee mother of mercy.[68] Thou, oh Mary, art so dear to God that he always graciously listens to thee; thy great mercy has never failed; thy most sweet condescension has never despised any sinner, however enormous his sins, who has had recourse to thee.[69] What! could the whole Church falsely and in vain name thee her advocate and the refuge of sinners?[70] No, never be it said that my sins prevent thee, oh my mother, from exercising the great office of mercy which thou dost hold, by which thou art at the same time the advocate and mediator of peace between God and man, and next to thy Son the only hope and refuge of sinners.[71] Whatever of grace and glory is thine, even the dignity of being mother of God itself, if I may so speak, thou owest to sinners, since for their sake the divine Word has made thee his mother.[72] Far from this divine mother who has brought forth unto the world the fountain of mercy, be the thought that she, could refuse her compassion to any sinner who recommends himself to her.[73] Since, then, oh Mary, thy office is that of peacemaker between God and man, may thy great mercy, which far exceeds all my sins, move thee to aid me.[74]

Console yourselves, then, oh ye faint of heart, I will say with St. Thomas

---

67. Revolve diligentius evangelicæ historiæ seriem universam, et si quid forte durum occurrerit in Maria, ad eam accedere verearis, Serm. in Sign. Magn.
68. Adibo te imo etiam conveniam, gloriossissima Dei genitrix, quam matrem misericordiæ vocat imo clamitat omnis eccles a sanctorum. De Reth. Div. c. 18.
69. Tu, inquam, cujus gratiositas nunquam repulsam patitur, cujus misericordia nulli unquam defuit; cujus benignissima humanitas nullum unquam deprecantem quantumcumque peccatorem despexit.
70. An falso aut inaniter vocat te omnis Ecclesia advocatam suam, et miserorum refugium?
71. Absit, ut peccata mea possint suspendere te a tam salubri officio pietatis; quo et advocata es, et mediatrix hominum, post filium tuum spes unica et refugium tutissimum miserorum.
72. Totum siquidem quod habes gratiæ, totum quod habes gloriæ, et etiam hoc ipsum quod mater es Dei, si fas est dicere, ob peccatores tibi collata sunt.
73. Absit hoc a matre Dei quæ fontem pietatis toti mundo peperit, ut cuique miserorum suæ misericordiæ subventionem unquam deneget.
74. Officium ergo tuum est te mediam interponere inter ipsum et homines. Moveat te gloriosa Dei mater, benignissima misericordia tua, quæ major est incogitabiliter omnibus vitiis meis et peccatis. Guill. Paris. d. c. 18, de Reth. Div.

of Villanova, take heart, oh miserable sinners; this great Virgin, who is the mother of your judge and God, is the advocate of the human race. Powerful and able to obtain whatever she wishes from God; most wise, for she knows every method of appeasing him; universal, for she welcomes all, and refuses to defend none.[75]

EXAMPLE

Our advocate has shown how great is her kindness towards sinners by her mercy to Beatrice, a nun in the monastery of Fontebraldo, as related by Cesarius,[76] and by Father Rho.[77] This unhappy religious, having contracted a passion for a certain youth, agreed to flee with him from the convent; and in fact she went one day before a statue of the blessed Virgin, there deposited the keys of the monastery, for she was portress, and boldly departed. Arrived in another country, she led the miserable life of a prostitute for fifteen years. It happened that she met, one day, the agent of the monastery in the city where she was living, and asked of him, thinking he would not recognize her again, if he knew sister Beatrice? "I knew her well," he said: "she is a holy nun, and at present is mistress of novices." At this intelligence she was confounded and amazed, not knowing how to understand it. In order to ascertain the truth, she put on another dress and went to the monastery. She asked for sister Beatrice, and behold, the most holy Virgin appeared before her in the form of that same image to which at parting she had committed her keys, and her dress, and the divine mother thus spoke to her: "Beatrice, be it known to thee that, in order to prevent thy disgrace, I assumed thy form, and have filled thy office for the fifteen years that thou hast lived far from the monastery and from God. My child, return, and do penance, for my Son is still waiting for thee; and strive by thy holy life to preserve the good name I have gained thee." She spoke thus and disappeared. Beatrice re-entered the monastery, resumed the habit of a religious, and, grateful for the mercy of Mary, led the life of a saint. At her death she made known the foregoing incident, to the glory of this great queen.

---

75. Consolamini pusillanimes; respirate miserabiles; Virgo Deipara est humani generis advocata; idonea, sapientissima, universalis. In Rog. pro exp. adv. Turc. susc.
76. L. 7, c. 25.
77. In Ex.

PRAYER

Oh great mother of my Lord, I now see that the ingratitude shown by me for so many years to God and to thee, would justly merit that thou shouldst abandon all care of me, for the ungrateful are no more worthy of favors. But, oh Lady, I have a great idea of thy goodness; I believe it to be far greater than my ingratitude; continue, then, oh refuge of sinners, to help a miserable sinner who confides in thee. Oh mother of mercy, extend thy hand to raise a poor fallen creature who implores thy mercy. Oh Mary, defend thou me, or tell me to whom I shall have recourse, and who can protect me better than thou. Can I find an advocate with God more merciful and more powerful than thou, who art his mother? Thou having been created for the mother of the Savior, art destined to save sinners, and hast been given me for my salvation. Oh Mary, save him who has recourse to thee. I do not merit thy love, but the desire thou hast to save the lost gives me the hope that thou dost love me; and if thou lovest me, how can I be lost? Oh my beloved mother, if, as I hope, I am saved by thee, I will no longer be ungrateful; I will make amends by perpetual praises and by all the affection of my soul for my past ingratitude, and will make some return for the love thou bearest me. In heaven, where thou reignest and wilt reign forever, I will always joyfully sing thy mercies, and forever I will kiss those loving hands that have freed me from hell as often as I have deserved it for my sins. Oh Mary, my liberator, my hope, my queen, my advocate, my mother, I love thee, I wish thee well, and will always love thee. Amen, amen; thus I hope, so may it be.

SECTION 3
Mary is the peace-maker between sinners and God

The grace of God is a treasure, very great and most earnestly to be desired by every soul. It is called by the Holy Spirit an infinite treasure, since by means of divine grace we are raised to the honor of being made the friends of God: "She is an infinite treasure to men, which they that use become the friends of God."[78] Whence it is that Jesus, our Redeemer and God, did not hesitate to call those who are in grace, his friends: You are my friends: "Vos amici mei estis."[79] Oh accursed sin that loosens the ties of this blessed friendship: "Your iniquities have divided between you and your God;"[80] for they make the soul hateful to God, and from a friend it becomes an enemy of the Lord: "To God the wicked and his wickedness are hateful alike."[81] What, then, must a sinner do who finds himself so unhappy as to have become an enemy of God? He must find a mediator who will obtain pardon for him and enable him to recover the lost friendship of God. Take courage, says St. Bernard, oh sinner, who has lost God. Thy Lord himself hath given thee a mediator, even his Son Jesus Christ who can obtain for thee whatever thou desirest.[82]

But, oh God, the saint here exclaims, why do men esteem severe this most merciful Savior, who hath given his life for our salvation? Why do they look upon him as terrible who is all loveliness? Distrustful sinners, say, why do you fear? If you fear because you have offended God, remember that Jesus with his own lacerated hands has nailed your sins to the cross, and having satisfied the divine justice for them by his death, he has removed them from your soul.[83] But if ever, adds the saint, you fear to have recourse to Jesus Christ because his divine majesty alarms you, since when he became man he did not cease to be God, if you ever wish for another advocate with this mediator, invoke Mary, for she will intercede for you with the Son, who will surely graciously listen to her, and the Son will intercede with the Father, who can refuse nothing to this Son.[84] And so, concludes St. Bernard, this divine mother, oh my children, is the ladder of sinners, by which they ascend anew to the height of divine grace. This is my greatest confidence—this is the whole ground of my hope.[85]

Let us hear what the Holy Spirit makes the blessed Virgin say in the

---

78. Infinitus est thesaurus, quo qui usi sunt, participes facti sunt amicitiæ Dei. Sap. vii. 14.
79. Joan. xv. 14.
80. Iniquitates vestræ diviserunt inter vos et Deum vestrum. Is. lix. 2.
81. Odio sunt Deo impius et impietas ejus. Sap. xiv. 9.
82. Jesum tibi dedit mediatorem; quid non apud talem patrem filius talis obtineat. Serm. de Aquæd.
83. Serverum imaginantur, qui pius est, terribilem, qui amabilis est. Quid timetis modicæ fidei? Peccata affixit cruci suis manibus.
84. Sed forsitan et in ipso majestatem vereare divinam, quod licet factus sit homo, manserit tamen Deus. Advocatum habere vis et apud ipsum? recurre ad Mariam; exaudiet utique matrem filius, et exaudiet filium Pater.
85. Filioli, hæc peccatorum scala, hæc maxima mea fiducia est, hæc tota ratio spei meæ. Cit. Serm. de Aquæd.

sacred Canticles:[86] I am, says Mary, the defense of those who have recourse to me, and my mercy is to them a tower of refuge for this I have been appointed by my Lord as a peacemaker between sinners and him. Cardinal Hugo, on the same text, says, that Mary is the great peacemaker who obtains from God, and gives peace to enemies, salvation to the lost, pardon to sinners, and mercy to the despairing.[87] For this reason she was called by her divine spouse: Beautiful as the curtains of Solomon: "Formosa sicut pelles Salomonis."[88] In the tents of David there was nothing treated of but war, but in the tents of Solomon peace alone was spoken of. The Holy Spirit giving us to understand by this, that the mother of mercy does not treat of war and of vengeance against sinners, but only of peace and the pardon of their offenses.

Again, Mary was prefigured by Noah's dove, who returned to the ark bearing in her beak the olive-branch, as a sign of the peace which God granted to men. Wherefore St. Bonaventure says: Thou art that most faithful dove, which, mediating with God, hath obtained for the world, which was lost, peace and salvation. Mary, then, was the heavenly dove who brought to the lost world the olive-branch, a sign of mercy;[89] for she gave us Jesus Christ, who is the fountain of mercy,[90] and thus obtained, by the price of his merits, all the graces which God gives us. And as through Mary the world received celestial peace,[91] as St. Epiphanius says, so by means of Mary sinners are constantly becoming reconciled to God. In the same way, the blessed Albertus Magnus says in her name: I am that dove of Noah, who brought to the Church universal peace.[92]

Moreover, the rainbow seen by St. John, that surrounded the throne of God, was also an exact type of Mary.[93] According to the explanation of Cardinal Vitalis, Mary is always before the divine tribunal to mitigate the sentence and punishment due to the sinner.[94] And St. Bernardine of Sienna says that it was of this rainbow that the Lord spoke, when he said to Noah that he would place in the clouds the bow of peace, that when

---

86. Ego murus; et ubera mea sicut turris, ex quo facta sum coram eo quasi pacem reperiens. Cant. viii. v. 10.
87. Ipsa reperit pacem inimicis, salutem perditis, indulgentiam reis, misericordiam desperatis.
88. Cant. i. 4.
89. Tu enim es illa fidelissima columba Noe, quæ inter Deum et mundum diluvio spirituali submersum mediatrix fidelissima extitisti.
90. Nam ipsa Christum nobis detulit fontem misericordiæ. P. Spinell.
91. Per te pax cœlestis donata est.
92. Ego sum columba Noe, Ecclesiæ ramum olivæ et pacis inferens universalis. In Bibl. Mar. lib. Cant. n. 16.
93. Et Iris erat in circuitu sedis. Apoc. c. iv. 3.
94. Iris in circuitu sedis est Maria, quæ mitigat Dei judicium et sententiam contra peccatores. In Spec. S. Script.

he should see it he might remember the eternal covenant that he had established with men.[95] And Mary, says St. Bernardine, is that very bow of eternal peace.[96] For as God, at the sight of the bow, remembers the peace promised to the earth, thus at the prayers of Mary he pardons sinners the offenses committed against him, and establishes peace with them.[97]

For the same reason Mary is also compared to the moon.[98] For, St. Bonaventure says, as the moon is in the midst between heaven and earth, so she continually interposes between God and sinners, that she may appease the Lord towards them, and enlighten them on their return to God.[99]

And this was the most important office given to Mary when she was placed upon the earth—of lifting the souls fallen from divine grace, and reconciling them to God. Feed thy kids: "Pasce hædos tuos."[100] This was said to her by the Lord when he created her. It is well known that sinners are represented by goats; and as the elect, represented by sheep, will be placed on the right hand in the valley of judgment, the goats will be placed on the left. Now these goats, says William of Paris, are committed to thee, oh great mother, that thou mayest change them into sheep, and that those who, by their sins, have merited to be banished to the left, by thy intercession may be placed on the right.[101] Hence the Lord revealed to St. Catherine of Sienna that he had created this his beloved child as a sweet bait, that would draw men, and especially sinners, to God.[102] And here we should note the beautiful reflection of William, the Englishman, on the passage above cited, who says, that God recommends to Mary her own goats, "hædos tuos;" because the Virgin does not save all sinners, but only those who serve and honor her. Those, on the contrary, who live in sin, and do not honor her with any special devotion nor recommend themselves to her in order to escape from their sins, are not the goats of Mary, but in the judgment will be placed miserably on the left among the damned.[103]

---

95. Arcum meum ponam in nubibus, et erit signum fœderis inter me et terram . . . Videbo illam, et recordabor fœderis sempiterni. Gen. ix. 13.
96. Ipsa est arcus fœderis sempiterni. Serm. 1, de No. Mar. Art. I. c. 3.
97. Fructus iridis est recordatio divini fœderis; sic per verginem gloriosam offensa eis remittitur, fœdus stringitur. Serm. in Apoc. c. 41.
98. Pulchra ut Luna. Cant. vi. 9.
99. Sicut Luna est media inter corpora cœlestia et terrena, et quod ab illis accipit ad inferiora refundit; sic et virgo regia inter nos et Deum est media, et gratiam ipsa nobis refundit. Serm. 14, de Nat. Dom.
100. Cant. i. 8.
101. Pasce hædos tuos, quos convertis in oves, et qui a sinistris in judicio erant collocandi, tua intercessione collocantur a dextris.
102. Hæc est a me electa tanquam esca dulcissima ad capiendos homines, potissimum peccatores. Ap. Blos. Mon. Spir.
103. Suos vocat quia non omnes hædi vocantur Mariæ, sed qui Mariam colunt ac venerantur, licet sceleribus contaminati. Qui vero peccatis irretiti sunt, nec B. Virginem speciali obsequio prosequuntur, nec preces fundunt in ejus cultum, ut aliquando resipiscant, hædi prefecto sunt non Mariæ, sed ad sinistram judicis sistendi.

A certain nobleman, who was despairing of his eternal salvation on account of his sins, was encouraged by a religious to have recourse to the most holy Virgin, by visiting her sacred image which was in a certain church. The nobleman went to the church, and on seeing the figure of Mary he felt himself, as it were, invited by her to cast himself at her feet

Courtesy of Felipe Barandiarán

Queen of Mercy. **17th century azulejo. Hospital de San José, Lisbon, Portugal.**

and trust. He hastens to do so, kisses her feet, and Mary, from that statue, extended her hand for him to kiss, and on it he saw these words written: "I will deliver thee from them that afflict thee."[104] As if she had said to him: My son, do not despair, for I will deliver thee from thy sins, and from the fears that oppress thee. It is related that on reading these sweet words, that sinner felt such sorrow for his sins, and conceived such a love for God, and for his sweet mother, that he died there at the feet of Mary. Oh, how many obstinate sinners does this magnet of hearts draw daily to God, as she herself said to St. Bridget: "As the magnet attracts to itself iron, thus I draw to myself the most obdurate hearts, that I may reconcile them to God;"[105] and this prodigy is not rarely, but daily experienced. I could myself testify to many cases that have occurred in our missions alone, where sinners who have remained harder than iron during all other sermons, while hearing that on the mercy of Mary, were touched with compunction, and turned to God. St. Gregory relates that the unicorn is so ferocious a wild beast, that no hunter can succeed in taking it; but at the voice of a maiden who calls upon him to surrender, he draws near, and without resistance allows himself to be bound by her. Oh, how many sinners, more fierce than wild beasts, who flee from God, at the sound of the voice of this great Virgin Mary, advance and allow themselves to be gently bound by her to God!

For this end, says St. John Chrysostom, the Virgin Mary was made mother of God, that those sinners who, by reason of their wicked life, could not be saved according to the divine justice, might obtain salvation through her sweet compassion and powerful intercession.[106] St. Anselm confirms this when he says that Mary has been exalted to be mother of God for sinners rather than for the just, since Jesus Christ announced that he came not to call the just, but sinners.[107] And so the holy Church sings: "Sinners thou dost not abhor, since but for them thou never wouldst have been worthy of such a Son."[108] William of Paris also says: Oh Mary, thou art obliged to help sinners, since for all the gifts, graces, and honors thou dost possess,

104. Ego eripiam te de affligentibus te.
105. Sicut magnes attrahit ferrum sic ego attraho dura corda. L. 3. Rev. c. 32.
106. Ideo mater Dei prælecta es ab eterno; ut quos justitia filii salvare non potest, tu per tuam salvares pietatem. Hom. de Præs. B. V.
107. Scio illam magis propter peccatores, quam propter justos, factam esse Dei Matrem; dixit enim ejus bonus filius se non venisse vocare justos, sed peccatores.
108. Peccatores non abhorres, sine quibus nunquam fores tanto digna filio.

which are comprehended in the dignity thou hast received of being the mother of God, for all, if I may so speak, thou art indebted to sinners, since for their sakes thou wert made worthy to have a God for thy Son.[109] If, then, concludes St. Anselm, Mary, for the sake of sinners, has been made mother of God, how can I, however great may be my sins, despair of pardon?[110]

The holy Church teaches us, in the collect of the Mass for the Vigil of the Assumption, that the divine mother has been removed from this earth that she might intercede for us with God, in sure confidence of being graciously heard.[111] Hence Mary is named by St. Justinian, Arbitress: "Sequestra." The Word employed Mary as arbitress.[112] *Sequester* signifies the same as arbiter, one to whom two contending parties refer all their questions; so that the saint means to say, that as Jesus is mediator with the eternal Father, so Mary is our mediatrix with Jesus, to whom the Son refers all the charges which, as judge he has against us.

Mary is called by St. Andrew of Crete, the confidence and security of our reconciliation with God.[113] And by this the saint intends to say, that God seeks a reconciliation with sinners by pardoning them, and that they may not despair of pardon, he has given them Mary as a pledge of it; hence he salutes her: Hail, oh peace of God with men; "Salve divina hominibus reconciliatio." Wherefore St. Bonaventure says, encouraging every sinner: If thou fearest, on account of thy sins, that an angry God may wish to avenge himself upon thee, what art thou to do? Go to the hope of sinners, namely, Mary; and if thou fearest that she will refuse to take thy part, know that she cannot refuse to defend thy cause, for God himself has assigned her the office of relieving the wretched.[114]

And what does the Abbot Adam say? Should a sinner fear being lost, to whom the mother of his judge offers herself as his mother and advocate?[115] And then the same writer adds: Oh Mary! who art mother of mercy, couldst thou refuse to pray thy Son, who is judge, for another son, who is the criminal? Canst thou refuse to intercede in behalf of a redeemed soul with the

---

109. Totum quod habes, si fas est dicere, peccatoribus debest omnia enim propter peccatores tibi collata sunt. De Reth. Div. c. 18.
110. Si ipsa propter peccatores facta est Dei mater, quomodo immanitas peccatorum meorum cogere poterit desperare veniam? De Exc. v. c. 1.
111. Quam idcirco de hoc sæculo transtulit, ut apud te pro peccatis nostris fiducialiter intercedat.
112. Verbum usum est Virgine sequestra.
113. Divinarum reconciliationem, quæ pignore accepto fit, fidejussio. Or. 2, de Aff.
114. Si propter tuas nequitias Dominum videris indignatum, ad spem peccatorum confugias; sibi pro miseris satisfacere ex officio commissum est.
115. Timere ne debet ut pereat, cui Maria se matrem exhibet, et advocatam.

Redeemer, who, for no other end than to save sinners, died on the cross?[116] No, thou wilt not refuse, but earnestly wilt employ thyself in praying for all those who invoke thee, well knowing that the same Lord who hath constituted thy Son mediator of peace between God and man, has at the same time made thee mediatrix between the Judge and the criminal.[117] Here St. Bernard takes up the subject, and says: Give then thanks to him who has provided thee with such a mediatrix.[118] Whoever thou art, oh sinner, plunged in the mire of guilt, hoary in sin, do not despair; thank thy Lord, who in order to show mercy to thee, has not only given thee his Son for an advocate, but, to increase thy confidence and courage, has provided thee with such a mediatrix, who, by her prayers, obtains whatever she wishes. Have recourse to Mary, and thou wilt be saved.

EXAMPLE

It is related by Rupensis,[119] and by Boniface,[120] that in Florence there lived a young girl, named Benedetta (the blessed), although she might better have been called Maladetta (the cursed), from the scandalous and wicked life she led. Happily for her, St. Dominic happened to preach in that city, and she, from mere curiosity, went one day to hear him. But the Lord touched her heart during the sermon, so that, weeping bitterly, she went to make her confession to the saint. St. Dominic heard her confession, gave her absolution, and directed her to say the rosary. But the unhappy girl, by the force of her evil habits, returned to her wicked life. The saint heard of it, and going to her, induced her to confess once more. God, in order to confirm her in her good life, one day showed hell to her, and some persons there who had been already condemned on her account. Then opening a book, he made her read in it the frightful record of her sins. The penitent shuddered at the sight, and, full of confidence, had recourse to Mary, asked her help, and learned that this divine mother had

---

116. Tu misericordiæ mater non rogabis pro filio filium, pro redempto redemptorem?
117. Rogabis plane quia qui filium tuum inter Deum et hominem posuit mediatorem, te quoque inter reum, et judicem posuit adjutricem.
118. Age gratias ei, qui talem tibi mediatricem providit. Serm. In Sign. Magn.
119. Ros. Sacr. p. 5, c. 60.
120. Stor. Virg. l. 1, c. 11.

already obtained from God for her time enough to mourn for her numerous sins. The vision disappeared, and Benedetta devoted herself to a good life; but seeing always open before her eyes that dark catalogue, she one day prayed in these words to her consoler: "Oh mother, it is true that for my sins I should now be deep in hell; but since thou, by thy intercession, hast liberated me from it, by obtaining for me time for repentance, most merciful Lady, I ask of thee one other favor. I will never cease to weep for my sins; but do thou obtain for me that they may be cancelled from that book." After this prayer, Mary appeared to her, and told her that in order to obtain what she asked, she must preserve an eternal remembrance of her sins, and of the mercy of God towards her; and still more, that she must meditate on the passion of her Son, which he suffered for love of her; and also that she must bear in mind that many had been damned who had committed fewer sins than she had done. She also revealed to her that a child of only eight years of age, for one mortal sin only, had been that day condemned to hell. Benedetta having faithfully obeyed the most holy Virgin, one day beheld Jesus Christ, who showed her that book, and said to her: Behold, thy sins are cancelled; the book is white, inscribe on it now acts of love and of virtue. Benedetta did this, led a holy life, and died a holy death.

PRAYER

Then, oh my most sweet Lady, if thy office is, as William of Paris says, to interpose as a mediatrix between the sinner and God,[121] I will say to thee with St. Thomas of Villanova: Ah, then, oh our advocate, fulfill thy office.[122] Fulfill at once thy office also in my behalf. Do not tell me that my cause is too difficult to be gained; for I know, and all tell me, that no cause, however desperate, if defended by thee, was ever lost; and will mine be lost? No, I fear not this. I have only to fear, when I behold the multitude of my sins, that thou wilt not undertake my defense; but considering thy vast compassion and the great desire that fills thy most loving heart to help the

---

121. Officium tuum est, te mediam interponere inter Deum et homines.
122. Eja ergo advocata nostra officium tuum imple.

vilest sinners, I no longer fear even this. And who was ever lost that had recourse to thee? I invoke, then, thy aid, oh my great advocate, my refuge, my hope, and my mother Mary. To thy hands I commit the cause of my eternal salvation. To thee I consign my soul; it was lost, but thou must save it. I always thank the Lord that he gives me this great confidence in thee, which, notwithstanding my unworthiness, I believe will secure my salvation. One fear alone remains to afflict me, my beloved queen: it is, that I may one day lose, through my neglect, this confidence in thee. Therefore I pray thee, oh Mary, by all thy love for thy Jesus, to preserve and increase more and more in me this most sweet confidence in thy intercession, by which I certainly hope to recover the divine friendship, which I have hitherto so foolishly despised and lost; and once having recovered it, I hope by thy means to preserve it; and preserving it, I hope finally through thee to go one day and thank thee for it in paradise, and there to sing the mercies of God and thine through all eternity. Amen. Thus I hope, so may it be, and so it *shall be*!

CHAPTER 7

Illos tuos misericordes oculos ad nos converte
Turn thy eyes of mercy towards us

SECTION 1
Mary is all eyes to pity and relieve our miseries

S t. Epiphanius calls the blessed Virgin, "Multoculam;" that is, one who has many eyes, that she may relieve our miseries on this earth. One day, when a person possessed was being exorcised, the devil was asked by the exorcist what Mary was then doing. The Evil One replied: "She is descending and ascending;"[1] by which he intended to say, that this gracious Lady does nothing else than descend upon the earth to bring graces to men, and ascend to heaven to obtain there the divine blessing on our supplications. Rightly, then, was the holy Virgin named by St. Andrew of Avellino, the active power of paradise; for she is continually employed in deeds of mercy, imploring favors for all, for the just and for sinners. "The eyes of the Lord are upon the just," says David;[2] but the eyes of our Lady are upon the just and upon sinners,[3] as Richard of St. Laurence says; for he adds: The eyes of Mary are the eyes of a mother; and the mother not only guards her child from falling, but if he falls, she hastens to raise him.[4]

Jesus himself revealed this to St. Bridget, whom the saint heard one day speaking to his mother, and saying: "Ask of me, oh my mother, whatever thou dost desire;"[5] and the Son is always in heaven saying this to Mary, pleased with granting his beloved mother whatever she asks. But what does Mary ask? St. Bridget understood the mother to answer him: I ask mercy for sinners: "Misericordiam peto pro miseris,"[6] as if she would say, my Son, thou hast already destined me for the mother of mercy, for the refuge of sinners, for the advocate of the miserable, now thou sayest to me that I may ask whatever I wish; but what would I ask of thee? I ask of thee that thou wilt have mercy on the sinner: "Misericordiam peto pro miseris." Thou art, oh Mary, so full of compassion, St. Bonaventure tenderly says

---

1. Ap. il P. Pep. to. 5, Lec. 235.
2. Oculi Domini super justos. Ps. xxxiii. 16.
3. Sed oculi Dominæ super justos et peccatores.
4. Sicut oculi matris ad puerum ne cadat, vel si ceciderit, ut cum sublevet.
5. Mater pete quod vis a me.
6. Rev. 1. 1. c. 46.

to her, thou art so watchful to relieve the wretched, that it seems thou hast no other desire, no other concern than this.[7] And because, among the wretched sinners are the most wretched of all, the venerable Bede affirms, that Mary is continually praying the Son in behalf of sinners.[8]

Even whilst on earth Mary was so kind and tender to men that, as St. Jerome says, there never was any person so afflicted by his own sufferings as Mary by the sufferings of others.[9] She plainly showed the compassion she feels for the sufferings of others at the nuptials of Cana (as has been mentioned in previous chapters), where, as when the wine failed, without being requested, as St. Bernardine of Sienna remarks, she assumed the office of a kind comforter.[10] And from mere compassion for the troubles of that family, she interceded with her Son, and obtained the miracle of changing the water into wine.

But, perhaps, says St. Peter Damian, since thou wast exalted to the dignity of queen of heaven, thou hast forgotten the wretched; and then he adds, let this never be thought of—it does not belong to a mercy so great as that which reigns in the heart of Mary, to forget such misery as ours.[11] The common proverb, honors change customs, "Honores mutant mores," certainly does not apply to Mary. It, indeed applies to worldlings who, when raised to dignity, become inflated with pride, and forget their old and poor friends: but not to Mary, who rejoices in her greater exaltation, because it gives her more power to assist others. Considering this point, St. Bonaventure applies to the blessed Virgin the words spoken to Ruth: "Blessed art thou, my daughter, and thy latter kindness has surpassed the former."[12] Meaning, as he afterwards explains, that if the pity of Mary for the unhappy was great when she lived on earth, much greater is it now when she is reigning in heaven.[13] The saint gives the reason for this by saying, that the divine mother shows now, by the innumerable favors she obtains for us, this her increased compassion, because now she better understands our miseries.[14] And he adds, that as the splendor of the sun exceeds that of the

---

7. Undique sollicita es de miseris, misericordia vallaris, solum misereri videris appetere. Sup. Salve Reg.
8. Stat Maria in conspectu filii sui non cessans pro peccatoribus exorare. In cap. i. Luc.
9. Nullum in hac vita adeo pœnæ torserunt propriæ sicut Mariam alienæ. Epist. ad Eust.
10. Officium piæ auxiliatricis assumpsit non rogata.
11. Nunquid, O Beata Virgo, quia ita glorificata es, ideo nostræ humilitatis oblita es? Absit, non convenit tantæ misericordiæ oblivisci. Serm. 1, de Nat. Virg.
12. Benedicta filia priorem misericordiam posteriore superasti. Ruth iii. 10.
13. Magna fuit erga miseros misericordia Mariæ adhuc exulantis mundo, sed multo major est regnantis in cœlo. In Spec. B. V. c. 8.
14. Majorem per innumerabilia beneficia nunc ostendit misericordiam; quia magis nunc videt hominum miserias.

moon, so the mercy of Mary, now that she is in heaven, exceeds the mercy she had for us when she was upon the earth.[15] And is there any one living on the earth who does not enjoy the light of the sun? —any one on whom this mercy of Mary does not shine?[16]

On this account she is called bright as the sun, "Electa ut sol;"[17] because no one is shut out from the heat of this sun,[18] as St. Bonaventure says. And St. Agnes revealed this from heaven to St. Bridget, when she said to her, that our queen, now that she is united with her Son in heaven, cannot forget her innate goodness; hence she exercises her compassion towards all, even towards the most impious sinners, so that as both the celestial and terrestrial bodies are illuminated by the sun, thus through the goodness of Mary, there is no one in the world who does not, if he asks for it, share in the divine mercy.[19] A great and desperate sinner, in the kingdom of Valencia, in order to escape justice, had resolved to become a Turk, and was actually going to embark, when by chance he passed a church, in which Father Jerome Lopez, of the Company of Jesus, was preaching, and preaching of the divine mercy; by that preaching he was converted, and confessed to the father, who inquired of him if he had practiced any devotion, for which God had shown towards him that great mercy; he answered that he had practiced no other devotion than praying the holy Virgin every day not to abandon him.[20] The same Father found in the hospital a sinner, who for fifty-five years had never been to confession, and had only practiced this little devotion, that when he saw an image of Mary he saluted it, and prayed to her that he might not die in mortal sin; and then he related that in a quarrel with an enemy, his sword was broken, and he turned to the Madonna, saying: "Alas, I shall be slain, damned; oh moather of sinners, help me." When he had said this, he found himself, he knew not how, transported into a secure place. He made a general confession, and died full of confidence.[21]

St. Bernard writes that Mary becomes all things to all men, and opens to all the bowels of her mercy, that all may receive of her; the captive his

---

15. Nam quemadmodum sol lunam superat magnitudine splendoris, sic priorem Mariæ misericordiam superat magnitudo superioris.
16. Quis est super quem misericordia Mariæ non resplendet? Loc. cit.
17. Cant. vi. 9.
18. Non est qui se abscondat a calore ejus.
19. Nunc autem conjuncta filio non obliviscitur innatæ bonitatis suæ, sed ad omnes extendit misericordiam suam, etiam ad pessimos; ut sicut sole illuminantur cœlestia et terrestria, sic ex dulcedine Mariæ nullus est qui non per eam, si petitur sentiat pietatem. L. 3, Rev. c. 30.
20. Patrign. Men. 2, Feb.
21. Patrign. Men. 2, Feb.

freedom; the sick man health; the afflicted consolation; the sinner pardon, and God glory: hence there is no one, since she is the sun, who does not partake of her warmth.[22] And is there any one in the world, exclaims St. Bonaventure, who will not love this lovely queen? She is more beautiful than the sun, and sweeter than honey; she is a treasure of goodness, and is kind and courteous to all.[23] I salute thee, then, thus the enamored saint goes on to say, oh my Lady and mother! my heart! my soul! Pardon me, oh Mary, if I say that I love thee: if I am not worthy of loving thee, thou art truly worthy of being loved by me.[24]

It was revealed to St. Gertrude,[25] that when any one repeats with devotion these words to the Virgin: "Turn, then, towards us, oh our advocate, thy pitying eyes,"[26] Mary never fails to listen to the prayer. Oh, let the immensity of thy mercy, oh great Lady, fill the whole earth, exclaims St. Bernard.[27] Whence St. Bonaventure says, that this loving mother has such a desire to do good to all, that she feels herself offended not only by those who offer her some positive injury, for there are souls to be found so perverse, especially gamesters, who sometimes, to vent their anger, blaspheme and insult this good Lady, but she looks upon herself as injured by those, also, who neglect to ask of her some favor.[28] So that, as St. Idelbert says, thou dost instruct us, oh Lady, to expect favors greater than our merits, for thou dost never cease to dispense graces that far exceed what we merit.[29]

The prophet Isaias predicted that by the great work of human redemption, a great throne of divine mercy would be prepared for us: "A throne shall be prepared in mercy."[30] Who is this throne? St. Bonaventure answers: This throne is Mary, in whom all, both the just and sinners, find the consolations of mercy;[31] and he afterwards adds: As the Lord is full of compassion, so also is our Lady; and as the Son, so the mother cannot withhold her mercy from those who ask it.[32] Hence Guerric, the abbot, represents

---

22. Maria omnia omnibus facta est; omnibus misericordiæ sinum aperit, ut de plenitudine ejus accipiant omnes, captivus, redemptionem, æger curationem, tristis consolationem, peccator veniam; ut non sit qui se abscondat a calore ejus. In Sig. Mag.
23. Quis te non diliget, O Maria, pulchriorem sole, dulciorem melle, omnibus amabilis, omnibus affabilis?
24. Ave ergo, Domina mea, mater mea; imo cor meum, anima mea, parce mihi, Domina, si me amare te dicam: si ego non sum dignus te amare, tu non es digna amari a me. Stim. p. 5, c. 19.
25. Rev. 1. 4, c. 53.
26. Eja ergo; advocata nostra, illos tus misericordes ocules ad nos converte.
27. Latitudo misericordiæ tuæ replet orbem terrarum. Serm. 4, Sup. Miss.
28. In te, Domina, peccant, non solum qui tibi injuriam irrogant, sed etiam qui te non rogant. In Spec. Virg.
29. Doce nos sperare majora meritis, quæ meritis largiri non desinis.
30. Præparabitur in misericordia solium ejus. Isa. xvi. 5.
31. Solium divinæ misericordiæ est Maria, in qua omnes inveniunt solatia misericordiæ. Spec. c. 8.
32. Nam sicut misericordiosissimum Dominum, ita misericordiosissimam Dominam habemus. Dominus noster multæ misericordiæ invocantibus se; et Domina nostra multæ misericordiæ invocantibus se.

Jesus thus speaking to Mary: My mother, upon thee I will establish the seat of my kingdom, for through thee will I bestow the graces that are asked of me: thou hast given me the human nature; I will give to thee, as it were, a divine nature, that is, my omnipotence, by which thou canst assist all who invoke thee to obtain their salvation.[33]

When St. Gertrude was one day devoutly repeating these words to the divine mother: "Turn towards us thy merciful eyes," she saw the Virgin pointing to the eyes of her Son whom she held in her arms, and she said to her: "These are the most merciful eyes that I can turn towards all those who invoke me for their salvation."[34] A sinner once weeping before the altar of Mary, and imploring her to intercede with God for his pardon, was given to understand that the blessed Virgin turned to the child whom she held in her arms, and said to him: "My son, shall these tears be in vain?"[35] And he learned that Jesus Christ at once pardoned him.

And how can any one ever perish who recommends himself to this good mother, when the Son, as God, has promised, for love of her, to exercise mercy, as far as it pleases her, towards all those that have recourse to her? Precisely this our Lord revealed to St. Bridget; permitting her to hear these words which he spoke to Mary: "By my omnipotence, venerated mother, I have granted thee the pardon of all sinners, in whatever way it pleases thee, who devoutly invoke the aid of thy mercy."[36] Hence the Abbot Adam Persenius, considering the great compassion that Mary has for all, full of confidence says to her: Oh mother of mercy, thy power is as great as thy pity. As thou art powerful to obtain, so thou art merciful to pardon.[37] And when, he adds, dost thou ever fail to have compassion on sinners, being the mother of mercy; or art thou unable to help them, being mother of omnipotence? Ah, thou canst as readily obtain whatever thou wilt, as thou canst listen to our woes.[38] Satiate thyself, then, says the Abbot Rupert, satiate thyself, oh great queen, with the glory of thy Son, and through thy compassion, not certainly

---

33. In te mihi regni sedem constituam, per te preces exaudiam. Communicasti mihi quod homo sum, communicabo tibi quod Deus sum. Serm. 2, de Assump.
34. Hi sunt misericordiosissimi oculi mei, quos ad omnes me invocantes possum salubriter inclinare. Rev. 1. 4, c. 53.
35. Fili, et istæ lacrimæ peribunt?
36. Ex omnipotentia mea, mater reverenda, tibi concessi propitiationem omnium peccatorum, qui devote invocant tuæ pietatis auxilium, qualicumque modo placeat tibi.
37. Mater misericordiæ, tanta est pietas tua, quanta potestas; tam pia es ad parcendum, quam potens ad impetrandum.
38. Quando non compatieris miseris, mater misericordiæ? Aut quando illi opem conferre non poteris, cum sis mater omnipotentæ? Eadem facilitate obtinens quodcumque vis; qua facilitate nostra innotescit miseria. Ap. P. Pep.

through our merit, be pleased to send down to us, thy poor servants here below, whatever fragments may remain.[39]

If our sins ever throw us into despair, let us say with William of Paris: Oh Lady, do not bring forward my sins against me, for I shall bring forward thy mercy in opposition to them. And let it never be said that my sins can rival, in the judgment, thy mercy, which is more powerful to obtain my pardon, than my sins are to obtain my condemnation.[40]

EXAMPLE

We read in the chronicles of the Capuchin Fathers,[41] that there lived in Venice a celebrated advocate, who, by fraud and evil practices, had become rich. His whole life was very bad, and it appears that he had but one good habit, that of reciting every day a certain prayer to the holy Virgin. Yet, even this little devotion saved him from eternal death, through the mercy of Mary. It happened in this way: Happily for himself, he had a great esteem for Father Matthew da Basso, and urged him so much to come and dine at his house, that one day the Father gave him this pleasure. Having arrived, the advocate said to him: "Now, Father, I will show you something that you have never seen. I have a wonderful ape, who is my valet, washes my glasses, lays the table, and opens the door." "This may not be an ape," answered the Father: "it may be something more than an ape; order him to come here." The ape was called again and again, search was made for him everywhere, and he could not be found. At length, he was discovered hidden under a bed in the lower part of the house, but he would not come out. "Come, then," said the religious, "let us go and see him;" and he went with the advocate to his hiding-place. "Infernal beast," he said, "come forth, and in the name of God I command you to tell me what you are." And behold, the ape answered that he was the devil, and that he was waiting until that sinner should omit some day to recite his accustomed prayer to the mother of God; for the first time he should omit it, God had given him leave to strangle him, and

---

39. O mater misericordiæ, saturare gloria filii tui, et dimitte reliquias tuas parvulis tuis. In Cant. lib. 5.
40. Ne alligaveris peccata mea contra me, qui misericordiam tuam allego contra ea. Absit, ut stent in judicio peccata mea contra misericordiam tuam, quæ omnibus vitiis fortior est. De Reth. Div. c. 18.
41. C. 11, p. 1.

take him to hell. At these words the advocate cast himself upon his knees to ask help of the servant of God, who encouraged him, and commanded the devil to depart from that house without committing any injury, only he gave him permission, as a sign that he had really gone, to break a piece of the wall. Scarcely had he finished speaking, when, with a great crash, a hole was made in the wall, which, although it was several times closed with stone and mortar, God willed that it should remain open for a long time; until, by the advice of the servant of God, it was filled up with a slab of marble, with an angel carved on it. The advocate was converted, and, it is to be hoped, persevered until death in his new course of life.

PRAYER

Oh creature, among all others the greatest and most sublime, most holy Virgin, I from this earth salute thee; I, a miserable, unhappy rebel to my God, who deserve punishment and not favors, justice and not mercy. Oh Lady, I do not say this because I distrust thy mercy. I know that thou dost glory in being merciful as thou art great. I know that thou dost rejoice in being so rich, that thou mayest share thy riches with us sinners. I know that the more wretched are those who seek thee the greater is thy desire to help and save them. Oh my mother, it is thou who once did weep for thy Son when he died for me. Offer, I pray thee, thy tears to God, and with these obtain for me a true sorrow for my sins. So much did sinners grieve thee, then, and so much did I, too, grieve thee by my iniquities. Obtain for me, oh Mary, that I at least from henceforth may no longer continue to afflict thee and thy Son by my ingratitude. What will thy tears avail me if I should continue to be ungrateful to thee? What would thy mercy avail me if I should again be faithless and be lost? No, my queen, do not permit it. Thou hast supplied all my deficiencies; thou canst obtain from God whatever thou wilt; thou graciously hearest every one that prays to thee. These two favors do I ask of thee, and at all events from thee do I hope and desire them: namely, that thou wilt obtain for me to be faithful to God by never more offending him, and to love him as much as I have offended him during the life that remains to me.

Our Lady of Confidence. Chapel of the Pontifical Roman Major Seminary, Rome, Italy.

CHAPTER 8

Et Jesum benedictum fructum ventris tui
nobis post hoc exilium ostende
*And after this our exile, show us the blessed
fruit of thy womb, Jesus*

SECTION 1
Mary rescues her servants from Hell

It is impossible that a servant of Mary who faithfully honors her and recommends himself to her should be lost. This proposition at first sight may appear to some persons extravagant. But I would beg them not to condemn it before reading what will hereafter be said on this point. When it is said that a devoted servant of Mary cannot be lost, those servants are not intended who abuse their devotion by sinning with less fear. Therefore it is unjust to say, as some do who disapprove extolling the mercy of Mary to sinners, that by so doing they are encouraged to sin the more; for such presumptuous persons for their presumption merit punishment and not mercy. It is understood, then, only of those of her servants who, with the desire to amend, faithfully honor and commend themselves to the mother of God. That these should be lost is, I say, morally impossible. And I find Father Crasset has affirmed the same thing in his book upon devotion to Mary;[1] and before him Vega,[2] Mendoza,[3] and other theologians. And that we may know that they have not spoken unadvisedly, let us see what the Doctors and Saints have said on this subject. Let no one be surprised if I here quote several sentences, of different authors, containing the same thing; for I have wished to record them all, in order to show how unanimously all writers agree on this point. St. Anselm says, that as he who is not devoted to Mary and protected by her cannot be saved, so it is impossible that he should be condemned who recommends himself to the Virgin, and is regarded by her with affection.[4] St. Antoninus asserts the same thing in nearly the same words: As it is impossible that those from whom Mary turns

---

1. Tom. 1. qu. 7.
2. Teologia Mariana.
3. Virid. l. 1, Probl. 9.
4. Virgo benedictissima, sicut impossibile est, ut a te aversus, et a te despectus salvetur, ita ad te conversus et a te respectus impossibile est ut pereat. De Exc. Virg. c. 11.

away her eyes of compassion should be saved, so it must be that all those towards whom she turns her eyes, and for whom she intercedes, shall be saved and glorified.[5] This saint adds, then, that the servants of Mary must necessarily be saved.

Let us note, however, the first part of the statement of these saints, and let those tremble who little esteem, or abandon, through negligence, devotion to this divine mother. They say that it is impossible for those to be saved who are not protected by Mary. And this is also asserted by others, as the blessed Albertus Magnus: All those who are not thy servants, oh Mary, shall perish: "Gens quæ non servierit tibi peribit."[6] St. Bonaventure, too: He who neglects the service of Mary shall die in sin.[7] And in another place: He who has not recourse to thee, oh Lady, will not reach paradise.[8] And on Psalm 99 the saint goes so far as to say that those from whom Mary turns away her face, not only will not be saved, but can have no hope of salvation.[9] And before this St. Ignatius, the martyr, said the same thing, asserting that a sinner cannot be saved except by means of the holy Virgin, who, on the other hand, saves by her merciful intercession many that would be condemned by the divine justice.[10] Some persons doubt whether this passage is from St. Ignatius; at least Father Crasset says that St. John Chrysostom has adopted it as his own.[11] It is also repeated by the Abbot of Celles.[12] And in the same sense the holy Church applies to Mary these words of Proverbs: All that hate me love death: "Omnes qui me oderunt, diligunt mortem."[13] For, as Richard of St. Laurence says, commenting on the words: She is like the merchant's ship:[14] all those who are out of this ship shall be submerged in the sea of this world.[15] Even the heretic Œcolampadius esteemed neglect of devotion in any one to the mother of God as a certain sign of reprobation; hence, he said: Let it never be heard of me that I am averse to Mary, to be ill affected toward whom I should think a certain sign of a reprobate mind.[16]

---

5. Sicut impossibile est, ut illi a quibus Maria oculos suæ misericordiæ avertit, salventur; ita necessarium quod hi, ad quos convertit oculos suos, pro eis advocans, salventur et glorificentur. Part 4, tit. 50.
6. Bibl. Mar. c. 60.
7. Qui neglexerit illam, morietur in peccatis suis. In Psal. cxvi.
8. Qui te non invocat in hac vita, non perveniet ad regnam Dei. In Psal. lxxxvi.
9. A quibus averteris vultum tuum, non erit spes ad salutem.
10. Impossibile est aliquem salvari peccatorum, nisi per tuum, O Virgo, auxilium et favorem, quia quos non salvat Dei justitia, salvat sua intercessione Mariæ misericordia infinita. Ap. celada in Jud. Fig. s. 10.
11. In Deprec. ad Virg.
12. In Comp. Virg. c. 5.
13. Prov. viii. 36.
14. Facta est quasi navis institoris. Prov. xxxi. 14.
15. In mare mundi submergentur omnes illi, quos non suscipit navis ista. De Laud. V. I. 11.
16. Nunquam de me audiatur, quasi averser Mariam, erga quam minus bene affici reprobatæ mentis certum existimem judicium. V. Ap. P. Pep. Lez. tom. 7.

On the other hand, Mary says: He that hearkeneth to me shall not be confounded.[17] He who has recourse to me, and listens to what I say to him, shall not be lost. From which St. Bonaventure said: Oh, Lady, those who are mindful to honor thee, shall be far from perdition.[18] Even when, as St. Hilary says, they have hitherto deeply offended God.[19]

Hence the devil strives so hard with sinners, in order that, having lost divine grace, they may also lose devotion to Mary. Sarah, seeing Isaac playing with Ishmael, who was teaching him evil habits, asked Abraham to send him away, and his mother Agar also: "Cast out this bond-woman and her son."[20] She was not satisfied that the son alone should leave the house without the mother, fearing lest the son would come to visit his mother, and thus continue to frequent the house. In like manner, the devil is not satisfied with seeing Jesus cast out from a soul, if he does not see the mother also cast out: "Cast out this bond-woman and her son." Otherwise he fears that the mother, by her intercession, may again obtain the return of her son. And he has cause to fear, for as the learned Father Paciucchelli remarks: He who is faithful in honoring the mother of God, through Mary will soon receive him.[21] Therefore rightly was the devotion to our Lady called by St. Ephrem: The passport of escape from hell: "Charta libertatis."[22] The divine mother was also named by him: The protectress of the condemned: "Patrocinatrix damnatorum." And with truth St. Bernard says, that Mary is neither wanting in the power nor the will to save us.[23] Not in the power, because it is impossible that her prayers should not be heard, as St. Antoninus asserts;[24] and St. Bonaventure says also, that her requests cannot be unavailing, but obtain for her what she wishes: Quod quærit invenit et frustrari non potest.[25] Not in the will to save us, for Mary is our mother, and desires our salvation more than we desire it ourselves. If this is then true, how can it ever happen that a servant of Mary should be lost? He may be a sinner, but if, with perseverance and a desire for amendment, he commends himself to this good mother,

17. Qui audit me non confundetur. Eccli. xxiv. 30.
18. Qui præstat in obsequio tuo, procul fiet a perditione. In Psalm. cxviii.
19. Quantumcumque quis fuerit peccator, si Mariæ devotus extiterit, nunquam in æternum peribit. Cant. 12, in Matt.
20. Ejice ancillam hanc, et filium ejus. Gen. xxi. 10.
21. Qui Dei genitrici perseveranter obsequitur, non multa mora et Deum ipsum in se recipiet. In Salv. Reg. Ex. 5.
22. Or. de Laud. V.
23. Nec facultas, nec voluntas illi deesse potest. Serm. de Assump.
24. Impossibile est Deiparam non exaudiri. P. 4, tit. 15, c. 17. v. 4.
25. Serm. de Aquæd.

she will take care to obtain for him light to guide him out of his bad state, contrition for his sins, perseverance in goodness, and finally a good death. And is there any mother who would not rescue her child from death, if she could do it by praying his judge for mercy? And can we believe that Mary, the most loving mother possible to her servants, would fail to rescue one of them from eternal death, when she can do it so easily? Ah, devout reader, let us thank the Lord if we find that he has given us the love of the queen of heaven, and confidence in her; for God, as St. John Damascene says, does not grant this grace except to those whom he wishes to save. These are the beautiful words of the saint, with which he would quicken his own and our hope: Oh mother of God, if I place my confidence in thee I shall he saved. If I am under thy protection, I have nothing to fear, because to be thy servant is to have certain arms of salvation, which God only grants to those whom he will save.[26] Hence Erasmus thus salutes the Virgin: Hail, terror of hell! hail, hope of Christians! confidence in thee secures salvation.[27]

Oh, how much it grieves the devil to see a soul persevering in its devotion to the divine mother! We read in the life of Father Alphonsus Alverez, who had a special devotion to Mary, that being in prayer, and finding himself tormented by impure temptations with which the devil afflicted him, the enemy said to him: Quit thy devotion to Mary, and I will cease to tempt thee.

The Lord revealed to St. Catherine of Sienna, as we read in Blosius, that he, in his goodness, had granted to Mary, from love to his only-begotten Son, whose mother she is, that not even one sinner, who commends himself devoutly to her, should be the prey of hell.[28] The Prophet David, too, prayed to be rescued from hell, for the honor in which he held Mary: "I have loved, oh Lord, the beauty of thy house; take not away my soul with the wicked."[29] He says of thy house, "Domus tuæ," because Mary was, indeed, that house of God, which he himself, when he became man, built on this earth for his habitation, and for the place of his rest, as we read in Proverbs: Wisdom hath built herself a house.[30] No, he surely will not be lost, says St. Ignatius, the martyr, who is constant in his devotion to this virgin mother.[31] And this is

---

26. Serm. de Nat. B. V.
27. Salve, inferorum formido, Christianorum spes, certa est fiducia tua. Orat. ad Virg.
28. Mariæ filii mei genitrici a bonitate mea concessum est propter Incarnati Verbi reverentiam, ut qui-cumque etiam peccator ad eam cum devota veneratione recurrit, nullo modo rapiatur de dæmone infernali. In Man. Spir.
29. Domine, dilexi decorem domus tuæ, ne perdas cum impiis animam meam. Psal. xxv. 8, 9.
30. Sapientia ædificavit sibi domum. Prov. ix. 1.
31. Nunquam peribit qui genitrici Virgini devotus sedulusque extiterit.

confirmed by St. Bonaventure, who says: Oh Lady, those who love thee enjoy great peace in this life, and in the other they shall not see eternal death.[32] No, for it never did, and never will happen, as the devout Blosius assures us, that a humble and constant servant of Mary will be lost.[33]

Oh, how many would have been eternally condemned, or remained in obstinacy, if Mary had not interceded with her Son to exercise mercy! thus says Thomas à Kempis.[34] And it is the opinion of many doctors, especially of St. Thomas, that the divine mother has obtained from God a reprieve for many persons who had even died in mortal sin, and their return to life to do penance. We have many examples of this given by writers of good authority. Among others, Flodoard, who lived about the ninth century, narrates, in his chronicles,[35] that one Adelman, a deacon, who appeared to be dead, was about to be buried, when he returned to life, and said, that he had seen the place in hell to which he had already been condemned, but that, through the intercession of the blessed Virgin, he had been sent back to earth to do penance. Surius also relates, that a Roman citizen, named Andrew, had died without doing penance, and that Mary had obtained his return to life that he might procure pardon.[36] Pelbart, more-over, relates, that in his time, when the Emperor Sigismund was crossing the Alps with his army, a voice was heard, proceeding from a dead body, of which only the bones remained, asking for confession, and saying, that the mother of God, to whom he had been devoted whilst he was a soldier, had obtained for him that he should live in those bones until he had made his confession. Having confessed, he died.[37] These and similar examples must not serve as encouragement for some rash person who would live in sin, in the hope that Mary would free him from hell, even if he should die in sin; for as it would be a great folly to throw one's self into a well, in the hope that Mary would save us from death, because the Virgin has rescued some persons under similar circumstances; thus a greater folly would it be for one to run the risk of dying in sin, on the presumption that the holy Virgin would rescue him from hell. But these examples should serve to strengthen our confidence by the consideration, that if the intercession

---

32. Pax multa diligentibus te, Domina; anima eorum non videbit mortem in æternum. In Psal. cxviii.
33. Fieri non potest ut pereat qui Mariæ sedulus et umilis cultor extiterit. In Cant. v. Spir. c. 18.
34. Quanti fuissent, æternaliter condemnati, vel permansissent in desperatione obstinati, nisi beatissima Virgo Maria interpellasset ad filium. Ap. Pep. Lez. tom. 7.
35. Ap. Crass, to. 1, q. 12.
36. L. 1, c. 35.
37. Stellar. Cor. B. V. 1. 12, p. 2, a. 1.

of this divine mother could deliver those from hell—even those who have died in sin—how much more will it prevent those from falling into hell who in life have recourse to her with the intention to amend and serve her faithfully?

Then, oh our mother, let us say with St. Germanus: What will become of us who are sinners, but who wish to amend and have recourse to thee, who art the life of Christians?[38] Let us, oh Lady, hear what St. Anselm says of thee, that he will not be lost for whom thou hast once offered thy prayers.[39] Pray, then, for us, and we shall be saved from hell. Who will tell me, says Richard of St. Victor, that when I am presented at the divine tribunal, the Judge will not be favorable to me, if I shall have thee to defend my cause, oh mother of mercy?[40] And the blessed Henry Suso declared, that he had placed his soul in the care of Mary, and he said, that if the Judge wished to condemn him, he would have the sentence pass through the hands of Mary.[41] For he hoped that when the sentence of condemnation should fall into the kind hands of the Virgin, its execution would certainly be prevented. I ask and hope the same for myself, oh my most holy queen. Whence I will always repeat with St. Bonaventure: Oh Lady, in thee I have placed all my hopes, therefore I securely hope not to be lost, but safe in heaven to praise and love thee forever.[42]

EXAMPLE

In the year 1604 there lived in a city of Flanders two young students, who, instead of attending to their studies, gave themselves up to excesses and dissipation. One night, having gone to the house of a woman of ill fame, one of them, named Richard, after some time returned home, but the other remained. Richard having gone home was undressing to go to rest, when he remembered that he had not recited that day, as usual, some "Hail Marys." He

38. Quid autem de nobis fiet, O sanctissima Virgo, O vita Christianorum. De Zona Virg.
39. Æternum væ non sentiet ille pro quo semel oraverit Maria.
40. Si accedam ad judicium, et matrem misericordiæ in causa mea habeo mecum, quis judicium denegabit propitium? In C. c. 15.
41. Si judex servum suum damnare voluerit, per manus tuas piisimas, O Maria, hoc faciat. Hor. Sap. l. 1, c. 16.
42. In te, Domina, speravi, non confundar in æternum. In Psal. Mar.

was oppressed with sleep and very weary, yet he roused himself and recited them, although without devotion, and only half awake. He then went to bed, and having just fallen asleep, he heard a loud knocking at the door, and immediately after, before he had time to open it, he saw before him his companion, with a hideous and ghastly appearance. "Who are you?" he said to him. "Do you not know me?" answered the other. "But what has so changed you? you seem like a demon." "Alas!" exclaimed this poor wretch, "I am damned." "And how is this?" "Know," he said, "that when I came out of that infamous house, a devil attacked me and strangled me. My body lies in the middle of the street, and my soul is in hell. Know that my punishment would also have been yours, but the blessed Virgin, on account of those few "Hail Marys" said in her honor, has saved you. Happy will it be for you, if you know how to avail yourself of this warning, that the mother of God sends you through me." After these words he opened his cloak, showed the fire and serpents that were consuming him, and then disappeared. Then the youth, bursting into a flood of tears, threw himself with his face on the ground, to thank Mary, his deliverer, and while he was revolving in his mind a change of life, he hears the Matins bell of a neighboring Franciscan Monastery. "It is there," he exclaimed, "that God calls me to do penance." He went immediately to the convent to beg the fathers to receive him. Knowing how bad his life had been, they objected. But after he had related the circumstance which had brought him there, weeping bitterly all the while, two of the fathers went out to search in the street, and actually found there the dead body of his companion, having the marks of strangulation, and black as a coal. Whereupon the young man was received. Richard from that time led an exemplary life. He went into India to preach the faith; from thence passed to Japan, and finally had the good fortune and received the grace of dying a martyr for Jesus Christ, by being burned alive.[43]

PRAYER

Oh Mary! Oh my most dear mother! in what an abyss of evil I should find myself, if thou, with thy kind hand, hadst not so often preserved me! Yea, how many years should I already have been in hell, if thou, with thy powerful

---

43. P. Alf. Andrada de Bapt. Virg.

prayers, hadst not rescued me! My grievous sins were hurrying me there; divine justice had already condemned me; the raging demons were waiting to execute the sentence; but thou didst appear, oh mother, not invoked nor asked by me, and hast saved me. Oh my dear deliverer, what return can I make thee for so much grace and so much love? Thou hast overcome the hardness of my heart, and hast drawn me to love thee and confide in thee. And oh, into what an abyss of evils I afterwards should have fallen, if thou, with thy kind hand, hadst not so many times protected me from the dangers into which I was on the brink of falling! Continue, oh my hope, continue to save me from hell, but first of all from the sins into which I might again fall. Do not permit that I shall have to curse thee in hell. My beloved Lady, I love thee, and how can thy goodness endure to see one of thy servants who loves thee, lost? Ah, obtain for me the grace to be no longer ungrateful to thee and to my God, who for love of thee hath granted me so many favors. Oh Mary, what dost thou say to me? Shall I be lost? I shall be lost if I leave thee. But who will any more venture to forsake thee? Shall I ever forget thy love for me? Thou, after God, art the love of my soul. I dare live no longer without loving thee. I bless thee! I love thee! and I hope that I shall always love thee in time and in eternity, oh creature most beautiful! most holy! most sweet! most amiable of all creatures in this world! Amen.

SECTION 2
Mary assists her servants in Purgatory

Too happy are the servants of this most kind mother, since not only in this world are they aided by her, but also in purgatory they are assisted and consoled by her protection. For succor being there more needed, because they are in torment and cannot help themselves, so much the more does this mother of mercy strive to help them. St. Bernardine of Sienna says, that in that prison of souls who are spouses of Jesus Christ, Mary has a certain dominion and plenitude of power to relieve them, as well as deliver them from their pains.[44]

And, in the first place, as to relieving them, the same saint, applying the words of Ecclesiasticus: I have walked in the waves of the sea: "In fluctibus maris ambulavi,"[45] adds, visiting and relieving the necessities and sufferings

---

44. Beata Virgo in regno purgatorii dominium habet. Serm 3, de Nom. Mar. a. 1, c. 3.
45. Cap. xxiv. v. 8.

of my servants, who are my children.[46] St. Bernardine says, that the pains of purgatory are called waves, because they are transitory, unlike the pains of hell, which never end: and they are called waves of the sea, because they are very bitter pains. The servants of Mary tormented by those pains are often visited and succored by her. See, then, how important it is, says Novarino, to be a servant of this good Lady; for she never forgets such when they are suffering in those flames. And although Mary succors all the souls in purgatory, yet she always obtains more indulgences and alleviations for those who have been especially devoted to her.[47]

This divine mother, in her revelations to St. Bridget, said: "I am the mother of all the souls in purgatory; and all the sufferings which they merit for the sins committed in life are every hour, while they remain there, alleviated in some measure by my prayers."[48] This kind mother sometimes condescends even to enter into that holy prison, to visit and console these her afflicted children. I have penetrated into the bottom of the deep: "Profundum abyssi penetravi," as we read in Ecclesiasticus;[49] and St. Bonaventure, applying these words, adds: I have penetrated the depth of this abyss, that is, of purgatory, to relieve by my presence those holy souls.[50] Oh, how kind and beneficent is the holy Virgin to those who are suffering in purgatory! says St. Vincent Ferrer; through her they receive continual consolation and refreshment.[51]

And what other consolation have they in their sufferings than Mary, and the help of this mother of mercy? St. Bridget one day heard Jesus saying to his mother: "Thou art my mother, thou art the mother of mercy, thou art the consoler of those who are in purgatory."[52] And the blessed Virgin herself said to St. Bridget, that as a poor sick person, suffering and deserted on his bed, feels himself refreshed by some word of consolation, so those souls feel themselves consoled in hearing only her name.[53] The name alone

---

46. Scilicet visitans et subveniens necessitatibus et tormentis devotorum meorum quia filii sunt. Serm. 3, de Nom. Mar. a. 1, c. 8.
47. Vide quam referat Virginem colere, cum cultorum suorum in purgatorii flammis existentium non obliviscatur. Et licet omnibus opem et refrigerium ferat, id tamen præcipue erga suos præstat. Nov. Virg. Umb. c. 15, exc. 86.
48. Ego mater omnium qui sunt in purgatorio, quia omnes pœnæ, quæ debentur illis pro peccatis suis, in qualibet hora propter preces meas quodammodo mitigantur. L. 4. Rev. c. 132.
49. Cap. xxiv. 8.
50. Abyssi, idest purgatorii, adjuvans illas sanctas animas.
51. Maria bona, existentibus in purgatorio; quia per eam habent suffragium. Ser. 2, de Nat.
52. Tu es mater mea, tu mater misericordiæ, tu consolatio eorum, qui sunt in purgatorio. Lib. 1, Rev. 19.
53. Qui sunt in purgatorio gaudent, nomine meo audito, quemadmodum æger jacens in lecto, cum audit verbum solatii. Ap. B. Dion. Cant. l. 3, de Laud. V.

of Mary, a name of hope and salvation, which these beloved children often invoke in that prison, is for them a great comfort. But, then, says Novarino, the loving mother, on hearing herself invoked by them, adds her prayers to God, by which these souls receive comfort, and find their burning pains cooled as if by dew from heaven.[54]

But not only does Mary console and succor her servants in purgatory; she also releases them from this prison, and delivers them by her intercession. From the day of her glorious assumption, in which that prison is said to have been emptied,[55] as Gerson writes; and Novarino confirms this by saying, that many weighty authors relate that Mary, when about to ascend to paradise, asked this favor of her Son, that she might take with her all the souls that were then in purgatory;[56] from that time, says Gerson, the blessed Virgin has possessed the privilege of freeing her servants from those pains. And this also is positively asserted by St. Bernardine, who says that the blessed Virgin has the power of delivering souls from purgatory by her prayers and the application of her merits, especially if they have been devoted to her.[57] And Novarino says the same thing, believing that by the merits of Mary, not only the torments of these souls are assuaged, but also abridged, the time of their purgation being shortened by her intercession:[58] and for this it is enough that she presents herself to pray for them.

St. Peter Damian relates,[59] that a certain lady, named Marozia, after death, appeared to her godmother, and told her that on the day of the Assumption of Mary she had been released by her from purgatory, with a multitude of souls exceeding in number the whole population of Rome. St. Denis the Carthusian relates, that on the festivals of the birth and resurrection of Jesus Christ, Mary descends into purgatory, accompanied by troops of angels, and releases many souls from their torments.[60] And Novarino believes that the same thing happens on every solemn festival of the holy Virgin.[61]

---

54. Virginis nomen illarum pœnarum refrigerium est; addit Virgo preces quibus veluti supero quodam rore cruciatus illi magni mitigantur. Nov. cit. c. 15, exc. 86.
55. Totum purgatorium fuisse evacuatum.
56. Ferunt quippe bonæ notæ auctores, Virginem in cœlum ituram a filio hoc petiisse, ut omnes animas quæ detinebantur in purgatorio, secum ad gloriam ducere posset. Cit. Exc. 86.
57. Ab his tormentis liberat beata Virgo, maxime devotos suos. Serm. 3. de Nom. Mar. a. 2, c. 3.
58. Crediderim omnibus qui in flammis purgantur, Mariæ meritis non solum leviores fuisse redditas illas pœnas, sed et breviores; adeo ut cruciatuum tempus contractum Virginis ope illius sit. Cit. Exc. 86.
59. Lib. 3, Ep. 10 et in ord. 50.
60. Beatissima Virgo singulis in annis festivitate nativitatis Christi ad purgatorii loca cum multitudine angelorum descendit, et multas inde animas cripit. Etiam in nocte dominicæ resurrectionis solet descendere ad purgatorium pro eductione animarum. Cart. Serm. 2, de Assump.
61. Facile autem crediderim in quocumque Virginis solemni feste plures animas ab illis pœnis eximi. In loc. cit.

Our Lady of Mount Carmel comforts the souls in Purgatory. **Carved relief in the Cathedral of San Sebastián, Spain.**

Every one has heard of the promise made by Mary to Pope John, to whom she appeared, and ordered him to make known to all those who should wear the sacred scapular of Carmel, that on the Saturday after their death they should be released from purgatory. And this was proclaimed by the same pontiff, as Father Crasset relates,[62] in a bull which he published. It was also confirmed by Alexander V, Clement VII, Pius V, Gregory XIII, and Paul V, who, in 1612, in a bull said: "That Christians may piously believe that the blessed Virgin will aid by her continual intercession, by her merits and special protection, after death, and principally on Saturday, which is a day consecrated by the Church to the blessed Virgin, the souls of the members of the confraternity of holy Mary of Mount Carmel, who shall have departed this life in the state of grace, worn the scapular, observing chastity according to their state of life, recited the office of the Virgin, and if they have not been able to recite it, shall have observed the fasts of the Church, abstaining from flesh meat on Wednesdays, except on Christmas-day." And in the solemn office of the feast of holy Mary of Mount Carmel, we read that it is piously believed, that the holy Virgin, with a mother's love consoles the members of the confraternity of Mount Carmel in purgatory, and by her intercession conducts them to their heavenly country.[63]

Why should we not also hope for the same graces and favors, if we are devoted to this good mother? And if with more special love we serve her, why cannot we hope to obtain the grace of going immediately after death to paradise, without entering into purgatory? as we read that the holy Virgin said to the blessed Godfrey, through brother Abondo, in these words: "Go and tell brother Godfrey to advance in virtue, for thus he will be a child of my Son, and mine also; and when his soul quits the body, I will not permit it to go to purgatory, but I will take it and present it to my Son."[64] And if we would assist the holy souls in purgatory, let us endeavor to remember them in all our prayers to the blessed Virgin, applying to them especially the holy rosary, which procures for them great relief, as we read in the following example.

---

62. Tom. 2, Div. d. B. Virg. tr. 6, prat. 4.
63. Materno plane affectu, dum igne purgatorii expiantur, solari, ac in cœlestem patriam obtentu suo quantocius pie creditur afferre. In Festo S. Mar. de M. Carm. 16, Jul.
64. In lib. de Gest. Vir. ill. Sol. Villar.

EXAMPLE

Father Eusebius Nierembergh relates,[65] that there lived in the city of Aragona a girl, named Alexandra who, being noble and very beautiful, was greatly loved by two young men. Through jealousy, they one day fought and killed each other. Their enraged relatives, in return, killed the poor young girl, as the cause of so much trouble, cut off her head, and threw her into a well. A few days after, St. Dominic was passing through that place, and, inspired by the Lord, approached the well, and said: "Alexandra, come forth," and immediately the head of the deceased came forth, placed itself on the edge of the well, and prayed St. Dominic to hear its confession. The saint heard its confession, and also gave it communion, in presence of a great concourse of persons who had assembled to witness the miracle. Then, St. Dominic ordered her to speak and tell why she had received that grace. Alexandra answered, that when she was beheaded, she was in a state of mortal sin, but that the most holy Mary, on account of the rosary, which she was in the habit of reciting, had preserved her in life. Two days the head retained its life upon the edge of the well, in the presence of all, and then the soul went to purgatory. But fifteen days after, the soul of Alexandra appeared to St. Dominic, beautiful and radiant as a star, and told him, that one of the principal sources of relief to the souls in purgatory is the rosary which is recited for them; and that, as soon as they arrive in paradise, they pray for those who apply to them these powerful prayers. Having said this, St. Dominic saw that happy soul ascending in triumph to the kingdom of the blessed.

PRAYER

Oh Queen of heaven and of earth, oh mother of the Lord of the world, oh Mary, creature most great, most exalted, most amiable, it is true that

---

65. Troph. Marian. l. 4, c. 29.

many on the earth do not love thee and do not know thee; but there are innumerable angels and saints in heaven who love and praise thee continually. On this earth, too, how many souls burn with love of thee, and live enamored of thy goodness! Ah, if I, too, might love thee, my most lovely Lady! Oh, that I might always be engaged in serving thee, in praising thee, in honoring thee, and in striving to awaken love of thee in others. A God hath been enamored of thee, who, by thy beauty, if I may so speak, hast drawn him from the bosom of the eternal Father, to come upon the earth and become man and thy Son; and I, a miserable worm, shall I not be enamored of thee? Yes, my most sweet mother, I also will love thee, love thee much, and do all in my power to make thee loved by others. Accept, then, oh Mary, the desire I have to love thee, and help me to fulfill it: I know that thy lovers are regarded with much favor by thy God. Next to his own glory, he desires nothing more than thy glory, in seeing thee honored and loved by all. From thee, oh Lady, I await all my blessings. Thou must obtain the pardon of all my sins, thou must obtain for me perseverance, succor in death, deliverance from purgatory, in a word, thou must conduct me to paradise. All this thy lovers hope from thee, and they are not deceived. This I also hope, who love thee with all my heart, and above all things next to God.

SECTION 3
Mary conducts her servants to Paradise

Oh, what a signal mark of predestination have the servants of Mary! The holy Church applies to this divine mother the words of Ecclesiasticus, and makes her say for the comfort of her servants: "In all these I sought rest, and I shall abide in the inheritance of the Lord."[66] Cardinal Hugo, commenting on this, remarks: Blessed is he in whose habitation the holy Virgin found rest: "Beatus in cujus domo beatæ Virgo requiem invenerit." Mary, through the love she bears to all, seeks to make devotion to her prevail in all hearts. Many do not receive it or do not preserve it; blessed is he who receives it and preserves it. In the inheritance of the Lord will I abide; that is, adds the learned Paciucchelli, in those who are the inheritance of the Lord.[67] Devotion to the Virgin abides in all those who are the inheritance of the Lord, that is, who

---

66. In omnibus requiem quæsivi, et in hereditate Domini morabor. Cap. xxiv. 11.
67.Et in hæreditate Domini morabor. idest in illis qui sunt hæreditas Domini.

will be in heaven praising him eternally. Mary continues in the passage above cited: "He that made me, rested in my tabernacle, and he said to me: Let thy dwelling be in Jacob, and thy inheritance in Israel, and take root in my elect."[68] My Creator has condescended to come and rest in my bosom, and has willed that I should inhabit in the hearts of all the elect, whom Jacob prefigured, and who are the inheritance of the Virgin; and he has ordained that devotion to me and confidence in me should take root in the hearts of the elect.

Oh, how many would have failed of being among the blessed in heaven, if Mary, by her powerful intercession, had not conducted them thither! "I made that in the heavens there should rise light that never faileth;"[69] thus Cardinal Hugo puts into her mouth these words of the same chapter of Ecclesiasticus: I have made to shine in heaven as many eternal lights as I have devoted servants. Whence the same author adds, commenting on this text: Many saints are in heaven by her intercession, who never would have been there without it.[70] St. Bonaventure says, that the gate of heaven will be opened to receive all those who trust in the protection of Mary.[71] Hence St. Ephrem called devotion to the divine mother the opening of paradise.[72] And the devout Blosius, addressing the Virgin, says to her: Lady, to thee are committed the keys and the treasure of the heavenly kingdom.[73] And, therefore, we should continually supplicate her in the words of St. Ambrose: Open to us, oh Virgin, heaven, for thou hast the keys of it.[74] Nay, thou art even the gate of it, as the holy Church names thee, "Janua cœli."

For this reason the great mother is also called by the holy Church: Star of the sea: "Ave, Maris stella." For as navigators, says the angelic St. Thomas, are guided to port by means of a star, thus Christians are guided to heaven by means of Mary.[75]

She is for this reason, finally, called by St. Peter Damian, the ladder of heaven: "Scala cœlestis;" for, as the saint says, by means of Mary, God has descended from heaven to earth, that by the same, or by her, men might merit to ascend from earth to heaven.[76] And for this reason, oh Lady, says

---

68. Qui creavit me, requievit in tabernaculo meo; et dixit mihi, in Jacob inhabita, et in Israel hæreditare, et in electis meis mitte radices.
69. Ego feci in cœlis, ut oriretur lumen indeficiens. Cap. xxiv. v. 6.
70. Multi sancti sunt in cœlis, intercessione ejus, qui nunquam, ibi fuissent nisi per eam.
71. Qui speraverit in illa, porta cœli reserabitur ei.
72. Reseramentum cœlestis Jerusalem. Orat. de Laud. Virg.
73. Tibi regni cœlestis claves thesaurique commissi sunt. Cimel. Endol. 1.
74. Aperi nobis, O Virgo, cœlum, cujus claves habes.
75. Dicitur stella maris, quia sicut navigantes ad portum diriguntur per stellam maris, ita Christiani diriguntur ad gloriam per Mariam. Opusc. 8.
76. Scala cœlestis, quia per ipsam Deus descendit ad terram, ut per ipsam homines mererentur ascendere ad cœlum.

St. Anastasius, thou art full of grace, that thou mightest be made the way of our salvation, and the ascent to the celestial country.[77] St. Bernard calls the blessed Virgin: The vehicle to heaven: "Vehiculum ad cœlum." And St. John the Geometrician salutes her: Hail, most noble chariot: "Salve clarissime currus;" by which her servants are conducted to heaven. And, St. Bonaventure addresses her thus: Blessed are those who know thee, oh mother of God! for to know thee is the path to immortal life, and to publish thy virtues is the way to eternal salvation.[78]

In the Franciscan chronicles[79] it is related of brother Leo, that he once saw a red ladder, upon which Jesus Christ was standing, and a white one, upon which stood his holy mother. He saw persons attempting to ascend the red ladder; they ascended a few steps and then fell; they ascended again, and again fell. Then they were exhorted to ascend the white ladder, and on that he saw them succeed, for the blessed Virgin offered them her hand, and they arrived in that manner safe in paradise. St. Denis the Carthusian asks: Who will ever be saved? Who will ever reign in heaven? They are saved, and will certainly reign, he himself answers, for whom this queen of mercy offers her prayers.[80] And this Mary herself affirms: By me kings reign: "Per me reges regnant."[81] Through my intercession souls reign first in the mortal life on this earth, by governing their passions, and then they go to reign eternally in heaven, where, as St. Augustine declares, all are kings: "Quot cives, tot reges." Mary, in a word, as Richard of St. Laurence says, is the mistress of paradise, since there she commands according to her pleasure, and introduces into it whom she will. Therefore, applying to her the words of Ecclesiasticus, he adds: "My power is in Jerusalem:"[82] I command what I will, and introduce whom I will.[83] And as she is the mother of the Lord of paradise, she is with reason, also, says Rupert, the Lady of paradise. She possesses, by right, the whole kingdom of her Son.[84]

This divine mother, with her powerful prayers and assistance, has obtained for us paradise, if we place no obstacle to our entrance there.[85]

77. Ave gratia plena, quod facta sis salutis via, ascensusque ad superos. Serm. 1, de Annunc.
78. Scire et cognoscere te, O Virgo Deipara, est via immortalitatis; et narrare virtutes tuas est via salutis. In Psal. lxxxv.
79. P. 1, t. 1, c. 35.
80. Quis salvatur? quis regnat in cœlo? Illi sunt, pro quibus regina misericordiæ interpellat.
81. Prov. viii. 15.
82. In Jerusalem potestas mea. C. 24, 25.
83. Imperando scilicet quod volo, et quos volo, introducendo. Rios. l. 4, de. L. V.
84. Totum jure possidet filii regnum. L. 3, in Cant. 4.
85. Cœleste nobis regnum suo interventu, auxiliis, et precibus impetravit. St. Antoninus, p. 4, tit. 15, c. 2, s. 1.

Wherefore those who are servants of Mary, and for whom Mary intercedes, are as secure of paradise as if they were already there.[86] To serve
Mary and to belong to her court, adds St. John of Damascus, is the greatest
honor we can attain; for to serve the queen of heaven is to reign already in
heaven, and to live in obedience to her commands is more than to reign.[87]
On the other hand, he says that those who do not serve Mary will not be
saved; whilst those who are deprived of the support of this great mother,
are deprived of the succor of the Son, and of all the celestial court.[88]

Forever praised be the infinite goodness of our God who has constituted Mary our advocate in heaven, that she, as mother of the judge and
mother of mercy may efficaciously by her intercession, order the great
affair of our eternal salvation. This sentiment is taken from St. Bernard.[89]
And James the Monk, esteemed a doctor among the Greek fathers, says
that God has made Mary a bridge of salvation, by which we are enabled to
pass over the waves of this world, and reach the blessed port of paradise.[90]
Hence St. Bonaventure exclaims: Hear, oh ye people who desire paradise;
serve and honor Mary, and you will certainly find life eternal.[91]

Not even those who deserve hell should despair of attaining the kingdom of the blessed, if they faithfully devote themselves to the service of
this queen. Sinners, says St. Germanus, have sought to find God by thy
means, oh Mary, and have been saved![92] Richard of St. Laurence remarks
that Mary is said by St. John to be crowned with stars.[93] On the other hand,
in the sacred Canticles, the Virgin is said to be crowned with wild beasts,
lions and panthers: "Come from Lebanon, my spouse, come from Lebanon,
come; thou shalt be crowned from the dens of the lions, from the mountains of the leopards."[94] What does this signify? Richard answers that those
wild beasts are those sinners, who, through the favor and intercession of

86. Qui Virgini famulatur, ita securus est de paradiso ac si esset in paradiso. Guerricus Abbas.
87. Summus honor servire Mariæ, et de ejus esse familia. Etenim et servire regnare est, est ejus agi frœnis
plusquam regnum. De Exc. Virg. c. 9.
88. Gens quæ non servierit illi, peribit. Gentes destitutæ tantæ matris auxilio, destituuntur auxilio Filii,
et totius curiæ cœlestis. Exc. Virg. c. 9.
89. Advocatam promisit peregrinatio nostra, quæ tanquam judicis mater, et mater misericordiæ, suppliciter et efficaciter salutis nostræ negotia pertractabit. Serm. 1, de Assump.
90. Eam tu pontem fecisti, quo a mundi fluctibus trajiciens, ad tranquillum portuum tuum deveniamus.
Orat. in Nat. Deip.
91. Audite, gentes, qui cupitis regnum Dei, Virginem Mariam honorate et invenietis vitam æternam. In
Psalt. Vir.
92. Peccatores per te, Deum exquisierunt et salvi facti sunt. Serm. de Dorm. Deip.
93. Et in capite ejus corona stellarum duodecim. Apoc. xii. 1
94. Veni de Libano, sponsa mea, veni de Libano, veni coronaberis de cubilibus leonum, de montibus pardorum. Cant. iv. 8.

Mary, have become stars of paradise, which are a crown more worthy of this queen of mercy, than all the material stars of heaven.[95] The servant of the Lord, sister Seraphina da Capri, as we read in her life, in her prayers to the most holy Virgin during the Novena of her assumption, asked of her the conversion of a thousand sinners; but as she feared that her demands were too extravagant, the Virgin appeared to her, and reproved her for this her vain fear, saying to her: "Why do you fear? am I not powerful enough to obtain for thee from my Son the salvation of a thousand sinners? Behold them, I have already obtained it." She showed her the soul of innumerable sinners who had merited hell, and had afterwards been saved by her intercession, and were already enjoying eternal bliss.

It is true that in this life no one can be certain of his eternal salvation: "Man knoweth not whether he be worthy of love or hatred, but all things are kept uncertain for the time to come."[96] David asked of God: Oh Lord, who will be saved? "Who shall dwell in thy tabernacle?"[97] St. Bonaventure, writing on these words, answers: Oh sinners, let us follow the footsteps of Mary, and cast ourselves at her blessed feet, and let us not leave her until she blesses us, for her blessing will secure to us paradise.[98] It is enough, oh Lady, says St. Anselm, that thou dost wish to save us, for then we cannot but be saved.[99] St. Antoninus adds, that souls protected by Mary are necessarily saved; those upon whom she turns her eyes are necessarily justified and glorified.[100]

With reason, says St. Ildephonsus, the most holy Virgin predicted that all generations would call her blessed;[101] for all the elect by means of Mary obtain eternal blessedness.[102] Thou, oh great mother, art the beginning, the middle, and the end of our felicity, says St. Methodius.[103] The beginning, because Mary obtains for us the pardon of our sins; the middle, because she obtains for us perseverance in divine grace; the end, because she finally obtains for us paradise. By thee, St. Bernard continues, heaven

95. Et quid est hoc? Nisi quia feræ per gratiam et orationes Mariæ sunt stellæ, quæ conveniunt tantæ reginæ. De Laud. Virg. cap. 3.
96. Nescit homo utrum odio vel amore dignus sit, sed omnia in futurum servantur incerta. Eccli. ix. 1, 2.
97. Domine quis habitabit in tabernaculo tuo? Psal. xiv. 1.
98. Amplectamur Mariæ vestigia, peccatores, et ejus beatis pedibus pervolvamur.Teneamus eam fortiter, nec dimittamus, donec ab ea mereamur benedici.
99. Tantummodo velis salutem nostram, et vere nequaquam salvi esse non poterimus. De Exc. Virg. c. 11.
100. Necessarium est quod hi ad quos convertit (Maria) oculos suos justificentur, et glorificentur. P. 4, tit. 55.
101. Beatam me dicent omnes generationes. Luc. 1, 48.
102. Beata jure dicitur, quia omnes ex ea beatificantur. Serm. 3, de Assump.
103. Tu felicitatis nostræ principium, medium et finis. Serm. in Hypant.

has been opened—by thee hell has been emptied—by thee paradise has been restored—by thee, in a word, eternal life has been given to many sinners who have merited eternal death.[104]

But above all, we should be encouraged in the certain hope of paradise, by the rich promise which Mary has herself made to those who honor her, and especially to those who, by their words and their example, strive to make her known and honored among others: "They that work by me shall not sin; they that explain me shall have life everlasting."[105] Oh happy, then, are they, says St. Bonaventure, who gain the favor of Mary! they will be welcomed by the blessed as being already their companions; and whosoever bears the seal of a servant of Mary, has his name already written in the book of life.[106] Of what avail is it, then, to trouble ourselves with the opinions of the schoolmen, on the question, whether predestination to glory precedes or follows the foreknowledge of merits? Whether or not our names are written in the book of life? If we are true servants of Mary and obtain her protection, we certainly are written there; for, as St. John of Damascus says, God gives the grace of devotion to his holy mother only to those whom he will save; in conformity with this, as the Lord seems to have declared expressly through St. John: "He that shall overcome, I will write upon him the name of my God, and the name of the city of my God."[107] And who is this city of God but Mary? as St. Gregory explains, commenting on this passage of David: "Glorious things are said of thee, oh city of God."[108]

We may, then, well say with St. Paul: "Having this seal, the Lord knoweth who are his."[109] Whosoever carries the seal of a servant of Mary is acknowledged by God as his own. We read in St. Bernard, that devotion to the mother of God is the most certain sign that we shall obtain eternal salvation.[110] And the blessed Alanus, speaking of the "Hail Mary," says that he who often invokes the Virgin with this angelical salutation, has a very certain sign of predestination.[111] And again he says of perseverance in the

---

104. Per te cœlum apertum est, infernus evacuatus, instaurata cœlestis Jerusalem, miseris damnationem expectantibus vita data est. Serm. 4, de Assump. Virg.
105. Qui operabunt in me, non peccabunt. Qui elucidant me, vitam æternam habebunt. Eccli. xxiv. 30, 31.
106. Qui acquirunt gratiam Mariæ, agnoscentur a civibus paradisi et qui habuerit caracterem ejus, adnotabitur in libro vitæ. In Spcc.
107. Qui vicerit . . . scribam super eum nomen Dei mei, et nomen civitatis Dei mei. Apoc. iii. 12.
108. Gloriosa dicta sunt de te, civitas Dei. Psal. lxxxvi. 3.
109. Habens signaculum hoc, cognovit Dominus qui sunt ejus. Tim. ii, 19.
110. Certissimum est signum salutis æternæ consequendæ.
111. Habentes devotionem hanc, signum est predestinationis permagnum ad gloriam. P. 2, Ros. c. 11.

daily recitation of the holy rosary: Let it be to thee a most probable sign of eternal salvation, if thou dost perseveringly honor the blessed Virgin by daily reciting her rosary.[112] Father Nierembergh still further remarks, that the servants of the mother of God not only are more privileged and favored in this world, but also in heaven will be more especially honored. And he adds, that in heaven they will have a peculiarly rich device and livery, by which they will be known as servants of the queen of heaven and as the people of her court, according to those words of Proverbs: "All her domestics are clothed with double garments."[113]

St. Mary Magdalen de Pazzi saw a small vessel in the midst of the sea, in which all the servants of Mary had taken shelter; she herself steering it, safely conducted them to port. By this the saint understood that they who live under the protection of Mary, are rescued, in the midst of all the dangers of this life, from the shipwreck of sin, and from damnation, for by her they are guided in safety to the port of paradise. Let us, then, strive to enter this blessed little vessel of the mantle of Mary, and there let us dwell secure of the kingdom of heaven; for the Church sings, "Holy mother of God, all those who are to be partakers of eternal joy dwell with thee, and live under thy protection."[114]

EXAMPLE

Cesarius relates,[115] that a certain Cistercian monk, who was a devoted servant of our blessed Lady, desired very earnestly a visit from his dear Lady, and was praying her continually to grant him this favor. He went one night into the garden, and while he stood there looking up to heaven, breathing forth to his queen in ardent sighs his desire to see her, a beautiful and radiant virgin descended, and said to him: "Thomas, wouldst thou like to hear me sing?" "Certainly," he answered, and then she sang so sweetly that it seemed to the devout religious that he was in paradise. Having finished her

---

112. Signum sit tibi probabilissimum æternæ salutis, si perseveranter in die beatam virginem in
      Psalterio salutaveris. P. 44, de Psalt. c. 44.
113. Omnes domestici ejus vestiti sunt duplicibus. xxxi, 21.
114. Sicut lætantium omnium habitatio est in te, sancta Dei genitrix.
115. Lib. 7, Dial. c. 3.

song, she disappeared, leaving him absorbed with an ardent desire to know who it could have been; and, soon after, another extremely beautiful virgin appeared to him, who, like the first, allowed him the pleasure of hearing her sing. He could not refrain from asking this one who she was, and the virgin answered: "She whom you saw a little while ago was Catherine, and I am Agnes, both martyrs for Jesus Christ, sent by our Lady to console you. Give thanks to Mary, and prepare for a greater favor." Having said this she disappeared, but left the religious with a greater hope of finally seeing his queen. Nor was he deceived, for shortly after he saw a great light and felt a new joy flowing into his heart, for in the midst of that light the mother of God appeared to him surrounded by angels, and of a beauty far surpassing that of the other two saints who had appeared to him. She said to him: "My dear servant and son, I have been pleased with the devotion which you have offered me, and have graciously heard your prayers: you have desired to see me; look on me, and I will also sing to you." Then the most holy Virgin began to sing with so great sweetness, that the devout religious lost his senses, and fell with his face upon the ground. The matin-bell sounded, the monks assembled, and not seeing Thomas, searched for him in his cell and other parts of the convent, and at last going into the garden they found him there, apparently lifeless. The superior commanded him to tell what had befallen him. And coming to himself, by the power of obedience, he related all the favors which the divine mother had bestowed upon him.

PRAYER

Oh queen of paradise! mother of holy love! for thou art of all creatures the most lovely, the most beloved of God and his first lover; ah, suffer the vilest and most ungrateful sinner on the earth to love thee, who sees himself released from hell by thy intercession, and without any merit of his own so blessed by thee, that he is enamored of thy goodness. I would wish if I could, to make known to all men who do not know thee, how worthy thou art to be loved, that all might love and honor thee. I would willingly die for love of thee, in defending thy virginity, thy dignity as mother of God, and thy immaculate conception; if it were ever needful for me to die in defense of these thy great privileges. Oh my most beloved mother, graciously accept this my affection, and do not permit that one of thy servants, who loves thee, should ever become an enemy of thy God, whom thou lovest so much. Ah, unhappy me, such once was I when I offended my Lord. But then, oh Mary, I did not love thee, and I sought little to be loved by thee. Now, after the grace of God, I desire nothing else than but to love thee, and to be loved by thee. I do not despair of this on account of my past offenses, for I know that thou, oh most benign and grateful Lady, dost not disdain to love even the most miserable sinners who love thee, and never dost allow thyself to be outdone in love by any one. Oh most lovely queen, I wish to go to thee in paradise, there to love thee. There, at thy feet, I shall better know how amiable thou art, and how much thou hast done to save me; therefore I shall love thee there with greater love, and shall love thee eternally, without the fear that I shall ever cease to love thee. Oh Mary, I have the certain hope of being saved through thee. Pray to Jesus for me. I have no other wish. It is thine to save me; thou art my hope. I will always exclaim, Oh Mary, my hope, thou must save me.

CHAPTER 9

O clemens, o pia!
Oh clement! Oh merciful!

SECTION 1
How great is the clemency and mercy of Mary

St. Bernard, speaking of the great mercy of Mary for us poor sinners, says that she is the very Land promised by God, flowing with milk and honey.[1] St. Leo says, that to the Virgin has been given such bowels of compassion, that she not only merits to be called merciful, but should be called mercy itself.[2] And St. Bonaventure, considering that Mary was made the mother of God for the sake of us sinners, and that to her was committed the charge of dispensing mercies; and considering, moreover, the great care she has for all those in misery, which renders her so rich in compassion, that she appears to desire nothing else than to relieve the necessitous, says, that when he looked on Mary, it seemed to him that he no longer beheld the divine justice, but only the divine mercy with which Mary is filled.[3]

In a word, the mercy of Mary is so great, that as Guerric the Abbot says: Her bowels of love can never for a moment cease to bring forth for us the fruits of mercy.[4] And what, exclaims St. Bernard, can flow but mercy from a fountain of mercy? "Quid de fonte pietatis nisi pietas?"[5] For this reason Mary was called the olive-tree: As a fair olive-tree in the plains: "Quasi oliva speciosa in campis."[6] For, as the olive-tree produces nothing but oil, the symbol of mercy, thus from the hands of Mary nothing but graces and mercies proceed. Hence, justly, says the venerable Louis da Ponte, is Mary called the mother of oil, since she is the mother of mercy.[7] If, then, we have recourse to this mother, and ask of her the oil of her mercy, we cannot fear

---

1. Terra repromissionis Maria lacte et melle manans. Serm. sup. Salv. Reg.
2. Maria adeo prædita est misericordiæ visceribus ut non tamen misericors, sed ipsa misericordia dici promereatur. Serm. 1. de Nat. Dom.
3. Certe, Domina, cum te aspicio, nihil nisi misericordiam cerno; nam pro miseris mater Dei facta es, et tibi officium miserendi commissum. Undique sollicita es de miseris, misericordia vallaris; solum misereri videris appetere. Stim. Am.
4. Cujus viscera nunquam desistunt fructum parturire pietatis. Serm. l, de Assump.
5. Serm. 1, in Dom. p. Ep.
6. Eccli. xxiv. 19.
7. Merito dici potest mater olei, nam est mater misericordiæ. Lib. 1, in Cant.

that she will refuse us, as the wise virgins refused the foolish, answering: "Lest there be not enough for us and for you."[8] No, for she is, indeed, rich in that oil of mercy, as St. Bonaventure remarks: Mary abounds in the oil of mercy: "Maria plena oleo pietatis."[9] She is called by the Church not only prudent, but most prudent, and by this we may understand, as Hugo of St. Victor says, that Mary is so full of grace and mercy that there is enough for all without exhausting her.[10]

But why, I would ask, is it said that this fair olive is in the midst of the plains, and not rather in a garden surrounded by walls and hedges? Cardinal Hugo answers to this question: In order that all may easily see her, and thus may easily have recourse to her, to obtain relief for their necessities.[11] St. Antoninus confirms this beautiful thought, when he says: That as all can go and gather the fruit of an olive-tree that is exposed in the open fields, so all, both the just and sinners, can have recourse to Mary to obtain mercy.[12] And then the saint adds: Oh how many sentences of punishment have been revoked through the merciful prayers of this most holy Virgin, in favor of sinners who have had recourse to her![13] And what more secure refuge can we find, says the devout Thomas à Kempis, than the compassionate heart of Mary? There the poor find shelter; the sick medicine; the afflicted consolation; the doubtful counsel; the abandoned help.[14]

Wretched should we be, if we had not this mother of mercy, mindful and solicitous to help us in our miseries! "Where there is no wife," says the Holy Spirit, "he mourneth that is in want."[15] This wife, remarks St. John Damascene, is certainly Mary, without whom the sick man suffers and mourns.[16] So, indeed, it is, since God has ordained that all graces should be dispensed by the prayers of Mary: where these are wanting, there is no hope of mercy, as our Lord signified to St. Bridget, saying to her: "Unless Mary interposes by her prayers, there is no hope of mercy."[17]

---

8. Ne forte non sufficiat nobis et vobis. Matth. xxv. 9.
9. Maria plena oleo pietatis. In. Spec. cap. 7.
10. Gratia plena, et in tantum plena, ut ex tua redundante oleo totus mundus hauriat. Si enim prudentes Virgines oleum acceperunt in vasis cum lampadibus, tu prudentissima Virgo gestasti vas redundans et indeficiens, ex quo, effuso oleo misericordiæ, omnium lampades illuminares.
11. Ut omnes eam respiciant, omnes ad eam confugiant.
12. Ad olivam in campis omnes possunt accedere, et accipere fructum ejus. Ad Mariam et justi et peccatores possunt accedere, ut inde misericordiam accipiant. P. 3, tit. 31, c. 4.
13. O quot sententias flagellorum propter peccata hæc sanctissima Virgo misericorditer revocavit.
14. Non est tutior locus ad latendum, quam sinus Mariæ. Ibi pauper habet domicilium, ibi infirmus invenit remedium, tristis solatium; ibi turbatus consilium, ibi destitutus acquirit juvamentum.
15. Ubi non est mulier ingemiscit egens. Eccli. xxxvi. 27.
16. Ingemiscit infirmus, ubi non fuerit hæc sanctissima mater.
17. Nisi preces Mariæ intervenirent, non esset spes misericordiæ. Rev. l. 6, c. 26.

But perhaps we fear that Mary does not see or pity our miseries. Oh, no! she sees them and feels them more than we do ourselves. And who among the saints can be found, says St. Antoninus, who pities us in our miseries as Mary does?[18] Hence, wherever she sees misery she cannot refrain from hastening to relieve it with her great compassion.[19] Thus Richard of St. Victor remarks, and Mendoza confirms it by saying: Therefore, oh blessed Virgin, wherever thou seest misery, there thou dost pour forth thy mercies.[20] And our good mother, as she herself declares, will never cease to exercise this office of mercy: And unto the world to come I shall not cease to be; and in the holy dwelling-place, I have ministered before him.[21] Upon which words Cardinal Hugo remarks: I will not cease, says Mary, even to the end of the world, to succor men in their miseries, and to pray for sinners, that they may be saved and rescued from eternal misery.[22]

Suetonius relates of the Emperor Titus, that he was so desirous to grant favors to those who asked them of him, that on those days when he had no opportunity of doing so, he would say, sorrowfully, I have lost a day: "Diem perdidi." This day has been lost to me, because I have passed it without benefiting any one. Probably Titus said this more through vanity, or a desire for esteem, than through a movement of charity. But our Empress Mary, if a day should ever pass in which she did not confer some favor, would say it only because she is full of charity, and of a desire to do us good; for as Bernardine de Bustis says, she is more desirous to confer favors on us, than we are to receive them from her.[23] And this same author adds, that when we have recourse to her, we shall always find her with her hands full of mercy and liberality.[24]

Rebecca was the type of Mary, who when the servant of Abraham asked her for a little water, answered that she would give him water enough not only for himself, but for his camels also.[25] Hence the devout St. Bernard

---

18. Non reperitur aliquis sanctorum ita compati in infirmitatibus, sicut mulier hæc beatissima Virgo Maria. P. 4, t. 15. c. 2.
19. Ubicumque fuerit miseria, tua currit et succurrit misericordia. In Cant. 4, 5.
20. Itaque, O B. Virgo, ubi miserias invenis, ibi tuas misericordias effundis. Cap. 4, 1, Reg.
21. Et usque ad futurum sæculum non desinam, ut in habitatione sancta coram ipso ministravi. Eccli. xxiv. 14.
22. Usque ad futurum sæculum, id est beatorum, non desinam miseriis subvenire, et pro peccatoribus orare.
23. Plus vult illa bonum tibi facere et largiri gratiam, quam tu accipere concupiscas. Mar. p. 1, Serm. 5, de Nov. Mar.
24. Invenies eam in manibus plenam misericordia et liberalitate. Loc. cit.
25. Quin et camelis tuis hauriam aquam, donec cuncti bibant Gen. xxiv. 19.

Our Lady of Hope Macarena. Seville, Spain.

addressing the blessed Virgin, says: Oh Lady, not to the servant of Abraham only, but also to his camels give from thy overflowing pitcher.[26] By which he intends to say: Oh Lady, thou art merciful and more liberal than Rebecca, therefore thou dost not rest contented with dispensing the favors of thy unbounded compassion to the servants of Abraham alone by whom are meant the faithful servants of God, but thou dost bestow them also on the camels, who represent sinners. And, as Rebecca gave more than she was asked, so Mary bestows more than we pray for. The liberality of Mary, says Richard of St. Laurence, resembles the liberality of her Son, who always gives more than is asked, and is therefore named by St. Paul: "Rich to all that call upon him;"[27] that is, giving abundantly his graces to all those that have recourse to him with their prayers. Hear the words of Richard: The bounty of Mary is like the bounty of her Son; she gives more than is asked.[28] Hence a devout author, addressing the Virgin, says: Oh Lady, pray for me, for thou wilt ask favors for me with greater devotion than I can do; and thou wilt obtain from God graces greater by far than I can pray for.[29]

When the Samaritans refused to receive Jesus Christ and his doctrine, St. James and St. John said to their Master: "Lord, wilt thou that we command fire to come down from heaven and consume them?" But the Savior answered: "You know not of what spirit you are."[30] As if he had said: I am of so mild and merciful a spirit, that I have come from heaven to save, not to punish sinners, and would you wish to see them lost? What fire? What punishment? Be silent, speak to me no more of punishment, that is not my spirit. But we cannot doubt that Mary, whose spirit is in everything so like that of her Son, is wholly inclined to exercise mercy; for, as she told St. Bridget, she is called the mother of mercy, and the mercy of God itself has made her so compassionate and sweet towards all.[31] Wherefore Mary was seen by St. John clothed with the sun: "And there appeared a great wonder in heaven, a woman clothed with the sun."[32] Upon which passage St. Bernard remarks, addressing the Virgin: Thou hast clothed the sun, and art thyself clothed with it.[33] Oh Lady, thou hast clothed the sun, the divine Word, with human

---

26. Domina, nec puero Abrahæ tantum, sed et camelis tribue de supereffluente hydria tua. Serm. Sup. Miss.
27. Dives in omnes qui invocant illum. Rom. x. 12.
28. Largitas Mariæ assimilat largitatem filii sui; dat amplius quam petatur. De Laud. Virg.
29. Majori devotione orabis pro me, quam ego auderem petere; et majora mihi impetrabis quam petere præsumam.
30. Noscitis cujus spiritus estis. Luc. ix. 55.
31. Ego vocor mater misericordiæ, et vero misericordia illius misericordem me fecit. Rev. l. 1, c. 6.
32. Et signum magnum apparuit in cœlo, mulier amicta sole. Apoc. xii. 1.
33. Vestis solem, et vestiris ab eo.

flesh, but he hath clothed thee with his power and his mercy.

So compassionate, then, and kind is this queen, says St. Bernard, that when a sinner recommends himself to her mercy, she does not begin to examine his merits, and whether he is worthy or not of being heard, but she graciously hears all and succors them.[34] Hence St. Idelbert remarks, that Mary is called fair as the moon: "Pulchra ut Luna;"[35] because, as the moon illuminates and benefits the smallest bodies upon the earth, so Mary enlightens and helps the most unworthy sinners.[36] And although the moon receives all her light from the sun, she moves more quickly than the sun; for, as a certain author remarks, what the sun does in a year, the moon does in a month.[37] Hence, says St. Anselm: Our relief is sometimes more immediate when the name of Mary is invoked than when we invoke the name of Jesus.[38] Wherefore Hugo of St. Victor tells us, that if by reason of our sins we fear to draw near to God, because he is an infinite majesty that we have offended, we should not hesitate to have recourse to Mary, because in her we shall find nothing to alarm us. She is indeed holy, immaculate, queen of the world, and mother of God; but she is of our flesh, and a child of Adam, like ourselves.[39]

In a word, says St. Bernard, whatever appertains to Mary is full of grace and mercy; for she, as mother of mercy, has become all things to all, and by her great charity has made herself a debtor to the just and to sinners, and open to all the bowels of her compassion, that all may share it.[40] As "the Devil," according to St. Peter, "goeth about seeking whom he may devour,"[41] so, on the contrary, says Bernardine de Bustis, Mary goeth about seeking to whom she can give life and salvation.[42]

We should understand that the protection of Mary, as St. Germanus says, is greater and more powerful than we can comprehend.[43] And how is it that the same Lord, who was under the old law so severe in punishing, exercises so

34. Non discutit merita, sed omnibus exorabilem se præbet, Serm. in Sign. Magn.
35. Cant. 6, 9.
36. Pulchra ut luna quia pulchrum est benefacere indignis. Epist. 26.
37. Quod sol facit in anno, luna facit in mense. Jo. di Minian. L. 1, de Cœl. c. 3.
38. Velocior nonnumquam est nostra salus, invocato nomine Mariæ, quam invocato nomine Jesu. De Excell. Virg. c. 6.
39. Si pertimescis ad Deum accedere, respice ad Mariam; non illis invenis quod timeas, genus tuum vides.
40. Quæ ad eam pertinent, plena omnia pietatis et gratiæ. Denique omnia omnibus facta est, sapientibus et insipientibus copiosissima charitate debitricem se fecit. Omnibus misericordiæ suæ sinum aperit, ut de plenitudine ejus accipiant omnes. Super Sign. Magn.
41. Circuit quærens quem devoret. Ep. 1, c. 5.
42. Ipsa semper circuit, quærens quem salvet. Marial. p. 3. Serm. 3.
43. Patrocinium tuum majus est, quam apprehendi possit. De Zona. Virg.

great mercy towards the greatest sinners? Thus asks the author del Pomerio;[44] and he also answers: He does all this for the love and merits of Mary.[45] Oh, how long since would the world have been destroyed, says St. Fulgentius, if Mary had not preserved it by her intercession![46] But we may with confidence go to God, as St. Arnold Carnotensis asserts, and hope for every blessing, now that the Son is our mediator with the divine Father, and the mother with the Son. How can it be that the Father will refuse to hear graciously the Son, when he shows him the wounds he has received for sinners? And how can it be that the Son will not graciously hear the mother, when she shows him the breasts from which she has nourished us?[47] St. Peter Chrysologus says with great energy, that this favored Virgin, having received God in her womb, demands in return, peace for the world, salvation for the lost, life for the dead.[48]

Oh how many, exclaims the Abbot of Celles, who merit to be condemned by the divine justice, are saved by the mercy of Mary! for she is the treasure of God and the treasure of all graces; therefore it is that our salvation is in her hands.[49] Let us always then have recourse to this mother of mercy, and confidently hope to be saved by means of her intercession; since she, as Bernardine de Bustis encourages us to believe, is our salvation, our life, our hope, our counsel, our refuge, our help.[50] Mary is that very throne of grace, says St. Antoninus, to which the apostle exhorts us to have recourse with confidence, that we may obtain the divine mercy, with all needed help for our salvation.[51] To the throne of grace, that is, to Mary, as St. Antoninus remarks.[52] Hence, Mary was called by St. Catherine of Sienna: The dispenser of divine mercy: "Administratrix misericordiæ."

Let us conclude, then, with the beautiful and sweet exclamation of St. Bernard upon the words: Oh clement, oh merciful, oh sweet Virgin Mary! "O clemens, O pia, O dulcis Virgo Maria." Oh Mary, thou art clement to the

---

44. Quare parcit nunc mundo ipse Deus, qui olim multo his minora peccata acrius punivit? Ap. P. Pepe. Grand, etc.
45. Totum hoc facit propter B. Virginem, et ejus merita.
46. Cœlum et terra jamdudum ruissent, si Maria suis precibus non sustentasset.
47. Securum accessum jam habet homo ad Deum, ubi mediatorem causæ suæ filium habet ante Patrem, et ante filium, matrem. Christus ostendit Patri latus et vulnera, Maria Christo pectus, et ubera. De Laud. Virg.
48. Una puella sic Deum in sui pectoris capit hospitio, ut pacem terris, salutem perditis, vitam mortuis, pro ipsa domo exigat pensionem. Serm. 140.
49. Sæpe quos justitia filii potest damnare, mater misericordiæ liberat. Thesaurus Domini est, et thesauraria gratiarum. Salus nostra in manu illius est. Prolog. in Contempl. Virg.
50. Hæc est nostra salus, vita, spes, consilium refugium, auxilium nostrum. P. l, Ser. 6, de Com. Mar.
51. Adeamus cum fiducia ad thronum gratiæ, ut misericordiam consequamur, ut gratiam inveniamus in auxilio opportuno. Hebr. iv. 16.
52. Ad thronum gratiæ, scilicet ad Mariam. P. 4, t. 15, c. 14, s. 7.

unhappy, merciful to those who pray thee, sweet to those who love thee: clement to the penitent, merciful to the advancing, sweet to the perfect. Thou showest thyself clement by rescuing us from punishment, merciful by bestowing on us graces, sweet by giving thyself to those who seek thee.[53]

EXAMPLE

Father Charles Bovius relates that in Domans, in France, lived a married man who had held a criminal connection with another woman. Now the wife being unable to endure this, continually besought God to punish the guilty parties; and one day in particular went to an altar of the blessed Virgin, which was in a certain church, to implore vengeance upon the woman who had alienated her husband from her; and this very woman went also every day to the same altar, to repeat a "Hail Mary." One night the divine mother appeared in a dream to the wife, who, on seeing her, began her accustomed petition: "Justice, mother of God, justice." But the blessed Lady answered: "Justice! do you seek justice from me? Go and find others to execute justice for you. It belongs not to me to do it for you. Be it known to you," she added, "that this very sinner offers every day a devotion in my honor, and that I cannot allow any sinner who does this, to suffer and be punished for his sins." The next day the wife went to hear mass in the above-named church of our Lady, and on coming out met her husband's friend; at the sight of her she began to reproach her and call her a sorceress, who had even enchanted with her sorceries the blessed Virgin. "Be silent," cried the people: "what are you saying?" "I be silent!" she answered: "what I say is only too true; this night the Virgin appeared to me; and when I implored justice of her, she answered me, that she could not grant it on account of a salutation which this wicked woman repeats daily in her honor." They asked the woman what salutation she repeated to the mother of God. She answered that it was the "Hail Mary;" and then on hearing that the blessed Virgin had dealt with her so mercifully in return for that trivial act of devotion, she cast herself on the ground

---

53. Clemens indigentibus, pia exorantibus, dulcis diligentibus. O clemens pœnitentibus, pia proficientibus, dulcis contemplantibus. O clemens liberando, O pie largiendo, O dulcis te donando. Sup. Salv. Reg.

before the sacred image, and there, in the presence of all the people, asked pardon for her scandalous life, and made a vow of perpetual continence. She afterwards put on a religious habit, built for herself a little cell near the church, where she retired, and persevered in continual penance until the day of her death.

PRAYER

Oh mother of mercy! since thou art so compassionate, and hast so great a desire to do good to us sinners, and to satisfy our demands, I, the most wretched of all men, to-day have recourse to thy mercy, that thou mayest grant my requests. Let others ask what they will, health of body, wealth, or temporal advantages; I come to ask of thee, oh Lady, those things which thou thyself dost most desire of me, and which are most conformable and most pleasing to thy sacred heart. Thou who wast so humble, obtain for me humility and love of contempt. Thou who wast so patient in the difficulties of this life, obtain for me patience in things contrary to my wishes. Thou who didst overflow with love to God, obtain for me the gift of a holy and pure love. Thou who wast all charity towards the neighbor, obtain for me charity towards all men, and especially towards those who are my enemies. Thou who wast wholly united to the divine will, obtain for me a perfect uniformity with the will of that God in all his dispositions concerning me. Thou, in a word, art the most holy of all creatures; oh Mary, obtain for me the grace to become a saint. Thy love is unfailing; thou canst and wilt obtain all things for me. Nothing, then, can hinder me from receiving thy graces but my neglect to invoke thee, or my want of confidence in thy intercession. But thou thyself must obtain for me the grace to seek thee, and this grace of confidence in thy intercession. These two greatest gifts I ask from thee—from thee will I receive them—from thee do I confidently hope for them. Oh Mary! Mary, my mother, my hope, my love, my life, my refuge, and my consolation. Amen.

Coronation of the Virgin Mary. Diego Velázquez. Museo del Prado, Madrid, Spain.

CHAPTER 10

O dulcis Virgo Maria!
Oh sweet Virgin Mary!

SECTION 1
How sweet is the name of Mary in life and in death

The great name of Mary, which was given to the divine mother, was not found on earth, neither was it invented by the mind or will of men, as were all other names that are in use among them; but it came from heaven, and was given to the Virgin by divine ordinance, as St. Jerome,[1] St. Epiphanius,[2] St. Antoninus,[3] and others attest. The name of Mary was drawn from the treasury of the divinity, as Richard of St. Laurence says: "De thesauro divinitatis Mariæ nomen evolvitur."[4] From the treasury of the divinity, oh Mary, came forth thy excellent and admirable name; for the Most Holy Trinity, the same author goes on to say, gave to thee this name, next to the name of thy Son, so superior to every name, and attached to it such majesty and power, that when it is uttered, all in heaven, earth, and hell must fall prostrate and venerate it.[5] Among all the other privileges which the Lord has attached to the name of Mary, let us see how sweet he has made it to the servants of this most holy Lady in life as well as in death.

To begin with life, the holy anchorite, Honorius, says, that the name of Mary is full of all divine sweetness.[6] And the glorious St. Anthony of Padua attributes to the name of Mary the same sweetness as St. Bernard attributed to the name of Jesus. The name of Jesus, said the latter, the name of Mary, said the former, is joy to the heart, honey to the mouth, melody to the ear of their devoted servants.[7] It is related in the life of the venerable Father John Ancina, Bishop of Saluzzo, that when he pronounced the name of Mary, he experienced so great a sensible sweetness that he

---

1. Lib. de Nat. Mar.
2. Or. de Præs. Deip.
3. Hist. tit. 4. c. 6.
4. De Laud. Virg. p. 14.
5. Dedit tibi, Maria, tota Trinitas nomen post nomen filii tui supra omne nomen; ut in nomine tuo omne genuflectatur, cœlestium, terrestrium, et infernorum. De Laud. v. l. 1, c. 2.
6. Hoc nomen Mariæ plenum est omni dulcedine ac suavitate divina.
7. Nomen Jesu . . . Nomen Mariæ jubilus in corde, mel in ore, in aure melos.

even tasted it on his lips. We also read that a certain woman in Cologne told the Bishop Marsillius, that whenever she pronounced the name of Mary she perceived in her mouth a taste sweeter than honey. Marsillius made the trial, and he also experienced the same sweetness. We read in the holy Canticles, that at the Assumption of the Virgin, the angels three times asked her name: "Who is she that goeth up by the desert as a pillar of smoke?"[8] "Who is she that cometh forth as the morning rising?"[9] And in another: "Who is this that cometh up from the desert, flowing with delights?"[10] Richard of St. Laurence inquires why the angels so often asked the name of this queen, and answers: The sound of the name of Mary was so sweet to the angels, and they repeated the question that they might hear it repeated also.[11]

But I do not here speak of this sensible sweetness, since it is not commonly granted to all, but I speak of the salutary sweetness of consolation, love, joy, confidence, and strength, which the name of Mary universally gives to those who, with devotion, pronounce it. Speaking on this subject, Francone the Abbot says, that next to the holy name of Jesus, the name of Mary is so rich in blessings, that no other name is uttered on earth or in heaven from which devout souls receive so much grace, hope, and sweetness.[12] For the name of Mary, he goes on to say, contains in itself something admirable, sweet, and divine, which, when it meets a friendly heart, breathes into it an odor of holy sweetness. And the wonder of this great name is, he concludes, that if heard a thousand times by the lovers of Mary, it is always heard as new, the sweetness they experience in hearing it spoken being always the same.[13]

The blessed Henry Suso, also speaking of this sweetness, says, that in pronouncing the name of Mary, he felt his confidence so much increased, and his love so joyfully enkindled, that amidst the joy and tears with which he pronounced the beloved name, he thought his heart would have leaped from his mouth; and he affirmed that this most sweet name, as honeycomb, melted into the depths of his soul. Whereat he exclaims: Oh most

8. Quæ est ista, quæ ascendit per desertum, sicut virgula fumi? C. iii. 6.
9. Quæ est ista, quæ progreditur, quasi aurora consurgens? C. vi. 9.
10. Quæ est ista, quæ ascendit de deserto deliciis affluens? viii. 5.
11. Forsitan, quia dulce nomen sibi desiderant responderi. De Laud. Virg. c. 2.
12. Neque enim post filii nomen aliud nomen cœlum et terra nominat, unde tantum gratiæ, spei, et suavitatis piæ mentes concipiant. De Grat. Nov. Test. tr. 6.
13. Nomen namque Mariæ mirum quid, suave, atque divinum in se continet, et cum convenit amicis cordibus, amicæ suavitatis odorem spiret. Et mirum illud est de nomine Mariæ, ut millies auditum semper audiatur quasi novum. De. Grat. Nov. Test. tr. 6.

sweet name! oh Mary, what must thou thyself be, if thy name alone is so lovely and sweet?

The enamored St. Bernard, too, addressing his good mother with tenderness, says to her: Oh great, oh merciful Mary, most holy Virgin, worthy of all praise, thy name is so sweet and lovely that it cannot be spoken without enkindling love to thee and to God in the heart of him who pronounces it; the thought of it alone is enough to console thy lovers, and inflame them with a far greater love to thee.[14] If riches are a consolation to the poor, because by them they are relieved of their miseries, oh how much more, says Richard of St. Laurence, does thy name console us sinners, oh Mary; far more than the riches of earth it relieves us in the troubles of the present life.[15]

In a word, thy name, oh mother of God, is full of grace and divine blessings, as St. Methodius says.[16] And St. Bonaventure affirms that thy name cannot be pronounced but it brings some grace to him who devoutly utters it.[17] So great is the virtue of thy name, oh most compassionate Virgin, says the Idiot, that no one can pronounce it, however hardened, however desponding may be his heart, and not find it wonderfully softened; for it is thou who dost console sinners with the hope of pardon and of grace.[18] Thy most sweet name, according to St. Ambrose, is a sweet ointment, which breathes the fragrance of divine grace.[19] The saint thus invokes the divine mother: May this oil of salvation descend into the depths of our soul; by which he intends to say: Oh Lady, remind us often to pronounce thy name with love and confidence; for thus to name thee, either is a sign that we already possess divine grace, or it is an earnest that we shall soon recover it.

For as Landolph of Saxony expresses it: The remembrance of thy name, oh Mary, consoles the afflicted, brings back the wanderer to the path of salvation, encourages the sinner, and saves him from despair;[20] and Father Pelbart remarks, that as Jesus Christ by his five wounds has prepared for

---

14. O magna, O pia, O multum laudabilis Maria, tu nec nominari potes quin accendas; nec cogitari, quin recrees affectus diligentium te. Ap. S. Bon. Spec. c. 8.
15. Mariæ nomen longe melius quam divitiæ, quia melius augustiam relevat. De Laud. Virg. c. 2.
16. Tuum, Dei genitrix, nomen divinis benedictionibus et gratiis ex omni parte refertum. Orat. in Hyp.
17. Nomen tuum devote nominari non potest sine nominantis utilitate. Spec. B. Virg. c. 8.
18. Tanta est virtus tui sacratissimi nominis, semper benigna Virgo Maria, quod mirabiliter emollit duritia cordis humani. Peccator per te respirat in spe veniæ et gratiæ. Idiot, in Alph. Mar. p. 827.
19. Unguentum nomen tuum. Descendat istud unguentum in animæ preæcordia, S. Maria, quo divinæ gratiæ spiramenta redoleam. De Instit. Virg. c. 13.
20. O Maria, tui recordatio nominis mœstos lætificat, errantes ad viam salutis revocat, et peccatores ne desperent confortat. In vita Christ, p. 2, c. 86.

the world the remedy for its woes, thus also Mary, with her most holy name, which is composed of five letters, confers every day pardon upon sinners.[21]

For this reason, the holy name of Mary in the sacred Canticles is compared to oil: Thy name is as oil poured out: "Oleum effusum nomen tuum."[22] The blessed Alanus, commenting on this passage, says: The glory of her name is compared to oil poured out. As oil heals the sick, diffuses odor, and kindles flame; thus the name of Mary heals sinners, rejoices hearts, and inflames them with divine love.[23] Hence Richard of St. Laurence encourages sinners to invoke this great name, because that alone will be sufficient to cure all their maladies; adding, that there is no disease so malignant that it will not at once yield to the virtue of this name.[24]

On the other hand, the devils, as Thomas à Kempis affirms, are in such fear of the queen of heaven that at the sound of her great name they flee from him who pronounces it as from burning fire.[25] The Virgin herself revealed to St. Bridget that there is no sinner living so cold in divine love, that if he invokes her holy name, with the resolution to amend, the devil will not instantly depart from him.[26] And she at another time assured her of this, telling her that all the demons so greatly venerate and fear her name, that when they hear it pronounced they immediately release the soul which they held in their chains.[27]

And as the rebel angels depart from sinners who invoke the name of Mary, thus, on the contrary, our Lady herself told St. Bridget, that the good angels draw more closely around those just souls who devoutly pronounce it.[28] And St. Germanus assures us, that as breathing is a sign of life, so the frequent utterance of the name of Mary is a sign that we are already living in divine grace, or that we shall soon receive that life; for this powerful name is effectual to obtain help and life for him who devoutly invokes it.[29] Finally,

---

21. Sic Maria suo sanctissimo nomine, quod quinque litteris constat, confert quotidie veniam peccatoribus. Stellar, a. 2.
22. Cant. i. 2.
23. Gloria nominis ejus oleo effuso comparatur. Oleum ægrotantem sanat, odorem parit, fiammam accendit. In Cant. 1, 2.
24. Peccator es? ad nomen Mariæ confugias; ipsum solum sufficit ad medendum. Nulla pestis, quæ ad nomen Mariæ non cedat continuo. De Laud. Virg. p. 14.
25. Expavescunt cœli reginam spiritus maligni, et diffugiunt, audito nomine sancto ejus, velut ab igne. Serm. 4, p. 3, ad Novit.
26. Nullus est in hac vita tam frigidus ab amore Dei, qui si invocaverit nomen meum, cum proposito pœnitendi, statim diabolus ab ipso non discedat. Rev. lib. 1, c. 9.
27. Omnes dæmones verentur hoc nomen, et timent, qui audientes hoc nomen Mariæ, statim relinquunt animam de unguibus, quibus tenebant eam. Rev. 1. 2, c. 19.
28. Angeli boni, audito nomine meo, justis magis propinquant. Ap. Dion. Cart. de Laud. V. cap. ult.
29. Quomodo corpus enim vitalis signum operationis habet respirationem, ita sanctissimum nomen tuum, O Virgo, quod in ore servorum tuorum versatur assidue, vitæ et auxilii non solum est signum, sed etiam ea procurat et conciliat. De Zona. Virg.

Richard of St. Laurence adds, that this admirable name is like a tower of strength, by taking shelter in which the sinner will be saved from death, since from this celestial tower the most abandoned sinners come forth securely defended and saved.[30]

A tower of strength, thus continues the same Richard, which not only shields sinners from punishment, but also defends the just from the assaults of hell; and he adds: Next to the name of Jesus there is no name which gives such support, and through which so great salvation is bestowed upon men, as this great name of Mary.[31] Especially is it every-where known, and the servants of Mary daily experience, that her great name gives strength to overcome temptations against chastity. The same author, remarking on the words of St. Luke: And the name of the Virgin was Mary: "Et nomen Virginis Maria,"[32] says, that these two names, of Mary and of Virgin, are united by the evangelist to show that the name of this most pure Virgin can never be separated from chastity.[33] Hence St. Peter Chrysologus says, that the name Mary is a sign of chastity: "Nomen hoc indicium castitatis;"[34] meaning, that whoever is in doubt whether he has yielded to temptations against purity, if he remembers having invoked the name of Mary may be sure that he has not violated chastity.

Let us, then, always follow the beautiful counsel of St. Bernard, who says: In every danger of losing divine grace let us think of Mary, let us invoke the name of Mary together with that of Jesus, for these names are always united. Let these two most sweet and powerful names never depart from our heart and our lips, for they will always give us strength to keep us from falling, and to conquer every temptation.[35] Very precious are the graces which Jesus Christ has promised to those who are devoted to the name of Mary, as he himself, speaking to his holy mother, gave St. Bridget to understand, revealing to her that whoever will invoke the name of Mary with confidence and a purpose of amendment, shall receive three special graces: namely, a perfect contrition for his sins, the grace to make satis-faction for them and strength to obtain perfection, and at last, the glory

---

30. Turris fortissima nomen Dominæ, ad ipsam fugiet peccator, et liberabitur. Hæc defendit quoslibet, et quantumlibet peccatores. De Laud. Virg. l. 11.
31. Non est in aliquo nomine tam potens adjutorium, nec est aliud nomen datum hominibus post nomen Jesu, ex quo tanta salus refundatur hominibus, sicut nomen Mariæ. De Laud. Virg. c. 2.
32. Luc. i. 27.
33. Hoc nomen semper cum castitate conjunctum esse debet. Loc. cit.
34. Serm. 146.
35. In periculis, in augustiis, in rebus dubiis Mariam cogita, Mariam invoca. Non recedat ab ore, non recedat a corde. Hom. 2, Sup. Miss.

of paradise;[36] for as the divine Savior added: "Thy words are so sweet and dear to me, oh my mother, that I cannot refuse thee what thou dost ask."[37]

Finally, St. Ephrem adds that the name of Mary is the key of the gate of heaven to him who devoutly invokes it;[38] and therefore St. Bonaventure rightly calls Mary the salvation of all those who invoke her: "O salus te invocantium;" as if it were the same thing to invoke the name of Mary and to obtain eternal salvation; for as the Idiot affirms: The invocation of this holy and sweet name leads to the acquisition of superabundant grace in this life, and sublime glory in another.[39] If you desire, then, brethren, concludes Thomas à Kempis, to be consoled in every affliction, have recourse to Mary, invoke Mary, honor Mary, recommend yourselves to Mary. Rejoice with Mary, weep with Mary, pray with Mary, walk with Mary, and with Mary seek Jesus; in a word, with Jesus and Mary desire to live and die. Do this, he adds, and you will always advance in the way of the Lord; for Mary will pray for you, and the Son will surely graciously listen to the mother.[40] Such are his beautiful words.

Very sweet, then, in life to her servants, is the most holy name of Mary, on account of the great graces which it obtains for them, as we have seen above; but sweeter still will it be to them in dying by the sweet and holy death she will obtain for them. Father Sertorio Caputo, of the Society of Jesus, exhorted all those who were called to the bedside of the dying, often to pronounce the name of Mary, saying that this name of life and of hope, pronounced in death, is alone sufficient to scatter the enemies and to comfort the dying in all their anguishes. St. Camillus de Lellis also strongly recommended it to his religious, that they should remind the dying often to invoke the name of Mary and of Jesus, as he always practiced it with others; but more sweetly he practiced it himself at the moment of his death, when, as we read in his life, he named with so much tenderness his beloved names of Jesus and Mary, that he inflamed also with love

---

36. Quicumque invocaverit nomen tuum, et in te sperabit cum proposito emendandi, tria illi dabuntur, contritio peccatorum, eorum satisfactio, et fortitudo ad proficiendum et insuper regnum cœlorum. Rev. l. 1, c. 10.
37. Tanta enim est in me dulcedo verborum tuorum, quod negare non valeo, quod tu petis.
38. Nomen Mariæ est reseratorium portæ cœli. In Deprec. ad Virg.
39. Devota invocatio hujus nominis ducit ad virorem gratiæ in præsenti, et ad virorem gloriæ in futuro. De Laud. Virg. 1. 2, c. 2.
40. Si consolari in omni tribulatione quæritis, accedite ad Mariam, Mariam invocate, Mariam honorate, Mariæ vos commendate; cum Maria gaudete, cum Maria dolete, cum Maria orate, cum Maria ambulate, cum Maria Jesum quærite; cum Maria et Jesu vivere et mori desiderate. Fratres, si ista exercetis, proficietis. Maria pro vobis libenter orabit, et Jesu libenter matrem suam exaudiet. Serm. par. 3, Serm. 2.

of them all those who heard him. And at length, with his eyes fixed on their adorable image, and his arms crossed, the saint expired in celestial peace, pronouncing with his last breath the most sweet names of Jesus and Mary. This short prayer of invoking the holy names of Jesus and Mary, says Thomas à Kempis, which it is as easy to retain in the memory as it is sweet to consider, is at the same time powerful to protect whoever uses it from all the enemies of our salvation.[41]

Blessed is he, says St. Bonaventure, who loves thy sweet name, oh mother of God.[42] Thy name is so glorious and admirable, that those who remember to invoke it at the moment of death, do not then fear all the assaults of the enemy.[43]

Oh, the happy lot of dying as Father Fulgentius of Ascoli, a Capuchin, died, who expired singing: Oh Mary, Mary, the most lovely of all beings, let me depart in thy company. Or, as blessed Henry the Cistercian, of whom it is related in the annals of the order, that he died with the name of Mary on his lips.[44] Let us pray, then, my devout reader, let us pray God to grant us this grace, that the last word we pronounce at death may be the name of Mary; as St. Germanus desired and prayed.[45] Oh sweet death, oh safe death, that is accompanied and protected by such a name of salvation, that God does not permit it to be invoked in death, except by those whom he will save!

Oh, my sweet Lady and mother, I love thee much, and because I love thee, I love also thy holy name. I purpose and hope with thy aid always to invoke it in life and death. For the glory, then, of thy name (let us conclude with the tender prayer of St. Bonaventure), when my soul departs from this world, wilt thou come to meet it, oh blessed Lady, and take it in thy arms?[46] Do not disdain, oh Mary, let us continue to pray with the saint, to come and comfort it, then, with thy sweet presence. Thou art its ladder and way to paradise. Wilt thou obtain for me the grace of pardon and eternal rest?[47] And the saint then terminates with saying: Oh Mary, our

---

41. Hæc brevis oratio, Jesu et Maria, facilis est ad tenendum, dulcis ad cogitandum, fortis ad protegendum.
42. Beatus vir qui diligit nomen tuum, Maria!
43. Gloriosum et admirabile nomen tuum; qui illud retinent, non expavescunt in puncto mortis. Spec. B. Virg.
44. Inter ipsam dulcissimi nominis articulationem. An. 1109.
45. Dei matris nomen sit mihi ultimus linguæ loquentis motus. Orat. 6, ad Ann. Virg.
46. Propter honorem nominis tui in exitu animæ meæ de hoc mundo occurre illi, domina, et suscipe eam. In Psalt. Deip.
47. Consolare eam vultu sancto tuo. Esto illi scala et iter ad paradisum; impetra ei indulgentiam pacis et sedem lucis.

advocate, to thee it belongs to shield thy servants, and defend their cause before the tribunal of Jesus Christ.[48]

EXAMPLE

It is related by Father Rho, in his Sabbati, and by Father Lireo, in his Trisagio Mariana, of a certain young maiden of Guelder-land [ed. Holland], who lived about the year 1465, that she was sent one day by her uncle to purchase something at the market of the city of Nimeguen, with the direction to go and pass the night at the house of her aunt, who lived in the town. The girl obeyed, but when she went at night to her aunt's house, she was rudely sent away by her, and she set out on her way homewards. Night overtaking her, she fell into a passion, and called loudly upon the devil to come to her aid. And behold, he suddenly appeared in the form of a man, and promised to assist her, provided she would do one thing. I will do any thing, answered the unhappy creature. I only wish, said the enemy, that henceforth you will not bless yourself with the sign of the cross, and will change your name. As to the cross, she answered, I will no longer sign myself with it, but my name of Mary is too dear to me, I will not change it. Then I will not help you, said the devil. At length, after much debate, it was agreed that she should be called by the first letter of the name of Mary, that is, Emme. They then went together to Antwerp, and the wretched girl remained there six years with her diabolical companion, living so sinful a life, that it was the scandal of the whole place. One day she told the devil that she wished to see her country again; the enemy objected, but finally was obliged to consent. When they entered together the city of Nimeguen, there was just then performing a public representation of the life of the most holy Mary. At such a sight the poor Emme, from that little devotion she had still preserved towards the mother of God, began to weep. "What are we doing here?" said her companion; "would you perform here another comedy?" He then seized her to take her away, but she resisted, and seeing that she was escaping from him, in a rage he raised her into the air and

---

48. Sustine devotos, suscipe causas reorum ante tribunal Christi.

Courtesy of Felipe Barandiarán

***The Divine Shepherdess.* Convento del Santo Cristo de El Pardo, Madrid, Spain.**

let her fall in the midst of the theatre. The poor girl then related what had happened to her. She went to the parish priest to confess, but he sent her to the Bishop of Cologne, and the bishop sent her to the Pope, who, having heard her confession, imposed it upon her as a penance, that she should wear three rings of iron, one around her neck, and two around her arms. The penitent obeyed, and having arrived at Maestricht, she retired into a convent of penitents, where she lived for fourteen years in severe penance. One morning she arose from her bed and found the three rings broken. Two years after she died in the odor of sanctity, and wished to have the rings buried with her, which had changed her from a slave of hell into the happy slave of Mary, her deliverer.

PRAYER

Oh great mother of God, and my mother Mary, it is true that I am unworthy to pronounce thy name, but thou who lovest me, and dost desire my salvation, thou must obtain for me, that, unclean as may be my tongue, I may yet always invoke thy most holy and most powerful name; for thy name is the support of the living, and the salvation of the dying. Ah, most pure Mary! ah, most sweet Mary! make thy name henceforth to be the breath of my life. Oh Lady, do not delay coming to my help when I call upon thee, since in all the temptations which may assail me, in all the necessities I may suffer, I shall never cease calling upon thee, always repeating Mary, Mary. Thus I hope to do in life, thus especially I hope to do in death, that I may afterwards come to praise eternally in heaven thy beloved name: O clemens! O pia! O dulcis Virgo Maria! Ah Mary! Mary most amiable! what comfort, what sweetness, what confidence, what tenderness does my soul feel only in pronouncing thy name, only in thinking of thee! I thank my God and my Lord that he has given thee, for my good, this name so sweet, so lovely, so powerful.

But, oh my Lady, I am not satisfied with merely pronouncing thy name, I would pronounce it also with love; I desire that my love may remind me to speak thy name at every hour, that I may exclaim with St. Anselm: Oh name of the mother of God, thou art my love. O amor mei nomen matris Dei.

Oh my dear mother Mary! oh my beloved Jesus! may your most sweet names always live in my own and in all hearts. May I forget all other names, that I may remember and always invoke none but your adored names. Ah Jesus, my Redeemer! and my mother Mary, when the moment of my death shall arrive, and my soul shall depart from this life, by your merits grant me the grace then to utter my last accents, repeating: *I love you, Jesus and Mary;* Jesus and Mary, I give you my heart and my soul.

VARIOUS PRAYERS

Virgin of the Grapes. **Pierre Mignard. Musée du Louvre, Paris, France.**

VARIOUS PRAYERS

Some Devout Prayers of Various Saints to the Holy Mother

The following prayers are added, not only for the use of the faithful, but also because they show the great idea which the saints entertained of the power and mercy of Mary, and their great confidence in her patronage.

PRAYER OF ST. EPHREM

Oh immaculate and wholly pure Virgin Mary! mother of God, queen of the universe, our most excellent Lady, thou art superior to all the saints, thou art the only hope of the Fathers, and the joy of the blessed. By thee we have been reconciled to our God. Thou art the only advocate of sinners, the secure haven of the shipwrecked. Thou art the consolation of the world, the redemption of captives, the joy of the sick, the comfort of the afflicted, the refuge and salvation of the whole world. Oh great princess! mother of God! cover us with the wings of thy compassion: have pity on us. We have no hope but in thee, oh most pure Virgin! We are given to thee, and consecrated to thy service; we bear the name of thy servants; do not permit Lucifer to draw us down to hell. Oh immaculate Virgin! we are under thy protection; therefore, unitedly we have recourse to thee, and supplicate thee to prevent thy Son, whom our sins have offended, from abandoning us to the power of the devil.

Oh full of grace! illuminate my intellect, loosen my tongue that it may sing thy praises, and especially the Angelic Salutation, so worthy of thee. I salute thee, oh peace! oh joy! oh salvation and consolation of the whole world! I salute thee, oh greatest of miracles! paradise of delight! secure haven of those who are in danger! fountain of grace! mediatrix of God and men!

PRAYER OF ST. BERNARD

We raise our eyes to thee, oh queen of the world. After having committed so many sins we must appear before our Judge, and who will appease him? None can do it better than thou, oh blessed Lady, who hast loved him so much, and hast been so tenderly beloved by him. Open thy heart, then, oh mother of mercy, to our sighs and prayers. We fly to thy protection; appease the anger of thy Son, and restore us to his favor. Thou dost not abhor the sinner, however loathsome he may be; thou dost not despise him, if he sends up his sighs to thee, and with contrition asks thy intercession; thou, with thy kind hand, dost deliver him from despair; thou dost encourage him to hope, dost comfort him, and dost not leave him until thou hast reconciled him to his Judge.

Thou art that only one in whom the Savior found his rest, and with whom he has deposited all his treasures. Hence all the world, oh Mary, honors thy chaste womb, as the temple of God, where the salvation of the world had its beginning. In thee was effected the reconciliation between God and man. Thou art the enclosed garden, oh great mother of God, whose flowers have never been gathered by the sinner's hand. Thou art the beautiful garden, in which God has placed all the flowers which adorn the Church, such as the violet of thy humility, the lily of thy purity, and the rose of thy charity. Who can be compared to thee, oh mother of grace and of beauty? Thou art the paradise of God. From thee hath sprung up the fountain of living water, that waters all the earth. Oh, how many favors hast thou bestowed upon the world, by meriting to be the channel of the waters of salvation!

Of thee the Holy Ghost speaks when he says: Who is she that arises like the dawn, fair as the moon, bright as the sun? Thou art, then, come into the world, oh Mary, as a resplendent dawn, preceding, with the light of thy sanctity, the coming of the Sun of Justice. The day in which thou didst appear in the world may truly be called the day of salvation, the day of grace. Thou art fair as the moon; for as there is no planet more like the sun, so there is no creature more like God than thou art. The moon illuminates the night with the light which it receives from the sun, and thou dost illuminate our darkness, with the splendor of thy virtues; and thou art fairer than the moon, because in thee is found neither stain nor shade. Thou art

Courtesy of Felipe Barandiarán

The Annunciation. **Mariano Salvador Maella. Monasterio de la Visitación, Madrid, Spain.**

bright as the sun, I mean as that Sun which hath created the sun; he has been chosen among all men, and thou among all women. Oh sweet, oh great, oh most lovely Mary, thy name cannot be pronounced by any one that thou dost not inflame with thy love; neither can those who love thee think of thee without feeling themselves encouraged to love thee more.

Oh blessed Lady, help our weakness. And who is more fit to speak to our Lord Jesus Christ than thou, who dost enjoy, so near to him, his sweet conversation? Speak, speak, oh Lady, because thy Son listens, and thou wilt obtain from him whatever thou shalt demand.

PRAYER OF ST. GERMANUS

Oh my only Lady, who art the sole consolation which I receive from God; thou who art the only celestial dew that doth soothe my pains; thou who art the light of my soul when it is surrounded with darkness;

thou who art my guide in my journeyings, my strength in my weakness, my treasure in my poverty; balm for my wounds, my consolation in sorrow; thou who art my refuge in misery, the hope of my salvation, graciously hear my prayer, have pity on me, as is befitting the mother of a God who hath so much love for men. Thou who art our defense and joy, grant me what I ask; make me worthy of enjoying with thee that great happiness which thou dost enjoy in heaven. Yes, my Lady, my refuge, my life, my help, my defense, my strength, my joy, my hope, make me to come with thee to paradise. I know that, being the mother of God, thou canst obtain this for me if thou wilt. Oh Mary, thou art omnipotent to save sinners, thou needest nothing else to recommend us to thee, for thou art the mother of true life.

PRAYER OF THE ABBOT OF CELLES, SURNAMED "THE IDIOT"

Draw me after thee, oh Virgin Mary, that I may run to the odor of thy perfumes. Draw me, for I am held back by the weight of my sins and by the malice of my enemies. As no one goes to thy Son unless the divine Father draws him, so I would dare to say, in a certain sense, that no one goes to him if thou dost not draw him with thy holy prayers. It is thou who teachest true wisdom; thou who dost obtain pardon for sinners, because thou art their advocate. It is thou who dost promise glory to him who honors thee, because thou art the treasurer of graces.

Thou hast found grace with God, oh most sweet Virgin, because thou hast been preserved from the stain of original sin, filled with the Holy Spirit, and hast conceived the Son of God. Thou hast received all these graces, oh Mary most humble, not only for thyself, but also for us, that thou mayest help us in all our necessities. And thou, indeed, dost so; thou dost succor the good by preserving them in grace; and the bad, by bringing them to receive the divine mercy; thou dost aid the dying by protecting them against the snares of the devil; and thou dost aid them also after death by receiving their souls, and leading them to the kingdom of the blessed.

PRAYER OF ST. METHODIUS

Thy name, oh mother of God, is full of all graces and divine blessings. Thou hast comprehended him who is incomprehensible, and nourished him who nourishes all living creatures. He who fills heaven and earth and is Lord of all, has chosen to have need of thee, since thou hast clothed him with that garment of flesh that he had not before. Rejoice, oh mother and handmaid of God! rejoice! rejoice! thou hast for a debtor him to whom all creatures owe their being. We are all debtors to God, but God is a debtor to thee. Hence it is, oh most holy mother of God, that thou hast greater goodness and greater charity than all the other saints, and more than all others hast near access in heaven to God, because thou art his mother. Ah, we pray thee that we may celebrate thy glories, and may know how great is thy goodness, being mindful of us and of our miseries.

PRAYER OF ST. JOHN DAMASCENE

I salute thee, oh Mary! thou art the hope of Christians; receive the petition of a servant who tenderly loves thee, especially honors thee, and places in thee all the hope of his salvation. From thee I have life, thou dost restore me to the favor of thy Son; thou art the certain pledge of my salvation. I implore thee, then, to deliver me from the burden of my sins; dispel the darkness of my mind; banish earthly affections from my heart; repel the temptations of my enemies, and so order my life, that I may reach, by thy means and by thy guidance, the eternal felicity of paradise.

PRAYER OF ST. ANDREW OF CANDIA

I salute thee, oh full of grace! the Lord is with thee. I salute thee, oh cause of our joy, by whom the sentence of our condemnation has been already revoked, and changed into a judgment of benediction. I salute thee, oh temple of the glory of God, sacred house of the King of Heaven. Thou art the reconciliation of God with men. I salute thee, oh mother of our joy. In truth thou art blessed, for thou alone, among all women, hast been found worthy of being the mother of thy Creator. All nations call thee blessed.

Oh Mary, if I put my confidence in thee I shall be saved; if I am under thy protection I have nothing to fear, for to be thy servant is to have the secure armor of salvation, which God does not grant except to those whom he will save.

Oh mother of mercy, appease thy Son. Whilst thou wast on earth thou didst only occupy a small part of it; but now that thou art raised above the highest heaven, the whole world considers thee as the propitiatory of all nations. We supplicate thee, then, oh holy Virgin, to grant us the aid of thy prayers with God; prayers which are dearer and more precious to us than all the treasures of earth;* prayers that render God inclined to forgive our sins; and wilt thou obtain for us abundant graces to receive the pardon of them and to practice virtue (*prayers that conquer our enemies, confound their designs, and triumph over their forces).

PRAYER OF ST. ILDEPHONSUS

I come to thee, oh mother of God, I supplicate thee to obtain for me the pardon of my sins, and that I may be purified from all the errors of my life. I pray thee to grant me thy grace, that I may unite myself with affection to thy Son and to thee; to thy Son as to my God, to thee as to the mother of my God.

PRAYER OF ST. ATHANASIUS

Hearken oh most holy Virgin, to our prayers, and remember us. Dispense to us the gifts of thy riches, and the abundant graces with which thou art filled. The archangel salutes thee and calls thee full of grace. All nations call thee blessed; the whole hierarchy of heaven blesses thee, and we, who are of the terrestrial hierarchy, also say to thee: "Hail, full of grace, the Lord is with thee;" pray for us, oh mother of God, our Lady and our Queen.

PRAYER OF ST. ANSELM

We pray thee, oh most blessed Lady, by that grace which God bestowed on thee when he so greatly exalted thee, rendering all things possible to thee with him; we pray thee to obtain for us that the fullness of grace which thou hast merited may make us to share thy glory. Be pleased, oh most merciful Lady, to procure for us the good for which God consented to become man in thy chaste womb. Be not slow to hear us. If thou wilt deign to supplicate thy Son, he at once will graciously hear thee. It is enough that thou wilt save us, for then we cannot but be saved. Who can restrain the bowels of thy compassion? If thou hast not compassion on us, thou who art the mother of mercy, what will become of us when thy Son shall come to judge us?

Come, then, to our succor, oh most compassionate mother, without regarding the multitude of our sins. Remember again and again that our Creator has taken human flesh from thee, not to condemn sinners, but to save them. If thou hadst been made mother of God only for thine own advantage, it might be said that it would be to thee of little importance whether we were saved or condemned; but God has clothed himself with thy flesh for thy salvation and for that of all men. What will it avail us that thou art so powerful and so glorious, if thou dost not render us partakers of thy felicity? Aid us and protect us; remember the need we have of thy assistance. We recommend ourselves to thee; save us from damnation, and make us serve and love eternally thy Son Jesus Christ.

PRAYER OF ST. PETER DAMIAN

Holy Virgin, mother of God, succor those who implore thy assistance. Turn to us. But, having been deified, as it were, hast thou forgotten men? Ah, certainly not. Thou knowest in what peril thou hast left us, and the wretched condition of thy servants; no, it is not befitting a mercy so great, to forget so great misery as ours. Turn to us with thy power, because he who is powerful hath given thee omnipotence in heaven and on earth. To thee nothing is impossible, for thou canst raise even the despairing to the hope of salvation. Thou must be compassionate as thou art powerful.

Turn to us, also, in thy love. I know, oh my Lady, that thou art all kindness, and dost love us with a love that no other love can surpass. How dost thou appease the anger of our Judge when he is on the point of punishing us for our offenses! All the treasures of the mercy of God are in thy hands. Ah, may it never happen that thou shouldst cease from doing us good: thou seekest but the occasion of saving all sinners, and of bestowing thy mercy upon them; for thy glory increases when, by thy means, penitents are pardoned, and the pardoned come to paradise. Turn, then to us, that we may come to see thee in heaven; for the greatest glory we can obtain next to seeing God, is to see thee, to love thee, and to be under thy protection. Ah, graciously hear us, since thy Son wishes to honor thee, by granting all thy requests.

PRAYER OF ST. WILLIAM, BISHOP OF PARIS

Oh mother of God, I fly to thee and I implore thee not to cast me off, for the whole Church of the faithful calls thee, and proclaims thee the mother of mercy. Thou art so dear to God, that thou art always graciously heard; thy compassion has never been wanting to any one; thy most gracious condescension has never despised any sinner, however enormous his sin, who has recommended himself to thee. Does the Church falsely and in vain call thee her advocate, and the refuge of the unhappy? No; let my sins never prevent thee from exercising thy great office of mercy by which thou art the advocate, the mediatrix of reconciliation, the only hope, and the most secure refuge of sinners. Let it never be that the mother, who, for the good of the whole world, brought forth him who is the fountain of mercy, should refuse her mercy to any sinner who has recourse to her. It is thy office to reconcile God to man; let then thy compassion move thee to help me, for it is greater than all my sins.

PRAYER TO THE MOST HOLY MARY
TO BE SAID EVERY DAY

Oh most holy, immaculate Virgin, and my mother Mary, to thee who art the mother of my Lord, the queen of the world, the advocate, the hope, the refuge of sinners, I, the most miserable of all, have recourse to-day. I venerate thee, oh great queen, and thank thee for all the favors thou hast hitherto granted me, especially for having delivered me from hell, which I have so often deserved. I love thee, oh most amiable Lady, and through the love I bear thee promise that I will always serve thee, and do all that I can that thou mayest also be loved by others. I place in thee all my hopes of salvation; accept me for thy servant, and receive me under thy mantle, oh thou mother of mercy. And since thou art so powerful with God, deliver me from all temptations, or obtain for me the strength to conquer them always until death. From thee I ask a true love for Jesus; from thee I hope to die a good death. Oh, my mother, by the love thou bearest to God, I pray thee always to help me, but most of all at the last moment of my life. Do not leave me until thou seest me actually safe in heaven, blessing thee, and singing thy mercies throughout all eternity. Amen. Thus I hope. Thus may it be.

American TFP Archive / Michael Gorre

Our Lady of Good Success. **Monasterio de la Limpia Concepción, Quito, Ecuador.**